A Peculiar Orthodoxy

REFLECTIONS
on THEOLOGY *and* THE ARTS

Jeremy S. Begbie

Baker Academic

a division of Baker Publishing Group
Grand Rapids, Michigan

In memory of Roger Lundin,
scholar, friend, and teacher extraordinaire

Published by Baker Academic
a division of Baker Publishing Group
PO Box 6287, Grand Rapids, MI 49516-6287
www.bakeracademic.com

Printed in the United States of America

Library of Congress Cataloging in Publication Data
Names: Begbie, Jeremy, author.
Title: A peculiar orthodoxy : reflections on theology and the arts / Jeremy S. Begbie.
Description: Grand Rapids, MI : Baker Academic, a division of Baker Publishing Group, 2018. |
    Includes bibliographical references and index.
Identifiers: LCCN 2017055432 | ISBN 9780801099571 (cloth : alk. paper)
Subjects: LCSH: Christianity and the arts.
Classification: LCC BR115.A8 B435 2018 | DDC 261.5/7—dc23
LC record available at https://lccn.loc.gov/2017055432

18   19   20   21   22   23   24   7   6   5   4   3   2   1

Contents

Introduction   v

1. Created Beauty: The Witness of J. S. Bach   1

2. Beauty, Sentimentality, and the Arts   25

3. Faithful Feelings: Music and Emotion in Worship   49

4. Openness and Specificity: A Conversation with David Brown on Theology and Classical Music   79

5. Confidence and Anxiety in Elgar's *The Dream of Gerontius*   93

6. The Holy Spirit at Work in the Arts: Learning from George Herbert   113

7. Natural Theology and Music   129

8. Room of One's Own? Music, Space, and Freedom   145

9. The Future of Theology amid the Arts: Some Reformed Reflections   181

Index   209

Introduction

One of the more encouraging signs in theological writing over the last thirty years or so has been a flourishing of activity at the interface of theology and the arts. When I first began working at this frontier in the early 1980s, although it was not hard to find material on poetry, music, and painting with overtly Christian subject matter, in many theological quarters that was about as far as the interest went. A few philosophically minded writers went out of their way to show how a Christian perception of the world might shape and in turn be shaped by our engagement with the arts. But this kind of activity tended to be confined to relatively small and isolated pockets. The majority of theologians in the United States and Europe tended to see the arts as a peripheral and specialist interest. There was little cross-disciplinary conversation, little recognition that the arts presented serious and fruitful territory for theological research, little in the way of college courses and programs, and very little of theological depth to help Christian laypeople come to terms with whatever art surrounded them day by day. And the resources for Christians who were making art "on the ground"—molding clay, stringing notes together, spinning words into verse—were scarce.

Things are dramatically different today. College courses abound, institutes and doctoral programs flourish, parachurch organizations prosper, and literature pours out in myriad forms: monographs, journals, magazines, websites, and social media. Admittedly, funding to support the best of this activity is often meager, but there can be little doubt that, like the confluence of two rivers, Christian theology and the arts are together generating a bubbling ferment that shows no signs of abating. And much of this spans a wide ecclesiastical spectrum—Protestant, Roman Catholic, Eastern Orthodox—generating cross-traditional conversation of a kind not witnessed to date.

Here we should not forget the dogged persistence of those who over many decades have kept the arts firmly on the radar of church and academy, amid what was often a climate of indifference (in some cases hostility). To the likes of Nicholas Wolterstorff, Calvin Seerveld, Jane and John Dillenberger, Wilson Yates, Frank Burch Brown, Sandra Bowden, Richard Viladesau, Greg Wolfe, Mako Fujimura, William Dyrness, and others, we owe an incalculable debt.

This burgeoning activity is surely in large part to be welcomed, auguring well for the future health of both theology and the arts. If I had reservations about the present-day scene, they would not concern the liveliness of the field or its seriousness or depth. My misgivings would rather involve the theological resources being drawn upon. I welcome the sheer range and variety of ecclesial traditions currently being deployed, but what often seems to be lacking is the sustained exercise of what some have called a "scriptural imagination"—a sustained immersion in biblical texts that enables us to perceive and live in the world in a way that is faithful to Scripture's theological coherence, and this together with an attention to the classic creedal traditions that seek to convey and foster such an imagination.[1] The reasons for this lack are many and varied. Undoubtedly one of them is that the Bible's overt references to the arts are few and far between, and the early church's patterns of belief were established with relatively little sustained reflection on the arts. In this light it is hardly surprising that many have turned to extrabiblical and extracreedal sources for the most promising primary sources of theological wisdom—an ancient metaphysical tradition perhaps, or a particular strand of modern or late modern philosophy. Others may put their confidence in a contemporary cultural movement or expression. Indeed, the tables can be turned here: some writers tell us that the arts themselves deliver theological wisdom that will make us question key elements in the biblical orthodoxy of yesteryear. The artist is typically an awkward customer, goading pastor and professor with questions they would rather ignore, questions that may well strike at the root of "the faith once delivered."

While fully appreciating the motivations and concerns underlying these convictions, I have come to believe that the most profoundly awkward and in the long run most life-giving questions that arise from a Christian engagement with the arts will be provoked through engaging the often strange and puzzling texts the church recognizes as its canon and from the creedal confessions that seek to be faithful to its testimony. It is this stubborn peculiarity of biblically based orthodoxy—centering on the embodiment of the world's Creator in

---

1. See, e.g., L. Gregory Jones and James J. Buckley, *Theology and Scriptural Imagination* (Oxford: Blackwell, 1998); C. Kavin Rowe, "The Formation of Scriptural Imagination," *Faith and Leadership* (2013), https://www.faithandleadership.com/features/articles/c-kavin -rowe-the-formation-scriptural-imagination.

a crucified king, and a God who is perplexingly threefold—that seems to be all too easily screened out or sanitized by those exploring the resonances between faith and the arts today. And it is worth emphasizing that in using "peculiar" in my title I have in mind both a strangeness ("he had a peculiar look in his eye") and a distinctiveness ("she had that look peculiar to academics"). That is, I am keen to encourage an awareness not only of the odd and puzzling character of orthodoxy but also of how unique and unparalleled it is, and thus also an awareness of the danger both of muting its witness and of trying to turn it into something it is not.

Orthodoxy, of course, necessarily deals with doctrine, and like orthodoxy, talk of doctrine may well raise hackles. Doctrine, it will be protested, is about tidying things up, things that need to be left open. In the church's deadening passion for control and conformity, for accurate propositions that supposedly give us a final hold on truth, mystery is dissolved, open-minded inquiry suppressed, conversation closed down. The arts move in a radically different world, so we are told, breathing a much fresher and healthier air. Here we will find openness, allusiveness, ambiguity, a resistance to that stifling pursuit of certainty that has plagued so much of the church's history. Indeed, at their best, the arts can help liberate the church from its misguided reliance on doctrinal correctness.

This kind of sentiment is more than understandable. The arts do indeed rely heavily on allusiveness for much of their potency. And few will need reminding of the ways in which the church has exploited Christian dogma in oppressive ways (the very term "dogma" easily suggests as much), ways that do indeed encourage hegemony, flatten irresolvable paradoxes, inhibit discussion, exclude much-needed voices, and—not least—asphyxiate the arts. At the same time, we need to question some of the assumptions behind this kind of resistance to doctrine. In particular, there is the notion that language—including propositional language—strives by its very nature to "close in" on its subject, like a shark seeking to seize its prey in one bite, the notion that language is *necessarily* an attempt to enclose, grasp, and control. Undoubtedly formulating doctrine always involves specifying and delineating. But if it is undertaken "according to the Scriptures"—that is, if it is open to the redeeming activity of the God of Israel and Jesus Christ—and if it is conceived as "direction for our fitting participation in the ongoing drama of redemption,"[2] then it will, potentially at least, be a vehicle of liberation.

2. Kevin J. Vanhoozer, "Into the Great 'Beyond': A Theologian's Response to the Marshall Plan," in *Beyond the Bible: Moving from Scripture to Theology*, ed. I. Howard Marshall and Kevin J. Vanhoozer (Grand Rapids: Baker Academic, 2004), 81–95, here 94.

Among other things, it will ensure that the gospel's mystery remains mystery, that its ambiguities persist as ambiguous. Doctrine is at its most orthodox when it enables the *skandalon* of the gospel to be heard more clearly as just that, good news—and good news precisely *because of* and *through* its stubborn refusal to be domesticated and controlled. Doctrine's prime ministry to the artist is to direct our eyes and ears to that *skandalon* above all, and the artist's ministry to the doctrinal theologian is perhaps above all to remind him or her that no formal or technical language can ever encompass or contain its subject matter, least of all language about God.

This book is a modest attempt to explore the fruits of the church's "peculiar orthodoxy" in the arena of the arts and in so doing recover a fresh confidence in its power. It has arisen through the encouragement of friends who suggested that I gather some scattered pieces of writing into one volume to make them more widely available. They span roughly ten years, and I have arranged them in chronological order.[3] I did consider updating the older ones substantially—with expansions, qualifications, and references to more recent scholarship—but with that kind of enterprise it is hard to know when to stop. So I decided to let each piece stand much as it first appeared. Each is for a particular time and occasion and should be read in that light.

I am very aware, despite what I have just said, that there is little detailed exegesis of particular scriptural texts in what follows. To be sure, much of the material depends on close readings of biblical material and on the labors of a host of biblical scholars from whom I have benefited over the years.[4] But a great deal more needs to be done along these lines. To that end, my *Redeeming Transcendence in the Arts: Bearing Witness to the Triune God* (Eerdmans, 2018) contains far more exegetical material, and I hope to extend this approach in future writings. The essays in the present volume are oriented in a preliminary way to that long-term task.

As far as recurring motifs and emphases are concerned, it is probably wise to leave it to others to point them out. But at least two key currents of thought

---

3. The original version of chap. 1 was written to precede chap. 2, but here I am using a slightly revised, and thus later, version of it.

4. It is worth noting that I am much encouraged by the movement known as "the theological interpretation of Scripture." See, e.g., J. Todd Billings, *The Word of God for the People of God: An Entryway to the Theological Interpretation of Scripture* (Grand Rapids: Eerdmans, 2010); Daniel J. Treier, *Introducing Theological Interpretation of Scripture: Recovering a Christian Practice* (Grand Rapids: Baker Academic, 2008); Bard East, "The Hermeneutics of Theological Interpretation: Holy Scripture, Biblical Scholarship and Historical Criticism," *International Journal of Systematic Theology* 19, no. 1 (2017): 30–52. It is unfortunate that this stream of writing seems to have had little influence so far in the theology-arts world.

are worth highlighting. First, it will be obvious that I believe the confession of the triunity of God cannot be treated as a merely intellectual nicety or an optional luxury, as icing on a prebaked methodological cake. That the God of Israel and Jesus Christ possess a threefold life will configure and reconfigure every dimension of Christian faith. And when unleashed in the arts, a trinitarian imagination will provoke a freshness and abundance of possibilities that in many places we are only just beginning to discover. Second, the reader will also notice an orientation to the Creator's particular and concrete historical engagement with the created world, climaxing in the new creation forged in Jesus Christ. In the incarnate, crucified, risen, and ascended Son, we are given a material promise of a future to this world, a future even now being realized by the Spirit among us and whose final splendor we can only barely imagine. In the artistic arena, the ramifications of this physically rooted hope are inexhaustible.

Because of these and other theological orientations, I have found myself less than enthusiastic about some of the more common default terms and habits of mind that shape many contemporary theological approaches to the arts. For example, I believe that the concept of beauty needs very careful handling if we are not to distort the way the arts actually operate in practice, and if we are to avoid being captive to intellectual schemes that cannot accommodate a narrative that culminates in a crucifixion and resurrection. (Chapters 1 and 2 in particular speak to this matter.) I am impressed with the wisdom that has come from associating the arts with the so-called transcendentals, but I am less impressed when a particular metaphysics is adopted that centers on, say, the beauty-truth-goodness triad and is then used without justification to set the entire stage for theological adventures in the arts. I am fascinated by the variety of senses associated with the terms "aesthetic" and "aesthetics," but I begin to ask questions when the arts are fastened on to one of them without any argument, and theologized accordingly. I welcome the way that the visual arts have recently been given much theological attention, but I become anxious when it is covertly assumed that what are distinctively visual casts of mind are equally applicable to all the arts.

Finally, some heartfelt acknowledgments are in order. I am immensely grateful to the scores of friends, colleagues, and scholars, past and present, who have helped shape the content of this book—there are too many to cite by name. But I should single out several whose recent influence has been especially important to me: Richard Bauckham, David Ford, Malcolm Guite, David Bentley Hart, Trevor Hart, Richard Hays, Roger Lundin (sadly missed), James MacMillan, Suzanne McDonald, W. David O. Taylor, Alan Torrance, Rowan Williams, Nicholas Wolterstorff, and Tom Wright. My warm thanks go also to my able research assistant, Alice Soulieux-Evans, for taking care of so many of the necessary detailed tasks; to Bob Hosack of Baker Books for his consistent support and advice; to Dan and Hillary Train for their seemingly boundless wisdom and support; and, as always, to my patient and long-suffering wife, Rachel.

1

Created Beauty

The Witness of J. S. Bach

When speaking with others about the arts in a theological setting, I have found that the topic of beauty tends to make an appearance very early in the discussion. There is little point in wishing this were not so, but we have every reason to ask about why the concept is invoked and about how it is informed (and re-formed) by the Christian faith. In this essay I attempt to sketch what I see as the main contours of a theology of beauty and relate them to the music of J. S. Bach. Crucial, I argue, is an orientation to the self-identification of the Christian God as triune. This means being wary of adopting concepts of beauty that, however ancient and venerated, turn on very different axes than those implicated in what has been played out in Jesus Christ, the one in whom and through whom all things are created (Col. 1:16). This essay should be read along with the next (they originally appeared together, arising from a conference at Wheaton College).

Among the millions of words spoken and written about J. S. Bach's *Goldberg Variations* of 1741, few are as intriguing as those of the musicologist Peter Williams when he stands back from this dazzling tour de force and reflects:

This chapter was originally published as Jeremy Begbie, "Created Beauty: The Witness of J. S. Bach," in *Resonant Witness*, ed. Jeremy Begbie and Steven Guthrie, 83–108 (Grand Rapids: Eerdmans, 2011).

I think myself that it "feels special" because, whatever antecedent this or that feature has, its beauty is both original—seldom like anything else, even in Bach—and at the same time comprehensible, intelligible, coherent, based on simple, "truthful" harmonies.[1]

Most of what I want to say in this essay is suggested by that observation (even though Williams himself would probably demur at the theological slant I shall be giving to his words). The matter he brings to the surface is the interplay between two types of beauty: on the one hand, the beauty that is in some sense already "there" in the nature of things (the beauty of "truthful harmonies"), and on the other, the beauty human beings make (the "original" beauty of a piece like the *Goldberg*). Put more theologically, there is the beauty directly given to the world by God and that which we are invited to fashion as God's creatures. Taking our cue from Williams, the question we shall pursue in this essay is, how might an engagement with Bach's music, especially as considered in its time and place, assist us in gaining a clearer theological perception and understanding of these two senses of created beauty and of the relation between them?

Theological Bearings

We shall turn to Bach in due course. The first task, however, is to say something about the concept of beauty itself, to clarify what we might intend by this fluid and much-contested notion and, in particular, what might be entailed in a specifically *theological* perspective on it. With limited space, I cannot attempt anything approaching a comprehensive "theology of the beautiful," but we do at least need to gain some theological bearings—that is, to highlight key features of the theological landscape that are especially relevant to a responsible Christian account of beauty and the ways in which such an account is shaped by them.

Our primary orientation will not be to an experience of the beautiful, nor to an aesthetics, but to the quite specific God attested in Scripture—the gracious, reconciling, self-revealing God of Jesus Christ. If an account of beauty is to be *theo-logical* in Christian terms, its *logos*, or rationale, will take its shape primarily from the being and acts of this *theos*. Crassly obvious as this may seem, even a casual survey of religious treatments and theologies of beauty over the last thirty years will frequently show a marked lack of attention to the

1. Peter F. Williams, *Bach: The Goldberg Variations* (Cambridge: Cambridge University Press, 2001), 1.

identity of the deity or deities being presumed. Difficulties are compounded if the de facto basic allegiance is to some prior and fixed conception of beauty, especially if it relies on a metaphysical scheme whose consonance with the testimony of Scripture is anything but clear. If we are to think of the phenomenon of beauty, at least initially, in terms of the main strands that inform the so-called great theory (and I see no compelling reason not to do so)—in other words, *proportion and consonance of parts, brightness* or resplendence, *perfection* or integrity, and *affording pleasure upon contemplation*[2]—then these strands need to be constantly re-formed and transformed, purged and purified by a repeated return to the saving self-disclosure of Scripture's God.

Needless to say, this approach will sound to some like an appeal for a sectarian retreat into a Christian ghetto, an isolationist "fideism" that rules out conversation with all but Christians. Nothing of the sort is intended. The point is not to close down dialogue about beauty with those outside or on the edges of the Christian tradition or with the vast corpus of philosophical writings on beauty. The issue is at root about the norms shaping our language. If a conversation about beauty is to be fruitful, one cannot *but* care about the criteria governing the deployment of such a historically loaded and polysemous word—for how can speech bear fruit if it has ceased to care about its primary responsibilities? And to care about these criteria, for the Christian at any rate, is ultimately to care about the God to whom the church turns for the shaping of all its words.

A Christian account of beauty, then, will be oriented to a particular God. Let me press the matter. According to the Christian tradition, this God has identified himself as irreducibly *trinitarian*. The deity celebrated in Christian faith is not an undifferentiated monad or blank "Presence" but a triunity of inexhaustible love and life, active and present to the world as triune and never more intensively than in the saving life, death, and resurrection of Jesus Christ. If, then, we are to speak of God as primordially beautiful—however we may want to qualify this—then strenuous care must be taken to ensure it is *this* God of whom we speak.[3] If we speak of divine proportion and consonance,

2. See Wladyslaw Tatarkiewicz, "The Great Theory of Beauty and Its Decline," *Journal of Aesthetics and Art Criticism* 31 (1972): 165–80. Nicholas Wolterstorff rightly points out that although Tatarkiewicz sees consonance of parts as identical with due proportion, not all the writers Tatarkiewicz cites presume this; Nicholas Wolterstorff, *Art in Action: Toward a Christian Aesthetic* (Grand Rapids: Eerdmans, 1980), 162. I am not suggesting, of course, that these strands together constitute a *definition* of beauty, but they do at least indicate some of the most prominent lines or themes in mainstream Western thinking about beauty. See also Jerome Stolnitz, "'Beauty': Some Stages in the History of an Idea," *Journal of the History of Ideas* 22, no. 2 (1961): 185–204.

3. It was a rigorous concern for the specificity of theology's God that made Karl Barth so circumspect about ascribing beauty to God—perhaps excessively so; see Karl Barth, *Church*

can these be any other than the proportion and consonance of this Triune God? If we speak of divine brightness, integrity, or perfection, can these be any other than the brightness, integrity, and perfection of the trinitarian life? Everything depends here on refusing all *a priori* abstractions and maintaining a resolute focus on the saving economy of God in Jesus Christ. Divine beauty is discovered not in the first instance by reference to a doctrine (still less to a philosophy of beauty) but by strict attention to a movement in history enacted for us—supremely the story of Jesus Christ the incarnate Son, living in the Father's presence in the power of the Spirit. Trinitarian beauty has, so to speak, been performed for us.[4]

To begin to unfold the implications of this notion: if beauty is to be ascribed primordially to the Triune God, and the life of God is constituted by the dynamism of outgoing love, then primordial beauty is *the beauty of this ecstatic love for the other*. God's beauty is not static structure but the dynamism of love. The "proportion and consonance" of God, his "brightness" or radiance, his "perfection" and his affording "pleasure upon contemplation"

Dogmatics, trans. G. W. Bromiley and T. F. Torrance, II/1 (Edinburgh: T&T Clark, 1957), 650–66. As so often with this theologian, this caution is motivated by fear of an intrusive *a priori* that in some manner constrains God, a "transcendental" to which God is made answerable—and the particular anxiety here is Hellenism. So Barth insists: "God is not beautiful in the sense that he shares in an idea of beauty superior to him, so that to know it is to know him as God. On the contrary, it is as he is God that he is also beautiful, so that he is the basis and standard of everything that is beautiful and of all ideas of the beautiful." Barth, *Church Dogmatics*, II/1, 656. Hence Barth will not allow beauty to be a "leading concept" in the doctrine of God. It is secondary to God's glory, an "explanation" of it; beauty is the "form" of God's glory—that about his self-revealing glory which attracts rather than repels, which redeems, persuades, and convinces, evokes joy rather than indifference. One might wish Barth had developed these views more extensively, especially in relation to creaturely beauty, but his *methodological* concerns, I would suggest, are to be seriously heeded. One of the most puzzling things about David Bentley Hart's substantial book on the aesthetics of Christian truth—*The Beauty of the Infinite: The Aesthetics of Christian Truth* (Grand Rapids: Eerdmans, 2003)—is that he is frequently very close to Barth methodologically, yet the few remarks he makes about Barth are extraordinarily dismissive. Among the reviews I have read, only Robert Jenson's points this out. Robert Jenson, "Review Essay: David Bentley Hart, *The Beauty of the Infinite: The Aesthetics of Christian Truth*," *Pro Ecclesia* 4, no. 2 (2005): 236.

4. So Hans Urs von Balthasar writes that we "ought never to speak of God's beauty without reference to the form and manner of appearing which he exhibits in salvation-history." And later: "God's attribute of beauty can certainly . . . be examined in the context of a doctrine of the divine attributes. Besides examining God's beauty as manifested by God's actions in his creation, his beauty would also be deduced from the harmony of his essential attributes, and particularly from the Trinity. But such a doctrine of God and the Trinity really speaks to us only when and as long as the *theologia* does not become detached from the *oikonomia*, but rather lets its every formulation and stage of reflection be accompanied and supported by the latter's vivid discernibility." See Hans Urs von Balthasar, *The Glory of the Lord: A Theological Aesthetics*, vol. 1, *Seeing the Form*, trans. Erasmo Leivà-Merikakis (Edinburgh: T&T Clark, 1982), 124, 125.

are all to be understood in the light of the endless self-donation of Father to Son and Son to Father in the ecstatic momentum of the Spirit. Hence we find Hans Urs von Balthasar insisting that we must go to the economy of salvation to discover God's beauty (and thus the ultimate measure of all beauty) since the incarnation, death, and raising of Jesus display God's love in its clearest and most decisive form; here, above all, we witness the mutual self-surrendering love of the Father and Son in the Spirit for the healing of the world.[5] This linking of beauty with outgoing love requires giving a full and crucial place to the Holy Spirit in connection with beauty. Insofar as the Spirit is the personal unity of the mutual outgoingness of Father and Son, the impulse toward self-sharing in God's life, we might well describe the Spirit as the "beautifier" in God.[6]

Giving the trinitarian character of God its formal and material due means that *we will resist the temptation to drive apart beauty and the infinite*, something that is very much a mark of modernity and postmodernity. Here we can sympathize somewhat with John Milbank and others who lament what they see as the modern rupture of beauty and the sublime, evident especially since the eighteenth century.[7] As understood in the tradition represented by Immanuel Kant (1724–1804), the experience of the sublime is an awareness of being overwhelmed by something uncontainable, beyond our grasp. In Kant this is either mainly "mathematical," when we are overwhelmed by size and are confronted with the limits of our sense perception (such as we

5. Speaking of God's saving economy, Balthasar writes: "Should we not . . . consider this 'art' of God's to be precisely the transcendent archetype of all worldly and human beauty?" Balthasar, *Glory of the Lord*, 1:70. In this respect we can also join Jonathan Edwards when he writes of "primary beauty," whose chief instance is God's own triune benevolence, the mutual generosity and "infinite consent" that constitutes the life of God. See Roland A. Delattre, *Beauty and Sensibility in the Thought of Jonathan Edwards: An Essay in Aesthetics and Theological Ethics* (New Haven: Yale University Press, 1968), chaps. 7–8; Amy Plantinga Pauw, *"The Supreme Harmony of All": The Trinitarian Theology of Jonathan Edwards* (Grand Rapids: Eerdmans, 2002); Edward Farley, *Faith and Beauty: A Theological Aesthetic* (Aldershot, UK: Ashgate, 2001), chap. 4.

We recall the woman pouring expensive ointment over Jesus's head. Jesus rebukes his disciples for complaining: "She has done a beautiful thing to me" (Matt. 26:10 NIV). Her "giving everything" has been provoked by, and perhaps even in some manner shares in, the divine self-giving in and through Jesus.

6. For a thorough exposition of the Spirit in relation to beauty, see Patrick Sherry, *Spirit and Beauty: An Introduction to Theological Aesthetics* (London: SCM, 2002).

7. John Milbank, "Beauty and the Soul," in *Theological Perspectives on God and Beauty*, ed. John Milbank, Graham Ward, and Edith Wyschogrod (Harrisburg, PA: Trinity Press International, 2003), 1–34; Milbank, "Sublimity: The Modern Transcendent," in *Religion, Modernity and Postmodernity*, ed. Paul Heelas (Oxford: Blackwell, 1998), 258–84; Frederick Bauerschmidt, "Aesthetics: The Theological Sublime," in *Radical Orthodoxy: A New Theology* (London: Routledge, 1999), 201–19; Hart, *Beauty of the Infinite*, 43–93.

might experience under a starry sky or when suddenly faced with a mountain massif), or "dynamical," when we are overwhelmed by a power that makes us acutely aware of our own finitude and physical vulnerability (such as we might feel in a raging storm).[8] On this reading, it should be stressed, the sublime is unrepresentable to the senses and the imagination, and as such can provoke not only awe and wonderment but also unease and even terror. Beauty, by contrast, is radically tied to the ordering of the mind. The experience of beauty, for Kant, is the experience of the cognitive faculties of the imagination and the understanding engaging in free play.[9] The Milbankian argument is that, in its approach to beauty and sublimity, the logic of postmodernism is essentially Kantian.[10] Beauty is downplayed (even "annihilated") as formed, tame, ordered, and controllable, affecting us through harmony and proportion, whereas the sublime is extolled as formless, untamable, indeterminate, and uncontrollable. Transposed into theology, infinite divine transcendence is understood in terms of negation: "Modernity and postmodernity tend strictly to *substitute* sublimity for transcendence. This means that all that persists of transcendence is sheer unknowability or its quality of non-representability and non-depictability."[11] As such, the sublime is a *formless* divine presence,[12] devoid of love or goodness, and thus potentially oppressive.[13] In response to these lines of thinking, it is insisted that the sublime should never have been divorced from beauty in the first place, that *beauty* should be associated with infinity, but that since this infinity is none other than the infinity of the Trinity, this beauty is not formless or shapeless or wholly unrepresentable, but the formful beauty of intratrinitarian love revealed in Jesus Christ, and

8. Immanuel Kant, *Critique of the Power of Judgement*, trans. Paul Guyer and Eric Matthews (Cambridge: Cambridge University Press, 2000), 128–59. See Paul Crowther, *The Kantian Sublime: From Morality to Art* (Oxford: Oxford University Press, 1991).

9. Kant, *Critique of the Power of Judgement*, 89–127.

10. "Even when Kant's sublime is not directly invoked, its logic (at least, construed in a certain way) is always presumed." Hart, *Beauty of the Infinite*, 44–45.

11. Milbank, "Sublimity," 259 (italics original). According to Hart, the key metaphysical assumption is "that the unrepresentable *is*; more to the point, that the unrepresentable . . . is somehow truer than the representable (which necessarily dissembles it), more original, and qualitatively *other*; that is, it does not differ from the representable by virtue of a greater fullness and unity of those transcendental moments that constitute the world of appearance, but by virtue of its absolute difference, its dialectical or negative indeterminacy, its no-thingness." Hart, *Beauty of the Infinite*, 52.

12. "It is just this attempt at once to reconcile and preserve a presumed incompatibility between form and infinity that recurs, almost obsessively, in postmodern thought." Hart, *Beauty of the Infinite*, 47.

13. Hart argues that the entire pathology of the modern and postmodern can be diagnosed in terms of "narratives of the sublime": the differential sublime, the cosmological sublime, the ontological sublime, and the ethical sublime. Hart, *Beauty of the Infinite*, 52–93.

as such can never be oppressive or dehumanizing but only life-enhancing. To quote Rusty Reno, "We are not overpowered by God as a sublime truth; we are romanced by God as pure beauty."[14]

Keeping in mind this primary orientation to the Triune God, whose own life is primordially beautiful, we can now turn more specifically to created beauty—and at this stage we will concentrate on created beauty in the first of our two senses, the beauty of the world as created by God.

First, a theological account of created beauty will speak of creation as testifying to God's beauty but in its own distinctive ways. Much here turns on doing full justice to a double grain in Scripture's witness: the Creator's faithful commitment to the cosmos he has made, and his commitment to the cosmos in its otherness. Creation testifies to God's beauty, but in its own ways, or perhaps better, God testifies to his own beauty through creation's own beauty.

Let us consider each side of this in turn, beginning with God's irreversible dedication to all that he has fashioned, a dedication grounded in the intra-trinitarian love, "the love that moves the sun and the other stars" (Dante). Basic to this is the Creator's commitment to physical matter, something that blazes forth above all in the incarnation and resurrection of Jesus. This means spurning any gnosticism that devalues created beauty (including that of the body) on the grounds, say, of its physicality or out of a mistaken belief in the inherent formlessness of matter. We will resist treating physical beauty as something through which we ascend to immaterial beauty if this means leaving creation's physicality behind as supposedly lacking reality or essential goodness in the sight of God. Creation's beauty is not, so to speak, something that lives in a land beyond the sensual or behind the material particular or beneath the surface or wherever—to which we must travel. Creation's beauty is just that, the beauty *of creation*. The beauty of a coral reef *is* its endless variety, its comedy of color and patterned relations; its beautiful forms are the forms *of its matter*.

No less important, however, is acknowledging God's commitment to the flourishing of the world as other than God, this otherness arising from and testifying to the otherness of the trinitarian persons.[15] Creation is indeed "charged" with divine beauty because the Creator is at work through his

14. R. R. Reno, "Review of *The Beauty of the Infinite: The Aesthetics of Christian Truth* by David Bentley Hart," *Touchstone*, September 2004, www.touchstonemag.com/archives /article.php?id=17-07-048-b.

15. Hart, *Beauty of the Infinite*, 249–53, 272–73. Wolfhart Pannenberg is one of many who want to trace the roots of the distinctiveness of the created world from God in the differentia-tion of God's intratrinitarian life. See Wolfhart Pannenberg, *Systematic Theology*, vol. 2, trans. Geoffrey W. Bromiley (Grand Rapids: Eerdmans, 1994), 20–35.

Spirit bringing things to their proper end in relation to the Father through the Son. But it is charged in its own creaturely ways, according to its own rationality and ordering processes.

There is therefore no need to deny *a priori* that the beauty of creation can correspond to God's beauty, reflect and bear witness to it, but care is needed if we are to do justice to creation's integrity. Special caution is needed if we find ourselves thinking along Platonic lines: of God as the Form of beauty in which beautiful particular things participate. If we attempt to discern creaturely signs of God's beauty in creation, we should be careful not to do so on the basis of some presumed necessity that created beauty resemble God's beauty or resemble it in particular ways, but only on the basis of what God has actually warranted us to affirm by virtue of his particular and gracious acts, climaxing in Jesus Christ. The naïveté of assuming we may simply "read off" God's beauty from creation is most obvious when we are confronted with creation's corruptions and distortions (however we are to account for these), and when we forget that our perception of creation *as* reflecting God's beauty depends on the work of the Holy Spirit.

For these reasons, if we are to speak of creation's beauty "participating" in God's beauty (on the grounds of creation as a whole "participating" in God), we will do so with some hesitation, despite the popularity of this language in some circles.[16] John Webster has drawn attention to the hazards of the "participation" metaphor, especially insofar as it is allowed to carry inappropriate Platonic overtones; for instance, that we will overlook the irreducible Creator-creature distinction and the asymmetry of the God-world relation, that we will fail to understand God's ways with the world through the lens of the particular saving acts of God in the history of Israel and Jesus Christ, that we will forget that any capacity of the creation to reflect or witness to the Creator is graciously given by the Creator.[17] Nevertheless, it is not at all obvious that we need reject the model of participation altogether, for

16. The notion of participation is central to the Radical Orthodoxy movement, with its commitment to a rehabilitated, Christianized Platonism and its eagerness to overcome any implication that a part of created territory can be considered independently of God. However, it is far from clear that Radical Orthodoxy's notion of the "suspension of the material" in the divine can do justice to a biblical, dynamic ontology of grace that upholds the irreducible Creator-creature distinction. For discussion, see James K. A. Smith, *Introducing Radical Orthodoxy: Mapping a Post-Secular Theology* (Grand Rapids: Baker Academic, 2004), 74–77, 189–95; Smith, "Will the Real Plato Please Stand Up? Participation versus Incarnation," in *Radical Orthodoxy and the Reformed Tradition*, ed. James K. A. Smith and James H. Olthius (Grand Rapids: Baker Academic, 2005), 61–72; Adrienne Dengerink Chaplin, "The Invisible and the Sublime: From Participation to Reconciliation," in *Radical Orthodoxy and the Reformed Tradition*, 89–106.

17. Webster's objections to the language of participation as applied to humans' fellowship with God are succinctly presented in "The Church and the Perfection of God," in *The

arguably it can be employed in ways that highlight effectively the gracious, prior agency of God and the contingency of the world upon God's triune life, without falling into the traps Webster and others fear.[18]

Second, a theological account of created beauty will return repeatedly to Jesus Christ as the one in whom creation has reached its eschatological goal. If Christ is the measure of divine beauty, so also is he of created beauty. In Jesus Christ, divine beauty has, so to speak, come to grips with the wounded and deformed beauty of the world; in the incarnate Son, crucified, risen, and now exalted, we witness God's re-creation of the world's beauty. The one through whom all things are upheld (Heb. 1:3), by whom all things are held together (Col. 1:17), by whose blood all things are reconciled to God (Col. 1:20), is "the firstborn of all creation . . . the beginning, the firstborn from the dead" (Col. 1:15, 18), the one in whom all things will finally be gathered up (Eph. 1:10). In the risen and ascended Christ, creation's beauty has reached its culmination. Here we see physical matter transformed into the conditions of the age to come, granting us a preview of that age when the earth will be filled with the glory of God.

Third, a theological account of created beauty will return repeatedly to the Holy Spirit as the one who realizes now in our midst what has been achieved in the Son, thus anticipating the future.[19] A Christian account of created beauty is thus charged with promise. It is chiefly determined not by a sense of a paradise lost but of a glory yet to appear, the old beauty remade and transfigured, the beauty of the future that has already been embodied in Christ: "The beautiful

---

Community of the Word: Toward an Evangelical Ecclesiology, ed. Mark Husbands and Daniel J. Treier (Downers Grove, IL: InterVarsity Press, 2005), 91–92.

18. See the trenchant treatment of Calvin's handling of the theme in Julie Canlis, "Calvin, Osiander and Participation in God," *International Journal of Systematic Theology* 6, no. 2 (2004): 169–84; and the wider discussion of participation in relation to theological language to be found in Alan J. Torrance, *Persons in Communion: An Essay on Trinitarian Description and Human Participation* (Edinburgh: T&T Clark, 1996), chap. 5. The critical point is that the first and primary control on the semantics of participation should be the New Testament notion of *koinonia*, not the Platonic concept of *methexis* (the participation of particulars in eternal forms)—whatever wisdom may be justifiably gleaned from the latter notion. The huge issue lurking in the background here is that of the "analogy of being" (*analogia entis*), the analogical correspondences between divine and created reality, a notion that in various forms has exercised considerable influence on philosophies and theologies of beauty. For an exceptionally clearheaded treatment of this matter, see Torrance, *Persons in Communion*, 356–71. Torrance properly urges that we do not presume an ontological continuity between the divine and created realms that is conceptualized apart from and independently of God's self-revelation in Christ.

19. This dimension is brought out strongly in Eberhard Jüngel's penetrating essay on beauty, "'Even the Beautiful Must Die'—Beauty in the Light of Truth: Theological Observations on the Aesthetic Relation," in *Theological Essays II*, ed. John Webster (Edinburgh: T&T Clark, 1995), 59–82.

is only the pre-appearance of the coming truth. . . . [It] carries within itself
the *promise* of truth to come, a future *direct* encounter with truth. . . . The
beautiful is a *pre-appearance directed to a goal.*"[20] Here there is much to be said
for the ancient wisdom of Basil the Great (ca. 330–379) for whom the Holy
Spirit "perfects" creation, enabling it to flourish in anticipation of the final
future.[21] Beauty we apprehend now is a Spirit-given foretaste of the beauty still
to be given, in the midst of a creation that languishes in bondage to corruption, groans in anticipation of a glory not yet revealed (Rom. 8:20–22). Hence
the dazzling mountain scene that takes our breath away should provoke us
not to try to seize and freeze the moment but to give thanks and look ahead
to the beauty of the new heaven and the new earth, of which this world's
finest beauty is but a minuscule glimpse. We delight in the world's beauty *as*
we lament its transience. To borrow William Blake's words:

> He who binds to himself a joy
> Does the winged life destroy;
> But he who kisses the joy as it flies
> Lives in eternity's sunrise.[22]

What is true of joy is no less true of beauty.

Fourth, a theological account of created beauty, oriented to Christ and the
Spirit and thus to a trinitarian God, will delight in a diversity of particulars.
If beauty's integrity involves a "proportion of parts," these parts are just
that, distinct parts or particulars in a variety of relations with one another.
And these particulars, in order for beauty to be manifest, are not normally
identical but will manifest diversity as they relate to one another, at least
at some level. In Gerard Manley Hopkins's words, creation's beauty is a
"pied" beauty: "dappled things," "skies of couple-colour as a brinded cow,"
"rose-moles all in stipple upon trout that swim," "fresh-firecoal chestnut-falls;
finches' wings"—all these things "praise him."[23] Creation sings *laus Deo* in
and through its irreducible diversity of particularities. Here again the ministry of the Spirit comes to the fore. The Spirit is the "particularizer" (sadly,
something not seen strongly in Hopkins), unifying and uniting, certainly, but

20. Jüngel, "'Even the Beautiful Must Die,'" 76 (italics original).

21. See Sherry, *Spirit and Beauty*, chap. 7. For a recent treatment of the Holy Spirit as the one
who frees creation, see Sigurd Bergmann, *Creation Set Free: The Spirit as Liberator of Nature*,
trans. Douglas Stott (Grand Rapids: Eerdmans, 2005).

22. "Eternity," in *The Complete Poems*, ed. W. H. Stevenson, 2nd ed. (London: Longman,
1989), 189.

23. Gerard Manley Hopkins, "Pied Beauty" (1877), in *Poems and Prose*, ed. W. H. Gardner,
2nd ed. (London: Penguin, 1963), 30.

in so doing liberating things to be the particular things they are created to be. The beautiful unity that the Spirit generates is not one of homogenized harmony or bland replication but one in which the unique particularity of things is enabled and promoted; it is the Spirit's office "to realise the true being of each created thing by bringing it, through Christ, into saving relation with God the Father."[24] The wellspring of this is, of course, to be found in the Godhead, whose unified life is not monadic sameness or oneness more fundamental than the persons but a life of "particulars-in-relation," in which the Spirit (to use language that would need much qualification) "particularizes" Father and Son.

Fifth, a theological account of created beauty will be wary of closed harmonies. We may indeed articulate beauty in terms of proportion and perfection or integrity, but if beauty is to be thought and rethought out of a center in the being and acts of the Triune God, we will approach cautiously accounts of created beauty that interpret such notions primarily or exclusively in terms of balance, symmetry, and equivalence. As far as divine beauty is concerned, if the "measure" of beauty is self-dispossessing love for the sake of the other, we will need to come to terms with *excess* or *uncontainability*, for the intratrinitarian life is one of a ceaseless overflow of self-giving. There is still proportion and integrity, but it is the proportion and integrity of abundant love.

Creation, by grace, is given to share in this "excess"—indeed, creation's very existence is the result of the overflow of divine love—albeit in its own creaturely ways. So God's beautiful extravagance takes creaturely form in the oversupply of wine at Cana, the welcome Jesus shows to outcasts and sinners, the undeserved forgiveness in the first light of Easter Day. This is how creation's deformed beauty is remade, not by a repair or return to the beginning but by a re-creation exceeding all balance, by a love that is absurdly lavish and profligate, outstripping all requirement, overflowing beyond anything demanded or expected, generous beyond measure.

This in turn means taking creation's contingency seriously, giving due recognition to the unpredictable, to that which does not simply flow out of the past but which is nonetheless consistent and fruitful, to the new developments that God is constantly bringing forth from the world. Those working at the borderlands of contemporary science and theology have not been slow to engage with such ideas, giving rise to various proposals for a metaphysics of "contingent order."[25] Whatever weight we give to this or that emerging

24. Colin E. Gunton, *The One, the Three and the Many* (Cambridge: Cambridge University Press, 1993), 189. This is a strand of pneumatology explored fully in chap. 6 below.
25. For different examples, see T. F. Torrance, *Divine and Contingent Order* (Edinburgh: T&T Clark, 1998); J. C. Polkinghorne and Michael Welker, *The End of the World and the Ends*

cosmology, the widespread questioning of closed mechanistic models in the natural sciences should at least give us pause for thought. Once again, a danger lurking here is a defective account of the Holy Spirit, in which we describe the Spirit's role chiefly (solely?) in terms of effecting return and closure, as if completing a circle. This notion has the unfortunate effect of neglecting the Spirit's role as improviser, bringing about a faithful novelty, fresh improvisations consistent with what has been achieved "once and for all" in Christ.[26] The other great danger of overly harmonious models of beauty is that they will be ill equipped to take the evilness of evil seriously, its sheer irrationality (a matter I address in the next essay).

Sixth, an account of created beauty will recognize that beauty elicits desire—a desire to dwell with and enjoy that which we experience as beautiful. This links with those currents in the "great theory" that speak of beauty's brightness (and thus attraction) and the pleasure it affords upon contemplation. There is, of course, massive literature in Christian history on the attractiveness of God's beauty and the love and desire (*eros*) that God's beauty evokes in us. Understandably, many are nervous about the alliance of beauty and desire, especially in a theological context. From a philosophical perspective, those in the Kantian tradition will suspect that desire destroys aesthetics (and, indeed, ethics), for to allow "interest" a role in aesthetic enjoyment is to undermine its character as contemplative dispassion. From a theological perspective, a sharp contrast is sometimes made between desire and love, *eros* and *agape*, the former understood in an instrumentalist sense as possessive and consuming, the latter as a selfless self-giving for the sake of the other as other. To allow *eros* a place in Christian faith, it is said, is to open the door to the suppression of the other, to an inevitable violation of the other's integrity.

Much recent writing has sought to counter these suspicions.[27] Without space to enter a complex field, we can at least say the following. Just as the Triune God lives as an endless momentum of attraction and joy, so God makes

of God: Science and Theology on Eschatology (Harrisburg, PA: Trinity Press International, 2000), chap. 1; A. R. Peacocke, *Creation and the World of Science* (Oxford: Clarendon, 1979); Jean-Jacques Suurmond, *Word and Spirit at Play: Towards a Charismatic Theology* (Grand Rapids: Eerdmans, 1994).

26. In this regard, with respect to human history, Ben Quash makes some pointed critical comments about Balthasar, especially in relation to his theodramatics, questioning whether he has allowed the "epic" character of his thought to engender an approach to history that cannot do justice to contingency. Ben Quash, *Theology and the Drama of History* (Cambridge: Cambridge University Press, 2005).

27. See, e.g., Karl Barth, *Church Dogmatics*, trans. G. W. Bromiley and T. F. Torrance, III/2 (Edinburgh: T&T Clark, 1960), 279–85; Timothy Gorringe, *The Education of Desire: Towards a Theology of the Senses* (London: SCM, 2001); Paul D. L. Avis, *Eros and the Sacred* (London: SPCK, 1989); Hart, *Beauty of the Infinite*, 19–20, 188–92.

himself available not as an object for dispassionate scrutiny but through an overture of enticement, through which by the Spirit's agency we are made to long for God's presence, indeed, thirst for God. God "attracts our attention" by the outgoing Spirit, enabling us to respond, catching us up into the divine life. Indeed, can we not say that to experience the allure of God *is* nothing other than to experience the Spirit reconciling us to the Father through the Son and thus reordering our desires?[28] No wedge need be driven between *agape* and *eros* provided the latter is not allowed to introduce notions of subsuming the "other" under manipulative restraint; indeed, as David Bentley Hart puts it, God's love, and hence the love with which we come to love God, is "eros and agape at once: a desire for the other that delights in the distance of otherness."[29] As far as created beauty is concerned, beauty in the world that glorifies this God will also evoke desire—a yearning to explore and take pleasure in whatever is beautiful. There need be no shame in this provided our delight is delight in the other *as other*, and as long as we regularly recall that our love for God is the *cantus firmus* that enables all other desires to flourish.[30]

Bach and Created Beauty

With these theological bearings in mind, expressed all too briefly, we turn to the music of J. S. Bach (1685–1750). How might an engagement with Bach's music, especially as considered in its time and place, help us gain a clearer theological perception and understanding of created beauty—beauty of the sort we have just adumbrated? To avoid methodological confusion, two preliminary points need to be made. First, in an exercise of this sort, music cannot provide the controlling truth criteria; Bach's works do not and cannot be allowed to provide norms for beauty that are more ultimate or determinative than those given in the self-disclosure of the Triune God in Jesus Christ. Nevertheless, and this is the second point, it is quite legitimate to ask whether, *within* the theological orientation provided by these criteria (some of which we have just outlined), music might make its own unique contribution to the perception and understanding of created beauty. And this is my concern here. Such an approach depends on (1) acknowledging that music is an art that is irreducible to the verbal forms of theological discourse, yet (2) allowing for

28. Compare Balthasar, *Glory of the Lord*, 1:121. Balthasar is rightly eager to reshape certain Platonic and neoplatonic conceptions of *eros* in light of God's self-communication in the economy of salvation.
29. Hart, *Beauty of the Infinite*, 20.
30. Dietrich Bonhoeffer, *Letters and Papers from Prison* (London: SCM, 1972), 303.

the possibility that it might nevertheless be able to engage the realities with which that discourse deals, and in ways that afford genuine discovery and lead to fresh, truthful articulation of them.[31]

We can focus our concern by asking, first of all: What kind of cosmos, under God, might Bach's music provoke us to imagine, and thus what vision of created beauty? Is there anything to support Hart's bold claim that "Bach's is the ultimate Christian music; it reflects as no other human artefact ever has or could the Christian vision of creation"?[32]

To begin with, we need to clarify some of the features of the way this composer typically operates. Of special importance is something that Laurence Dreyfus has recently argued was central to Bach's art, namely, "invention" (*inventio*).[33] Many pianists' first introduction to Bach will be one of his two-part "inventions."[34] The composer tells us that these were designed to serve as models for "good inventions" and "developing the same satisfactorily." What does he mean?

The word *inventio* derives from classical rhetoric and in Bach's time was widely used as a metaphor for the basic musical idea, the unit of music that formed the subject matter of a piece. It could also denote the process of discovering that fundamental idea. The key for Bach was to find *generative* material, an idea that was capable of being developed in a variety of ways, for "by crafting a workable idea, one unlocks the door to a complete musical work."[35] So the method of finding an invention was inseparable from thinking about how it might be developed—*elaboratio*, to use the rhetorical term. Hence Bach's concern to show us models of good inventions *and* of their development.

So, for example, the first of the two-part inventions begins:

31. For discussion of what is entailed here, see Jeremy Begbie, *Theology, Music and Time* (Cambridge: Cambridge University Press, 2000), chap. 10; Begbie, "The Theological Potential of Music: A Response to Adrienne Dengerink Chaplin," *Christian Scholar's Review* 33, no. 1 (2003): 135–41.

32. Hart, *Beauty of the Infinite*, 283.

33. Laurence Dreyfus, *Bach and the Patterns of Invention* (Cambridge, MA: Harvard University Press, 2004).

34. See J. S. Bach, "Inventions and Sinfonias," *Aufrichtige Anleitung* (BWV 772–801).

35. Dreyfus, *Bach and the Patterns of Invention*, 2.

Section "A" marks an invention.[36] Bach has found that the opening figure of this invention can be turned upside down (inverted) in a musically convincing way. Thus the seven-note figure in the first measure

in the third measure becomes

Indeed, this inversion is itself part of a secondary invention (beginning in the third measure). Both these core inventions have been chosen with a view to what can be elaborated from them. They can be subjected very effectively to voice exchange, melodic inversion, switching from major to minor, and so forth—as Bach goes on to demonstrate. I cannot here trace all the elaborations displayed in this one piece.[37] What needs stressing, however, is Bach's intense interest and skill in this elaborative dimension. The evidence suggests that most of his contemporaries viewed *elaboratio* as among the least exciting parts of composing and could treat it almost casually. Bach appears to have thought about extensive elaboration from the start, when choosing the initial material. As Dreyfus puts it, "One might even be tempted to say that in Bach's works both invention and elaboration are marked by an almost equally intense mental activity. . . . In no other composer of the period does one find such a fanatical zeal directed so often toward what others considered the least interesting parts of a composition."[38] Indeed, Bach seems to have had an almost superhuman eye for how relatively simple sets of notes would combine, cohere, and behave in different groupings. His son, C. P. E. Bach, famously testified to how his father used to hear the main theme of a fugue played or sung by someone else, predict what would be done with it, and then elbow his son gleefully when he was proved right.[39] In short, as Christoph

36. An invention is thus not a "theme" in the modern sense of the word; in this case the invention includes the same theme played twice. An invention is the entire unit of music that will provide material for development.

37. For a full treatment, see Dreyfus, *Bach and the Patterns of Invention*, 10–26.

38. Dreyfus, *Bach and the Patterns of Invention*, 22, 24.

39. "When [J. S. Bach] listened to a rich and many-voiced fugue, he could soon say, after the first entries of the subjects, what contrapuntal devices it would be possible to apply, and which of them the composer by rights ought to apply, and on such occasions, when I was standing next to him, and he had voiced his surmises to me, he would joyfully nudge me when his expectations were fulfilled." C. P. E. Bach, in *The New Bach Reader: A Life of Johann Sebastian*

Wolff observes, the principle of elaboration, "determines like nothing else Bach's art and personal style."[40]

With these preliminary remarks about *inventio* and *elaboratio* in mind, we can begin to open up the theological dimensions of our inquiry by highlighting certain features typical of the musical fabric of a vast number of Bach's pieces.

First, we hear an elaboration governed not chiefly by an external, pre-given logic but first and foremost by the musical material itself. Dreyfus's research has shown that, whatever the precise order in which Bach composed a piece, it is highly inappropriate to envision him starting with a fixed, precise, and unalterable "form" and then proceeding to fill it with music; rather we would be better imagining him searching for inventions with rich potential and accordingly finding an appropriate form. In other words, this is an art in which the musical material is not forced into preconceived strict grids but structured according to the shapes that appear to be latent in it and thus apt for it. For Bach, we recall, *inventio* and *elaboratio* were the chief disciplines; *dispositio*—the disposition or arrangement of the elaborations in a particular order—was a subsidiary process (as was *decoratio*, the art of decorating or embellishing).[41] This is not, of course, to claim that Bach had only a passing interest in large-scale structure or that he never worked with basic formal outlines. The point is rather that he seems to be driven chiefly not by prior structural schemes that require strict adherence but far more by the local and specific material he handles. A fugue, for instance, turns out to be more like a texture with conventions than a PowerPoint template.[42]

This aspect of Bach has been obscured by some scholars' fascination with number schemes and mathematics. There is little doubt that Bach was greatly charmed by numbers, that he used some number symbolism in his music, and that some of this symbolism is theological.[43] But this fact has not only led some scholars to construct elaborate and fanciful theories on the flimsiest of

---

Bach in Letters and Documents, ed. Hans T. David, Arthur Mendel, and Christoph Wolff (New York: Norton, 1998), 396.

40. Christoph Wolff, *Johann Sebastian Bach: The Learned Musician* (New York: Norton, 2000), 469.

41. "If a passage was to be transformed several times during the course of a piece, Bach must have planned at least some of its transformations in advance." In other words, "there is every reason to suppose that he composed some of it *out of order*." Dreyfus, *Bach and the Patterns of Invention*, 13 (italics original).

42. This is why genre was far more important than large-scale form for Bach and why so many of Bach's pieces modify and even disrupt traditional forms; "form was seen . . . as an occasional feature of a genre, and not the general theoretical category subsuming the genres that it later became." Dreyfus, *Bach and the Patterns of Invention*, 28.

43. The "Sanctus" ("Holy, Holy, Holy") from the *Mass in B Minor*, to cite one instance, is pervaded with threeness. Calvin Stapert remarks: "If Bach did not use number symbolism,

evidence;[44] it has also led to a neglect of the extent to which Bach, even in his most "mathematical" pieces, includes material that is anything but mathematically elegant. For instance, although we find ample evidence in the *Goldberg Variations* of mathematical sequences and symmetries, these are interlaced with striking and surprising irregularity.[45]

In sum, Bach seems far more intent on exploring the logic and potential of the musical material in hand than being driven by extramusical schemes of organization.[46] If we allow this aspect of his music to provoke a vision of the creation as God's handiwork possessed of beauty, it is one in which creation is not, so to speak, a text that hides a more basic group of meanings. Rather than theological schemes in which forms are given an eternal status in God's mind,[47] or schemes in which God initially creates ideas or forms and then subsequently creates the world, or schemes in which matter is created first and then shaped into forms, is it not more true to the biblical affirmation of the goodness and integrity of creation to affirm that it is created directly out of nothing, such that it has its own appropriate forms, forms that God honors and enables to flourish as intrinsic to the matter itself?[48] This links directly to what I have said about creation possessing its own creaturely beauty to which the Creator is wholly committed; creaturely beauty testifies to God's trinitarian beauty, certainly, but in its own distinctive ways. Creation's forms are beautiful as the forms *of its material*; only

---

there are a remarkable number of remarkably apt coincidences in his music." Stapert, "Christus Victor: Bach's St. John Passion," *Reformed Journal* 39 (1989): 17.

44. Some, for example, hold that Bach frequently employs a number alphabet, each number corresponding to a letter, such that the number of notes, rests, bars, or whatever carry theologically coded messages or allusions. This notion has been roundly criticized, and in any case, the particular connections drawn between numbers and music in Bach are often of meager theological value. For further discussion, see Ruth Tatlow, *Bach and the Riddle of the Number Alphabet* (Cambridge: Cambridge University Press, 1991).

45. Williams helpfully lists some of them: "The opening and closing irregularity of the dance-arabesque-canon sequences; the sheer difference in musical genre between the movements, irrespective of their part in the sequence (e.g., whether or not they are canons); the exploring of both twos and threes, both to the ear and the eyes; the irregular placing of the minor variations and slow movements; the variety in the arabesques (not always two voices) and canons (not always threes); the absence of other symmetries that would have been easy to organize (e.g., if the canons at the perfect fourth and fifth are *inversus*, why not the canon at the perfect octave?)." Williams, *Bach*, 46.

46. To borrow some words of John Milbank on baroque music, "structural supports are . . . overrun by the designs they are supposed to contain." Milbank, *Theology and Social Theory: Beyond Secular Reason* (Oxford: Blackwell, 1990), 429.

47. See the perceptive discussion in Colin E. Gunton, *The Triune Creator: A Historical and Systematic Study* (Edinburgh: Edinburgh University Press, 1998), 77–79.

48. I am not, of course, suggesting that Bach was creating out of nothing; the point is about "working with the grain of the universe," seeing form as intrinsic to matter.

after acknowledging this can we ask how these might witness to the beauty of the Triune God.

Second, we are provoked to hear, in a way that has perhaps never been surpassed, difference as intrinsic to unity. Bach's skill in deriving so much music from such tiny musical units means that he can offer intense demonstrations of the simultaneous combination of extreme unity and extreme complexity. Indeed, Bach is adept at helping us perceive rich complexity *in* the apparently simple. In the *Goldberg Variations*, we are given thirty variations on a lyrical and stately sarabande. After an hour and a quarter of *elaboratio*, he asks for the aria to be played at the end, *da capo*, note for note. Now we cannot hear it apart from the memory of all the variations in which it has been elaborated. In other words, we now hear the aria *as* varied, full of light and shade, wit and sorrow. At this point, the aria, we might say, *is* its elaboration; it is not more real than its variations. (For Bach, we recall, *elaboratio* is no less important than the invention. If Dreyfus is right, Bach heard simplicity *as* elaborated simplicity.)

The links with our earlier theological material on creation's beauty—seen through the double lens of Christ and the Spirit—will be clear. The diverse particulars of creation are not an expansion of some more profound, more basic, uniform simplicity, any more than the threefoldness of the triune Creator is the expression of a more basic singularity. In Hart's words, "the 'theme' of creation is the gift of the whole."[49] And this diversity of particulars-in-unity is not negated in the new heaven and the new earth but there finds its full and final glory: the beauty of that endless day is surely the beauty not of one note but of an eternally proliferating polyphony.

Third, we are provoked to hear the simultaneous presence of radical openness and radical consistency. With almost any Bach piece—although perhaps most of all in the solo instrumental works—the music will sound astonishingly contingent, free of necessity. Not only does Bach constantly adapt and reshape the forms and styles he inherits; even within the constraints he sets for himself for a piece, there is a remarkable contingency—Peter Williams even uses the word "caprice" to describe this aspect of the *Goldberg Variations*.[50] There is a wildness about Bach's beauty.

For this reason, I have deliberately avoided the word "organic." Tempting as it might be to say that the elaborations organically emerge from the inventions like plants from seeds, there is in fact rarely anything organic about Bach's music—in the manner of a quasi-inevitable, smooth, continuous unfolding

49. Hart, *Beauty of the Infinite*, 282.
50. Williams, *Bach*, 46.

of an idea or motif. Dreyfus ruthlessly exposes the inappropriateness of "organicism" as applied to Bach, arguing that such a model is far too closed, too prone to the logic of necessity, suppressing the place of human agency and historical circumstance.[51] Even without demonstration of this sort, however, we can perform a simple experiment to grasp the point: listen to almost any of the pieces for solo violin, stop the recording midway through a movement, and unless one happens to know the piece well, it is virtually impossible to predict what comes next. Yet what is heard is filled with sense: "each note is an unforced, unnecessary, and yet wholly fitting supplement" to the one that has come before it.[52]

It is this enticing interplay between constraint and contingency that has enthralled so many Bach scholars and players. An 1805 review of the first edition of Bach's works for solo violin described these pieces as "perhaps the greatest example in any art form of a master's ability to move with freedom and assurance, even in chains."[53] Put differently, much of Bach's music sounds improvised. This quality was one of the things about Bach that so intrigued the nineteenth-century composer and virtuoso Franz Liszt (1811–1886)—who himself transcribed and arranged many of Bach's works[54]—and that captivates many jazz musicians. (It is no accident that Bach was a superb improviser.) Again, I hardly need to point out the links with what I said earlier about the danger in thinking of beauty in terms of "closed harmonies," about the particularizing, proliferating ministry of the Holy Spirit, effecting faithful but unpredictable improvisations on the harmony achieved in Jesus Christ.

Fourth, a closely related observation: we are provoked to hear the potential boundlessness of thematic development. Even at the end of the *Goldberg Variations*—to take one of numerous examples—the music is by no means structured toward giving the impression that it *has* to stop when it does. Although these pieces do involve mathematical structures that require specifically timed closures (both on the small and the large scale), as I noted earlier, there is much in the music that works against this. The logic seems to be open, as if the variations were only samples from a potentially limitless range of options. It is thus not surprising that some speak of a kind of infinity evoked in pieces of this sort. This would need careful qualification, but we might say,

51. Dreyfus, *Bach and the Patterns of Invention*, esp. chap. 6.
52. Hart, *Beauty of the Infinite*, 283.
53. *Jenaische Allgemeine Literaturzeitung* (1805), 282, quoted in Wolff, *Johann Sebastian Bach*, 471.
54. Martin Zenck, "Reinterpreting Bach in the Nineteenth and Twentieth Centuries," in *The Cambridge Companion to Bach*, ed. John Butt (Cambridge: Cambridge University Press, 1997), 228.

cautiously, that insofar as there is an evocation of infinity to be heard here, it is not the infinity of monotonous continuation but much more akin to the infinity of proliferating novelty, the ever-new and ever more elaborate richness and bounty generated by the Holy Spirit as creation shares in the excess of God's own abundant differentiated infinity, and this itself might be heard as a glimpse of the nontransient novelty of the future transformed creation, "in which new occurrences are added but nothing passes away."[55]

Fifth, Bach's music can provoke us to hear a beauty that can engage with and transform dissonance. I have already alluded to this aspect of creation's beauty, and I will say much more about it in the next essay. Here we need only note that one of the marvels of Bach is the way in which he treats dissonance, in some pieces exploring it to quite unprecedented and alarming degrees (such as the famous twenty-fifth variation of the *Goldberg Variations*), yet never in such a way as to grant it any kind of ultimacy.

Sixth and finally, to state the obvious, and picking up on our earlier point about beauty and desire, Bach's music, as a creaturely reality, has proved an endless source of delight for three hundred years; its beauty has a rare attraction, provoking a desire among millions to be "with" the music whether as listener, dancer, jogger, singer, player, or analyst.

Standing back, then, we ask, what kind of cosmos, under God, might this music provoke us to imagine, and thus what vision of created beauty? A cosmos and a vision, it would seem, highly congruent with the sort we brought into relief in the first part of this chapter. This is not to claim, of course, that all of Bach's music has this capacity—were the argument to be developed, we would need to be far more specific—nor is it to claim that no other composer's music could do similar things; nor is it to deny that features of some of Bach's music move in rather different directions. The claim is only that there is music here that can justifiably be said to embody some of the main features of a theological vision of created beauty and as such, in its own musical ways, help us perceive and understand that vision more deeply and clearly.

It may well be asked, if we are on the right lines, are the links merely fortuitous? Bach, after all, even if not remarkably or exceptionally devout, was a strong Lutheran, biblically well educated. Is there anything to suggest that he himself would have conceived his music as giving voice to creation's beauty, or indeed that this might have been part of what he intended? This kind of question, of course, is deeply unfashionable these days. And to demonstrate what Bach might have believed about his music does not of

---

55. Richard Bauckham, "Time and Eternity," in *God Will Be All in All: The Eschatology of Jürgen Moltmann*, ed. Richard Bauckham (Edinburgh: T&T Clark, 1999), 186.

itself imply that such beliefs are correct; as we are often reminded, "The road to hell is paved with authorial intention."[56] Nevertheless, here we need only register that even a modicum of historical-theological research in the case of Bach shows that our invitation to hear his music in a certain way does at least have historical propriety—it would not have been fanciful to Bach himself and may in some respects reflect his intention—and this can be highly illuminating.[57] For the linking of music and the cosmos at large was anything but foreign to the Lutheranism of his period. As Joyce Irwin has shown, among theologians the ancient tradition of seeing music as articulating the divinely gifted order of the cosmos may have weakened considerably by Bach's time, but among musicians it was by no means dead.[58] Although Bach was not a theorist or theologian of music (how interested he would have been in detailed metaphysics is moot),[59] there is plenty to suggest that the notion of music bringing to sound an engrained God-given cosmic beauty and thus offering "insight into the depths of the wisdom of the world" (words used on Bach's behalf)[60] would have been anything but foreign to him.[61] In this light it is not at all inappropriate to listen to the

56. The phrase comes from N. T. Wright, *The New Testament and the People of God* (London: SPCK, 1992), 55.

57. To those who cry "intentional fallacy" at this point, it is worth remembering that when William K. Wimsatt and Monroe C. Beardsley offered their classic exposition of the intentional fallacy, their main point was that the "intention of the author is neither available nor desirable as a standard for judging the success of a work of literary art." Wimsatt and Beardsley, "The Intentional Fallacy," in *The Verbal Icon: Studies in the Meaning of Poetry*, ed. W. K. Wimsatt (Lexington: University of Kentucky Press, 1954), 3. That is quite different from claiming that research into what a composer may have believed and intended is always doomed to failure or is invariably irrelevant to understanding or benefiting from a musical text. One of the refreshing things about Dreyfus's work is his refusal to be hidebound by theorists who turn limited, instructive insights into inflated, all-encompassing claims (the "death of the author" etc.). See Dreyfus, *Bach and the Patterns of Invention*, 171.

58. Joyce L. Irwin, *Neither Voice nor Heart Alone: German Lutheran Theology of Music in the Age of the Baroque* (New York: Peter Lang, 1993), esp. chaps. 4, 11.

59. Dreyfus, *Bach and the Patterns of Invention*, 9.

60. J. A. Birnbaum, quoted in Wolff, *Johann Sebastian Bach*, 338.

61. See John Butt, *Music Education and the Art of Performance in the German Baroque* (Cambridge: Cambridge University Press, 1994), 33; Wolff, *Johann Sebastian Bach*, 1–11, 465–72. For example, a much-quoted saying is attributed to Bach about the "thoroughbass," a foundational bass line with accompanying chords, very common in baroque music, that relates this device to the God-given created order. John Butt calls this a "late flowering of the Pythagorean view of well-composed music as natural harmony." Butt, "Bach's Metaphysics of Music," in *The Cambridge Companion to Bach*, ed. John Butt (Cambridge: Cambridge University Press, 1997), 46–71, here 54. Relevant also is the witness of J. A. Birnbaum, almost certainly acting as Bach's mouthpiece, who appeals to "the eternal rules of music" and of polyphonous music as an exemplar of the unity and diversity pervading the cosmos (Butt, "Bach's Metaphysics of Music," 55–58); Wolff, *Johann Sebastian Bach*, 5–6. (Some elements in the Birnbaum document,

forty-eight preludes and fugues of *The Well-Tempered Clavier*, for example, as a stunning exploration of the properties and possibilities of a God-given sonic order, for they are derived from that physical "universal" built into the physical world: the harmonic series.

Yet matters cannot be left there. The implication would be that all Bach is doing, or thinks he is doing, is bringing to light and representing the order of the natural world. It is patently obvious that he is doing much more. If he is eliciting creation's own beauty, he is doing so through an active process of making, principally through *inventio* and *elaboratio*, both of which are themselves constructive exercises, involving combining tones, making music. Inventions do not tumble out of nature like apples off a tree; they have to be worked at, constructed, and the elaborations likewise. Indeed, frequently we find Bach having to adjust the elaborations slightly to make them "fit" his constraints. Even at the very basic acoustic level, there are modifications: *The Well-Tempered Clavier* is indeed based on the twelve-note chromatic scale that does indeed derive from the "natural" fact of the harmonic series, but the scale he uses and the slightly differently tuned

---

however, suggest that he believes nature was sometimes *lacking* beauty, something that does not seem to trouble Wolff et al.) In 1747 Bach joined a learned group, the Corresponding Society of the Musical Sciences, one of whose members wrote: "God is a harmonic being. All harmony originates from his wise order and organisation. . . . Where there is no conformity, there is also no order, no beauty, and no perfection. For beauty and perfection consist in the conformity of diversity" (quoted in Wolff, *Johann Sebastian Bach*, 466). During his last years, Bach wrote music that would seem to be highly consonant with the theories current in this circle, especially that of music as "sounding mathematics"—e.g., the *Canonic Variations on "Vom Himmel hoch da komm ich her"* and most famously, the *Art of Fugue*. Malcolm Boyd, *Bach* (Oxford: Oxford University Press, 2000), 205–6.

Nevertheless, to align Bach closely with the rationalist cosmologies of the German Enlightenment, as some have attempted, is highly questionable. Recently, Wolff has contended that Bach's output is usefully interpreted in light of the concept of musical "perfection," a characteristically Enlightenment notion used in Birnbaum's defense of Bach. See Wolff, *Johann Sebastian Bach*, 466–67; see also John Butt, "'A Mind Unconscious That It Is Calculating?' Bach and the Rationalist Philosophy of Leibniz and Spinoza," in Butt, *Cambridge Companion to Bach*, 60–71; Ulrich Leisinger, "Forms and Functions of the Choral Movements in J. S. Bach's *St. Matthew Passion*," in *Bach Studies 2*, ed. Daniel R. Melamed (Cambridge: Cambridge University Press, 1995), 70–84. However, Dreyfus shows that these lines of argument pay insufficient attention to the role of human agency in Bach's practice—I have already spoken about the dangers of interpreting Bach in terms of closed systems. (See Dreyfus, *Bach and the Patterns of Invention*, 26–27, and chap. 8.) And the contention that Bach would have leaned heavily on Enlightenment thinkers such as Leibniz and Wolff I find unconvincing. (Even Leisinger has to admit that "no documentary evidence can be presented that Johann Sebastian Bach ever possessed or read any of Leibniz's or Wolff's treatises"; see "Forms and Functions," 84.) As far as aesthetics is concerned, Dreyfus argues that Bach is better understood as a subtle *critic* of Enlightenment thought than as a solid supporter of it (see *Bach and the Patterns of Invention*, chap. 8).

one we commonly use today are in fact adjustments, "temperings" of what nature has given us.[62]

In fact, Bach reshaped almost everything he touched, from simple motifs to whole styles and genres. He is one of the least passive composers in history. Thus we are led to the second main sense of created beauty I distinguished at the start: the beauty humans make. If cosmic beauty is being discovered and turned into sound by Bach, this happens *as* it is shaped and reshaped, formed and re-formed, through the ingenious use of a vast array of often highly sophisticated techniques.

We are thus confronted with perhaps the central paradox of a Christian view of creativity: in and through the act of strenuous making, we discover more fully what we have not made. The inability to hold these two together in our thinking—"given" beauty and "generated" beauty (in this case, artistic beauty)—the tendency to see them as inherently opposed, is, I submit, one of the cardinal marks of modernity, captivated as it has so often been by the notion of the godlike artist, forging order where supposedly none can be trusted or even found. Postmodernity has fared no better, typically collapsing given beauty into generated beauty without remainder (what beauty could there be except that which we construct?). Reactions to both of these visions sometimes take the form of a "return to nature," as if any modification of nature is to be seen as a corruption of it. But this trades on essentially the same competitive, binary outlook—human creativity as necessarily pitted against the natural world. Bach's music would seem to point us toward—and arguably embodies—a vision of the relation between given and artistic beauty that does not assume an intrinsic tussle between them. Significantly, Bach's obituary spoke of his "ingenious and unusual ideas" *and* his extraordinary grasp of the "hidden secrets of harmony" without so much as a hint that the two had to be at odds.[63]

This is why attempts to align Bach with the German Enlightenment's aesthetics of his day—with its ideals of transparency and representation, where music is thought to be best when it shows the least human artifice—are so questionable. Bach seems less interested in representing than he is in shaping his materials respectfully and *in that way* expanding our awareness of those materials, the world we live in, and our place in it.[64] At the same time,

62. For explanation, see Stuart Isacoff, *Temperament: How Music Became a Battleground for the Great Minds of Western Civilization* (New York: Alfred A. Knopf, 2001).

63. David, Mendel, and Wolff, *New Bach Reader*, 305.

64. This is arguably where Christoph Wolff goes astray (*Johann Sebastian Bach*). He acknowledges that Bach shows astonishing novelty and originality, but he is still overenamored with trying to show Bach's supposed indebtedness to certain Enlightenment notions of music's

though of course Bach was astonishingly "original," we should avoid interpreting him through the lens of the self-conscious creativity of the Romantic *Künstler*, the individual genius who mediates order to the world through his or her unique art.

What Bach's music provokes us to imagine, then, when set in its context is a subtle relationship between natural and artistic beauty, where the two are not seen as fundamentally incompatible, but where natural beauty is the inhabited environment, trusted and respected, in which artistic beauty is born, even if through sweat and struggle. The vision of making beauty is not one that sees the artist as striving for creation out of nothing, fashioning and foisting order where none is given, or pursuing a fetish for originality (a wholly underived act); still less is it one of defiantly challenging God.[65] But nor is it one in which we simply "let nature be," merely follow its resonances and rhythms the way one might follow a river through a valley or gaze at the grain of a piece of wood. The vision is rather of the artist, as physical and embodied, set in the midst of a God-given world vibrant with a dynamic beauty of its own, not simply "there" like a brute fact to be escaped or violently abused but there as a gift from a God of overflowing beauty, a gift for us to interact with vigorously, shape and reshape, form and transform, and in this way fashion something as consistent and dazzlingly novel as the *Goldberg Variations*, art that can anticipate the beauty previewed and promised in Jesus Christ.

---

transparency to nature's harmony and order, and with these the notion that Bach's elaboration is a quasi-scientific exploration and discovery of nature's beauty (fueled by a comparison with Newton that is probably more questionable than illuminating). For discussion, see John Butt, "The Saint Johann Sebastian Passion," *New Republic* 10 (2000): 33–38; and of the wider issues, Dreyfus, *Bach and the Patterns of Invention*, chap. 8.

65. In a review of Wolff's book, Edward Said suggests that Bach (however unconsciously) appears to be engaged in a kind of rivalry with God. Is there not a "cosmic musical ambition" here, Said asks, "epic" in nature, even "demonic," especially in the late pieces where the composer unleashes such an awesome array of creative powers that we are bound to question (or at least qualify) traditional views of Bach's devotion to and reverence for God? "One can't help wondering whether all the piety and expression of humility before God weren't also Bach's way of keeping something considerably darker—more exuberant, more hubristic, verging on the blasphemous—at bay." Edward Said, "Cosmic Ambition," *London Review of Books* 23, no. 14 (July 19, 2001): 13. Said does not seem to notice how anachronistic the guiding assumption behind this kind of suspicion is: Bach and most of his contemporaries would not have seen anything unusual in holding at one and the same time that God provides the already-structured materials for the composer *and* that this same God invites and delights *in* an energetic elaboration of these materials on the part of a composer. And why should we?

2

Beauty, Sentimentality, and the Arts

Beauty has often been associated with sentimentality, with perceptions of the world that evade or trivialize evil, with superficial emotion, and with the avoidance of costly action in the world. Developing the previous essay's christological and trinitarian focus, here I argue that if we are not to fall into these traps, at the deepest level a theological imagination of beauty will need to be shaped by the momentum of Good Friday, Holy Saturday, and Easter Day.

Beauty . . . disappeared not only from the advanced art of the 1960s, but from advanced philosophy of art of that decade as well. . . . [It] rarely came up in art periodicals from the 1960s without a deconstructionist snicker.

Arthur C. Danto, *The Abuse of Beauty*

Why the embarrassed chuckle so often heard when beauty is mentioned in the presence of art connoisseurs? Is this merely condescending elitism, a disdain for anything with popular appeal? "Beautiful" art, after all, sells very well. I suspect that in most cases, in the midst of the scoffing will be a

An earlier version of this chapter appears in *The Beauty of God*, ed. Daniel J. Treier, Mark Husbands, and Roger Lundin. Copyright © 2007 by Daniel J. Treier, Mark Husbands, and Roger Lundin. Used by permission of InterVarsity Press, P.O. Box 1400, Downers Grove, IL 60515, USA.

profound misgiving about beauty, and one we would do well not to brush aside—a suspicion of sentimentality to which beauty, it will often be assumed, inevitably opens the door. In this essay, I argue that sentimentality is neither a superficial nor an inconsequential matter but rather a deep, pernicious strand in contemporary culture and in the church, and that the arts have often played a leading part in encouraging it. However, I contend that though it may often be associated with beauty, the tie is not a necessary one. What I stressed in the previous essay needs to be restressed here: all depends on being prepared to think and rethink beauty in light of the acts and being of the Triune God. Doing so will mean paying particular attention to the narrative of Good Friday, Holy Saturday, and Easter Day. Only in this way can we disentangle the pursuit of beauty from sentimentality and, moreover, begin to discern how the arts might contribute to generating a counter-sentimentality in our day.

The Pathology of Sentimentality

First, we need to examine what sentimentality involves. There has been a flurry of philosophical writing on the theme in the last two or three decades,[1] including a major book,[2] and some treatments of it as a phenomenon of Western

1. Michael Tanner, "Sentimentality," *Proceedings of the Aristotelian Society* 77 (1976–1977): 127–47; Mary Midgley, "Brutality and Sentimentality," *Philosophy* 54 (1979): 385–89; Anthony Savile, *The Test of Time: An Essay in Philosophical Aesthetics* (Oxford: Oxford University Press, 1982), chap. 11; Mark Jefferson, "What Is Wrong with Sentimentality?," *Mind* 92 (1983): 519–29; Marcia Eaton, "Laughing at the Death of Little Nell: Sentimental Art and Sentimental People," *American Philosophical Quarterly* 26, no. 4 (1989): 269–82; Robert C. Solomon, "In Defense of Sentimentality," *Philosophy and Literature* 14 (1990): 304–23; "On Kitsch and Sentimentality," *Journal of Aesthetics and Art Criticism* 49, no. 1 (1991): 1–14; Anthony Savile, "Sentimentality," in *Arguing about Art*, ed. Alex Neill and Aaron Ridley (New York: McGraw Hill, 1995), 223–27; Joseph Kupfer, "The Sentimental Self," *Canadian Journal of Philosophy* 26, no. 4 (1996): 543–60; Deborah Knight, "Why We Enjoy Condemning Sentimentality: A Meta-Aesthetic Perspective," *Journal of Aesthetics and Art Criticism* 57, no. 4 (1999): 411–20; Ira Newman, "The Alleged Unwholesomeness of Sentimentality," in Neill and Ridley, *Arguing about Art*, 320–22. A classic earlier treatment can be found in I. A. Richards, *Practical Criticism: A Study of Literary Judgement* (London: Kegan Paul, Trench & Trubner, 1929), chap. 6.

2. Robert C. Solomon, *In Defense of Sentimentality* (Oxford: Oxford University Press, 2004). Solomon's concern is with defending not sentimentality as I understand it here but what he calls the "tender" emotions: pity, sympathy, fondness, adoration, compassion. The "minimal definition" of sentimentality that controls his discussion is "an expression of and appeal to the tender emotions." He explains: "My central argument, here and throughout this book, is that no conception of ethics can be adequate unless it takes into account such emotions, not as mere 'inclinations' but as an essential part of the substance of ethics itself" (9). According

cultural life.[3] Like beauty, it is a somewhat sprawling concept and is probably best understood as "the name of several kinds of disease of the feelings."[4] At the very least, I suggest it involves three major traits or elements, closely bound up with one another. I shall treat each of these traits primarily as they are manifested in people (since sentimentality is a phenomenon properly applied in the first instance to persons), and only secondarily as they are evident in the arts, in artistic practices and artworks. The sentimentalist, I shall argue, (1) misrepresents reality by evading or trivializing evil, (2) is emotionally self-indulgent, and (3) avoids appropriate costly action. Let us take each in turn.

The Evasion or Trivialization of Evil

The sentimentalist *misrepresents reality* by *evading or trivializing evil.*[5] It involves pretense, an attachment to a distorted set of beliefs, above all "the

---

to Solomon, the key weakness of standard attacks on sentimentality is a low view of emotion in general and of the tender emotions in particular.

This minimal construal of sentimentality is in many respects strange. I suspect that despite earlier uses of the word (when the term first emerged in the eighteenth century, it was a term of commendation), most today would understand sentimentality negatively, as an emotional pathology, not merely something that (in a nonevaluative way) denotes a particular field of emotions. (Deborah Knight argues, *pace* Ira Newman, that there can be no such thing as a purely, descriptive nonevaluative sense of sentimentality or laudable instances of sentimentality; see "Why We Enjoy Condemning Sentimentality," 414–15; Newman, "Alleged Unwholesomeness of Sentimentality.") As Knight rightly observes, "What Solomon wants to defend is not really sentimentality, but rather the sentiments, especially the gentle ones" ("Why We Enjoy Condemning Sentimentality," 417).

3. See, e.g., *Faking It: The Sentimentalisation of Modern Society*, ed. Digby Anderson and Peter Mullen (London: Penguin, 1998); and in effect on the same theme, Stjepan G. Mestrovic, *Postemotional Society* (London: SAGE, 1997).

4. Tanner, "Sentimentality," 140.

5. In my view, unless we see something akin to the evasion or trivialization of evil as belonging to the center of sentimentality, we are unlikely to get very far in understanding its dynamics, at least insofar as we are concerned with how the word is commonly used and understood. One of the striking features of the philosophical literature on sentimentality is that this aspect is regularly either bypassed or marginalized (even allowing for an understandable hesitation about using a word as strong as "evil"). Mark Jefferson is one of the exceptions ("What Is Wrong with Sentimentality?"). He rightly criticizes Mary Midgley's contention that it is the misrepresentation of reality for the sake of indulging emotion that makes sentimentality morally objectionable, regardless of the emotion being exercised ("the central offence lies in self-deception, in distorting reality to get a pretext for indulging *any* feeling" [Midgley, "Brutality and Sentimentality," 386]). What matters, says Jefferson, is what *kind* of misrepresentation we are speaking about: "The qualities that sentimentality imposes on its objects are the qualities of innocence." Jefferson, "What Is Wrong with Sentimentality?," 527. The editors of a somewhat controversial collection of essays, *Faking It*, are much blunter: "Most of all the sentimentalist is frightened by the idea that men have a natural capacity for evil. For to admit evil, and the will to evil, is to destroy his world which rests upon the supposition that utopia may be ushered in by the mere adoption of the right

fiction of innocence."[6] Unable to deal with the phenomenon of evil, innocence
is projected onto the world. So Anthony Savile speaks of sentimentality as the
"false-coloring" of an object: we see things, including human nature, through
rose-tinted spectacles.[7]

This disjunction from reality plays out in various ways. On the cultural
level, one of the most obvious examples is the Western doctrine of progress.[8]
A heady mix of economic growth and confidence, technological achievement,
medical advance, sometimes allied with various theories of biological development and a certain kind of Darwinism, has for many generated a climate
of thought that imagines a steady march of the human race toward freedom
and justice, sustained often by a childlike belief in Western innocence and the
basic common sense and goodness of humankind. I recall Professor Nicholas
Lash once remarking that it was hardly an exaggeration to say that Western
modernism (as a worldview) could be defined by the twin belief that humanity's deepest problems not only *can* be solved but eventually *will* be. But faced
with the horrors and terrors of history[9]—the vast quantities of pain, suffering,
and loss in the story of humankind (not least in modernity) and the fear of a
future that cannot be wholly predicted and controlled—this misrepresentation
of reality proves singularly ill equipped. Intractable and starkly irrational evil,
from Stalin's gulag to the rape of a twelve-week-old baby (reported on the
national news as I was writing this), exposes the bankruptcy of all schemes
that trade on the supposed increasing purity of human nature. Likewise, the
resistance of "Mother Nature" to attempts to tame her and her capacity to
be hostile and cruel toward us mock simplistic views of the world's harmony.

It is hardly surprising, then, to find that two very common ways of reacting
to evil or the will to evil (of whatever sort) are evasion and trivialization. Evasion involves selection; we restrict ourselves to the pleasing or nondisturbing
aspects of a situation and disregard the rest. For example:

> Western politicians knew perfectly well that al-Qaeda was a danger, but nobody
> took it too seriously until it was too late. Countries bordering the Indian Ocean
> knew about tsunamis, but hadn't bothered to install early warning systems.
> We all know that Third-World debt is a massive sore on the conscience of the

---

plan." Digby Anderson and Peter Mullen, "The Idea of a Fake Society: Introduction and
Summary," in *Faking It*, 5–6.

6. Jefferson, "What Is Wrong with Sentimentality?," 526.

7. Savile, "Sentimentality," 225.

8. See Peter Mullen, "All Feelings and No Doctrine: The Sentimentalisation of Religion,"
in *Faking It*, 9–10.

9. See Richard Bauckham and Trevor A. Hart, *Hope against Hope: Christian Eschatology
at the Turn of the Millennium* (Grand Rapids: Eerdmans, 1999), 10–20.

world, but our politicians don't want to take it too seriously, because from our point of view the world is progressing reasonably well and we don't want to rock the economic boat—or to upset powerful interests.[10]

Sometimes, this evasion goes with an exaggeration of what is good or pleasing, as when we insist on seeing someone's kindness as far greater than it actually is, or on the social level, when we overstate the advantages of economic growth or overplay the benefits of medical advance.

In the case of trivialization, the evil is acknowledged but in some manner deflated, rendered less angular or stark. The sentimentalist typically remarks, "They aren't that bad really" or "Things aren't that bad" when they actually are. There is a drive toward simplicity, reducing the complexities and ambiguities that evil brings in its wake. There is a tendency toward premature harmony: in some forms of theodicy (justifying God in the face of the existence of evil), for example, the pains and losses of the world are presented as necessary darkness in order that the light of goodness may shine.

Almost any piece of art can be used to serve the evasion or trivializing of evil (certainly not "popular" art alone, as is often thought), and sometimes the art will have formal features or content that encourage this.[11] It is almost impossible not to mention greeting cards in this connection, especially those that treat death as nothing but a friend in disguise, merely a door into "the next room" (Scott Holland). This carries forward the tradition represented by the account of the death of Little Nell in Charles Dickens's *The Old Curiosity Shop*, a passage that epitomized Victorian sentimentality for many later critics.

> Dickens would have us accept a child who is not only uncomplaining [in the face of death], but whose only displayed emotions are increasing earnestness and gratitude. . . . Even had he succeeded in avoiding trite phrases and images, Dickens could not write in a way that would convince us that death or the dying are like this, for they are not. . . . At the very least, the onlookers suffer.[12]

In the same circle of ideas, Robert Solomon cites a painting by Adolph Bouguereau (1825–1905), a portrait of two pretty little girls in rosy pink and soft pastels, set against an expansive sky ("Childhood Idyll"). He comments:

10. N. T. Wright, "God, 9/11, the Tsunami, and the New Problem of Evil," *Response*, Seattle Pacific University, www.spu.edu/depts/uc/response/summer2k5/features/evil.asp.

11. We ought to be hesitant about pointing to a piece of art and calling it "sentimental," since our interpretation and use of it *as* sentimental often depend hugely on matters of context—our state of mind and body, memories and associations, social and cultural conventions, and so forth. Nevertheless, we may justifiably speak of features of an artifact that lend themselves more readily to sentimental interpretation and use than others.

12. Marcia Eaton, "Laughing at the Death," 276.

These girls don't do any of the nasty things that little children do. They don't whine. They don't tease the cat. They don't hit each other. They don't have any bruises. They aren't going to die. The art gives us a false portrait, a carefully edited portrait that limits our vision and restricts our sense of reality. . . . Above all, there is no discomfort, no ugliness.[13]

I need not dwell on this aspect of sentimentality now, but I can at least anticipate our later discussion by quoting words from the end of George Steiner's intellectual autobiography, *Errata*. Writing as one who struggles to believe in God, he finds he is engulfed by a sense of the evilness of evil, of some calamitous "break" with goodness:

There are those who tear out the eyes of living children, who shoot children in the eyes, who beat animals across their eyes. These facts overwhelm me with desolate loathing. . . . At the maddening centre of despair is the insistent instinct—again, I can put it no other way—of a broken contract. Of an appalling and specific cataclysm. In the futile scream of the child, in the mute agony of the tortured animal, sounds the "background noise" of a horror after creation. . . . Something—how helpless language can be—has gone hideously wrong. . . . I am possessed, as by a midnight clarity, by the intuition of the Fall. Only some such happening, irretrievable to reason, can make intelligible, though always near to unbearable, the actualities of our history on this wasted earth.[14]

Emotional Self-Indulgence

Evading or trivializing evil does not, however, amount to sentimentality. Sentimentality is, after all, an emotional pathology. And so to the second trait: typically, the sentimentalist is *emotionally self-indulgent*. Emotion is exercised according to the misrepresentation of reality I have just described and, at least in part, for the pleasure of exercising the emotion (whether through active deliberation or more passively).[15] Milan Kundera's much-cited definition of kitsch captures this well:

Kitsch causes two tears to flow in quick succession. The first tear says: How nice to see children running on the grass!

13. Solomon, "On Kitsch and Sentimentality," 5.
14. George Steiner, *Errata: An Examined Life* (London: Phoenix, 1997), 168–69.
15. Hence Mary Midgley's claim that being sentimental is "misinterpreting the world in order to indulge our feelings." Midgley, "Brutality and Sentimentality," 521. Compare Karsten Harries: "Kitsch creates illusion for the sake of self-enjoyment"; love is kitsch "if love has its center not in the beloved but within itself. Kitsch creates illusion for the sake of self-enjoyment." Harries, *The Meaning of Modern Art* (Evanston, IL: Northwestern University Press, 1968), 80.

> The second tear says: How nice to be moved, together with all mankind, by
> children running on the grass!
>   It is the second tear that makes kitsch kitsch.[16]

In other words, sentimentalists appear to be moved by something or someone beyond themselves but are to a large extent (perhaps primarily) concerned
with the satisfaction gained in exercising their emotions. (It is worth adding
that part of this satisfaction comes from knowing the impression the emotion
makes on others. We like others to realize that we are compassionate, tender,
and so forth. And even if others are not around, there can be something deeply
gratifying about exercising feelings that most would admire.)[17]
    This explains why the sentimentalist cannot engage in depth with another's
pain *as pain* (hence the strong link some see between sentimentality and
cruelty)[18] or face up to another's negative features. We only need think of the
friend who flatters us ceaselessly, regardless of our glaring faults, enjoying the
pleasure it affords, or the obsessive counselor, often found in churches, waiting
to descend on someone in crisis in order to feed his or her own emotional need
to be needed. Inasmuch as sentimentality is directed at other people, the other
person becomes a means to an end—he or she is absorbed into the subjectivity
of the sentimentalist. The sentimentalist loves or hates, grieves or pities not
for the sake of the other but for the sake of enjoying love, hate, grief, or pity.
    In much discussion of sentimentality, it is presumed that the emotions
indulged in this way are tender—pity, sympathy, fondness, and so on. But

16. Milan Kundera, *The Unbearable Lightness of Being* (New York: Harper & Row, 1984),
251. Kitsch is normally regarded as sentimental, but there is much sentimental art that would
not be labeled "kitsch" (some of Dickens, for example). Kitsch has a shorter history than
sentimentality and would seem to be tied to certain socioeconomic conditions associated with
the Industrial Revolution and modernization, e.g., mass production, technological progress,
urbanization, and the influx of peasant populations to the towns; and to romanticism, e.g.,
a stress on the dramatic, on pathos, immediate emotional appeal, and so forth. For further
discussion, see especially Thomas Kulka, *Kitsch and Art* (University Park: Pennsylvania State
University Press, 1996). See also Hermann Broch, "Notes on the Problem of Kitsch," in *Kitsch:
The World of Bad Taste*, ed. Gillo Dorfles (New York: Universe Books, 1968), 49–76; Gillo
Dorfles, *Kitsch: An Anthology of Bad Taste* (London: Studio Vista, 1968); Kathleen Higgins,
"Sweet Kitsch," in *The Philosophy of the Visual Arts*, ed. Philip Alperson (Oxford: Oxford
University Press, 1990), 568–81; Solomon, "On Kitsch and Sentimentality"; Betty Spackman,
A Profound Weakness: Christians and Kitsch (Carlisle, UK: Piquant, 2005).
    17. See Patrick West, *Conspicuous Compassion: Why Sometimes It Really Is Cruel to Be
Kind* (London: Civitas, 2004). "Sentimental emotions are *artefacts*: they are designed to cast
credit on the one who claims them. The sentimentalist is courting admiration and sympathy.
That is why there is sentimental love, sentimental indignation, sentimental grief and sympathy;
but not sentimental malice, spite, envy or depression, since these are feelings no-one admires."
Roger Scruton, *The Aesthetics of Music* (Oxford: Clarendon, 1997), 486 (italics original).
    18. Tanner, "Sentimentality," 143–44.

sentimentality can also implicate the harsher emotions—anger and rage, for example.[19] This might seem odd at first, given that the sentimentalist supposedly evades or trivializes evil. If we feel fury when we see an innocent mother in East Africa unable to feed her children because her country is torn apart by civil war, how can this be sentimental? The answer is: insofar as we are more concerned with indulging the anger than the plight of the woman and her family, and especially insofar as we take no action to alleviate her suffering. Indeed, sentimentalists show their true colors when they make it clear that they do not want the object of anger to be removed (think of the committee member who *has* to have someone to oppose and who is disappointed when people start getting on with one another).[20]

Again, the arts can easily be drawn into this process. To take only one example, a certain kind of art seems to "wallow"—as the saying goes—in some negative emotional field and perhaps encourages us to do the same. Some might cite the grief of the last movement of Tchaikovsky's Sixth (*Pathétique*) Symphony in this regard. Here, arguably, an emotional field is being rehearsed and churned over to the point that it becomes more important than anything toward which it could ever be directed, perhaps even all-consuming. The same kind of thing can happen to almost any art. In a book about romantic love in contemporary North America, Laura Smit writes of the results of interviews she conducted as part of her research:

> Sometimes music [was] used not as a tool for moving on but rather as a tool for remaining in the pathos of the painful experience, for reliving the rejection, for keeping alive a fantasy that should have been allowed to die. One woman told of the pain she experienced during her senior year in high school when the boy she was in love with began to date her best friend. She listened to a particular CD over and over, and now, she says, "I really can't listen to it without feeling like it's the spring of graduation year."[21]

The Absence of Costly Action

We may distinguish a third element in sentimentality: the sentimentalist *fails to take appropriate costly action.* Because her emotional engagement is

19. See, e.g., Savile, *Test of Time*, 223–27.

20. Patrick West writes of the way crowds gather outside the courts that try alleged child murderers. "Two children had been murdered and people were at Peterborough, ostensibly, to express their anger at this crime. Yet it suspiciously appeared to be an excuse for a good, adrenaline-fueled day out—a chance to prove one's 'human' credentials in the comfort of the crowd." West, *Conspicuous Compassion*, 16.

21. Laura A. Smit, *Loves Me, Loves Me Not: The Ethics of Unrequited Love* (Grand Rapids: Baker Academic, 2005), 165.

not with reality X but a falsification of reality X and to a large extent for the pleasure of exercising the emotion, it cannot generate action that is appropriate to reality X. To echo Oscar Wilde, the sentimentalist wants emotion on the cheap, the pleasure of an active emotional life without the price.[22] In this light a number of characteristics associated with sentimental people quickly make sense. Sentimentalists typically resist any challenge to their way of life.[23] They are more often moved by strangers than by those close to them since the former require no personal sacrifice.[24] They feel at home with ethical generalities (love, peace, justice, etc.) but struggle with the demands of awkward individuals. (Recall Linus: "I love mankind; it's people I can't stand.")[25] They are classically impatient; the cost of long-term commitment to someone in pain, for example, is just too great.[26] They display righteous indignation at a picture of a child dying of AIDS but will do nothing about it. The sentimentalist will rely on routine banalities and clichés ("I'll always be there for you"; "you know you mean more to me than anyone else") since it takes too much time and effort to find just the right words for this or that particular person.

This aspect of sentimentality also has its cultural forms. The Croatian sociologist Stjepan Mestrovic has described the postmodern condition as "postemotional."[27] Drawing on the works of David Riesman, Émile Durkheim, George Ritzer, George Orwell, and others, he contends that emotions are the primary object of manipulation in postmodern culture. Emotion has increasingly been divorced from the intellect and judgment, and thus from responsible *action*: "postemotional types," as he puts it,

> know that they can experience the full range of emotions in any field, domestic or international, and never be called upon to demonstrate the authenticity of their emotions in *commitment* to appropriate action. . . . Today, everyone knows that emotions carry no burden, no responsibility to act, and above all, that emotions of any sort are accessible to nearly everyone.[28]

22. The sentimentalist "desires to have the luxury of an emotion without paying for it. . . . They always try to get their emotions on credit, and refuse to pay the bill when it comes in." Oscar Wilde, "Letter to Lord Alfred Douglas," in *The Letters of Oscar Wilde*, ed. Rupert Hart-Davis (London: Hart-Davis, 1962), 501.
23. "In appreciating a sentimental ideal we are able to enjoy ourselves, just as we are, without challenge to our beliefs, values, or patterns of emotional response." Kupfer, "Sentimental Self," 546–47.
24. Scruton, *Aesthetics of Music*, 486.
25. "Sentimentality . . . steers us away from the twists and turns of particularity toward the bold line of generality." Kupfer, "Sentimental Self," 549.
26. Sentimentality is a "creed for people with no patience." Anderson and Mullen, "Idea of a Fake Society," 10.
27. Mestrovic, *Postemotional Society*.
28. Mestrovic, *Postemotional Society*, 56 (italics original).

Emotions are thus eviscerated of their power: "Postemotionalism refers to the use of *dead*, abstracted emotions by the culture industry in a neo-Orwellian, mechanical, and petrified manner."[29] Mestrovic speaks about our society's love of staged "collective effervescence" (Durkheim), alluding to phenomena such as the O. J. Simpson trial[30] (though *The Jerry Springer Show* might come more quickly to mind). Though Mestrovic's book appeared too early to note it, the reaction to the death of Princess Diana in 1997 is hard to avoid mentioning here: an upsurge of "conspicuous compassion" that led to very little in the way of positive, practical action.[31] In any case, Mestrovic believes that postemotionalism opens the way to manipulation by the unscrupulous on a vast scale, to a totalitarianism that is "so 'nice' and charming that it cannot lead to indignation or rebellion."[32]

Once again, it is not hard to see how the arts can be pulled into these dynamics. The arts have been and still are widely used to offer a rich emotional experience that will screen out the darker dimensions of life and thus prevent certain forms of action, turning the aesthetic into an anesthetic, so to speak.[33] This may be legitimate in some contexts, but in others it can take cruel and heartless forms. Classic examples are William James's depiction of a wealthy matron shedding tears at the plight of characters on stage while her servants freeze outside, or Auschwitz commandant Rudolf Hoess weeping at the opera staged by condemned Jewish prisoners (needless to say, weeping over the characters portrayed, not the performers). Most macabre of all, perhaps, is the thought of the camp band at Auschwitz playing Schubert marches for the arriving truckloads of Jews, deceiving the newcomers into thinking they were entering some kind of pleasure camp.[34] Indeed, the links between the arts, sentimentality, and totalitarianism can be very strong, something

29. Mestrovic, *Postemotional Society*, 26 (italics original).

30. Mestrovic, *Postemotional Society*, 5, 11, 56.

31. West, *Conspicuous Compassion* (esp. chap. 2). The most notorious treatment of the Diana phenomenon as sentimental ("the elevation of feeling, image and spontaneity over reason, reality and restraint") is that by Anthony O'Hear. O'Hear, "Diana, Queen of Hearts," in *Faking It*, 181–90. Some have argued that the outpouring of emotion at events like this may signal genuine emotional distress at deeper levels; gestures such as lighting candles en masse could be read as reactions to a sense of powerlessness felt by many in the face of life's "tragic" dimensions. Perhaps, but I am not convinced that this significantly weakens the case of those who see such phenomena as potent and concentrated expressions of sentimentality.

32. Mestrovic, *Postemotional Society*, 146.

33. Knight, "Why We Enjoy Condemning Sentimentality," 417.

34. Fania Fenelon and Marcelle Routier, *The Musicians of Auschwitz*, trans. Judith Landry (London: Joseph, 1977); Guido Fackler, "'Des Lagers Stimme': Musik in den frühen Konzentrationslagern des NS-Regimes (1933–1936)" (PhD diss., University of Freiburg, 1997); Fackler, "Musik im Konzentrationslager," *Informationen* 20, no. 41 (1997): 25–33.

alluded to by Mestrovic and highlighted by many others. To spotlight an example, during the rise of the Third Reich in the 1930s, one might imagine the radio waves being filled with rousing songs and upbeat patriotic marches. In fact, it seems that much of the music broadcast was light music, typified by syrupy love songs akin to the cliché-ridden material that dulled people to the bleakness of the Weimar Republic—an ideal sugarcoating for the cruel propaganda broadcast with it.[35]

Sentimentality in Christian Worship

Enough has been said, I hope, to show that sentimentality, far from being a trifling matter, can constitute a "deep threat"[36] in culture at large and in the arts and thus "deserves to be taken more seriously than it takes itself."[37]

It would be tempting for the church to distance itself from the currents we have traced, but Christians have been implicated in them as much as any others and not slow to deploy the arts in the process.[38] It is likely that "Christian kitsch" will come to mind, especially in the visual arts. Betty Spackman has recently offered an impressive treatment of this phenomenon, showing how it involves economics, class, and culture as much as any formal properties of the art itself. She stresses that kitsch is frequently the vehicle of deep and heartfelt faith (hence her title, *A Profound Weakness*)—quick dismissals are

35. Peter Wicke, "Sentimentality and High Pathos: Popular Music in Fascist Germany," *Popular Music* 5 (1985): 149–58, www.tagg.org/others/pw3reich.html. See also Saul Friedlander, *Reflections of Nazism: Essay on Kitsch and Death* (New York: Harper & Row, 1984). It might well be asked, does not all art to some extent fictionalize reality, distance us from the "real" world to the detriment of costly involvement with it? In Nicholas Wolterstorff's words, we can easily begin to "prize the world of a work of art for its falsehood in various respects to what we believe actuality to be like. We want for a while to burrow into a world significantly different from our actual world. We want for a while to escape the drudgery and the pain, the boredom, perplexity, and disorder of real life." Nicholas Wolterstorff, *Art in Action: Toward a Christian Aesthetic* (Grand Rapids: Eerdmans, 1980), 147. The arts do indeed "frame" things artificially, and they do frequently encourage us to envision or imagine a world distinct from the actual world. However, this process does not necessarily mean we are thereby drawn irrevocably away from the truth of that actual world and from responsible action in it. Even in fiction, "*by way of* fictionally projecting his distinct world the fictioneer may make a claim, true or false as the case may be, about our actual world." Wolterstorff, *Art in Action*, 125 (italics original). Does not the best and most enduring "fantasy" art take us out of ourselves *in order* that we may "return" to a deeper appreciation of the reality in which we have our ordinary existence and thus, where appropriate, to a deeper sense of ethical obligation?

36. Kupfer, "Sentimental Self," 545.

37. Tanner, "Sentimentality," 146.

38. For a somewhat extreme attack on sentimentality in contemporary Christianity, see Mullen, "All Feelings and No Doctrine," chap. 6.

out of place. Nonetheless, it is not hard to see links between much of the art she discusses and the strands of sentimentality we have marked out above.

Here I restrict myself to a few brief comments about another field, music in worship. Over the last thirty years or so, in many churches we have witnessed a burgeoning of a certain kind of devotional song, often directed to the risen Christ: a direct and unadorned expression of love, with music that is metrically regular, harmonically warm and reassuring, easily accessible, and singable. It would be disingenuous to seek to exclude these songs from worship on the grounds of their aesthetic simplicity. The New Testament witnesses to the joy of an intimate union with Christ, and most Christian traditions have quite properly found room in their worship for such heartfelt adoration. However, questions have to be asked if it is assumed that this kind of song exhausts the possibilities of "singing to Jesus" or if these sentiments are isolated from other dimensions of relating to him. Devotion to Jesus, after all, entails being changed into his likeness by the Spirit—a costly and painful process. It certainly involves discovering the embrace of Jesus's Father, Abba, but this is the Father we are called to obey as we are loved by him, the Father who judges us just because he loves us, and the Father who at salvation's critical hour was sensed by his Son as one who can forsake the beloved. If we ignore this wider trinitarian field, we are too easily left with a Jesuology that has ignored Jesus as the incarnate Son of the Father, left no room for the wide range of the Spirit's ministries, and encouraged us to tug Jesus into the vortex of our self-defined (emotional) need. Rowan Williams, while very sympathetic to much contemporary songwriting, writes about the dangers of what he calls "sentimental solipsism," where the erotic metaphors of medieval and Counter-Reformation piety reappear but without the theological checks and balances of those older traditions, where "Jesus as object of loving devotion can slip into Jesus as fantasy partner in a dream of emotional fulfilment."[39]

These comments should not be taken as a wholesale attack on this or that style of worship (in fact, most traditions have fallen into these traps at some stage). But our three strands of sentimentality are not that hard to detect in this genre, whatever particular form it takes. In a quite proper concern for intimacy with God through Jesus, reality can be misrepresented (the first strand); if sin is evaded and trivialized, God is shorn of his freedom and disruptive judgment and taken hostage to my emotional requirements. Most

---

39. Rowan Williams, "A History of Faith in Jesus," in *The Cambridge Companion to Jesus*, ed. Markus Bockmuehl (Cambridge: Cambridge University Press, 2001), 231. For a very fine, balanced treatment of these matters, see Robin Parry, *Worshipping Trinity: Coming Back to the Heart of Worship* (Cambridge: Lutterworth, 2013).

of us have attended services where we were invited to experience through music what Colin Gunton used to call "compulsory joy"—perhaps authentic for some on certain occasions but often disturbingly out of touch with what others have to endure in a world so obviously far from its final joy, the very world Christ came to redeem. Most of us have experienced worship services where music has been deployed as a narcotic, blurring the jagged memories of the day-to-day world, rather than as a means by which the Holy Spirit can engage those memories and begin to heal them. Emotional self-indulgence (the second strand) I have said enough about already. The failure to take appropriate costly action (the third strand) is sadly all too evident among those of us who sing most loudly. Comforting and immediately reassuring music may have its place, but something is amiss if this is the *only* function music is called on to exercise. A widespread dependence on musical clichés in the church should also give us pause for thought, even if there is a quite proper place for borrowing familiar idioms.[40] When Amos attacked music (Amos 5:23–24), he did so because it was (so to speak) too easy, blinding God's people to the downtrodden in their midst. We would do well to have Bonhoeffer's words (uttered in the midst of a racist regime) ringing in our ears: "Only he who cries out for the Jews may sing Gregorian chants."[41]

Sentimentality and Beauty

But what of the relation between sentimentality and beauty? I began by observing that for many people beauty is ineradicably associated with sentimentality. Why should this be? The reasons are many, but it is worth singling out three. First, the pursuit of beauty is suspected as an offense against truth, encouraging a lie in the midst of a world so obviously *not* beautiful. Reality, in other words, is misrepresented by evading the truth about evil. The artist Thomas Kinkade may say, "I like to portray a world without the Fall,"[42] but we know such a world is a daydream. The symphony with its closing fortissimo major chords, it is said, plays out the deceit of a harmonious reconciliation beyond

40. Kathleen Higgins writes of the way kitsch typically depends on "icons" that guarantee a wholly predictable and instant response—elements or symbols that conjure up a cultural "archetype" of beliefs and desires. Higgins, "Sweet Kitsch," 572. This is precisely how numerous chord changes and riffs function in much worship music.

41. Dietrich Bonhoeffer, quoted in Eberhard Bethge, *Dietrich Bonhoeffer: A Biography* (Minneapolis: Fortress, 2000), 607.

42. Thomas Kinkade, quoted in Gregory Woolfe, "Editorial Statement: The Painter of Lite™," *Image* 34 (2002): 5. Woolfe rightly says, "In refusing to see the world as it is, sentimentality reduces hope to nostalgia," that is, the longing for a supposedly pre-fallen state (6).

life's conflicts.[43] We know enough now to be certain that the entire space-time continuum is heading for a bleak and empty future. Beauty with a capital B, in the arts as much as anywhere else, is an illusory consolation—our quest for it springs from a primal human urge for order in a world we cannot bear to admit is destined for futility. When attempted in art, it raises hopes where none should be had. Thus many will claim it is best to be done with beauty's beguiling deception, give up the pretense of a necessary link between beauty and truth, and allow art to awaken us to a cosmos in turmoil with a hopeless future.

Second, the pursuit of beauty is suspected as an offense against goodness, in that it distracts us from our ethical obligations to others in need and distracts those unjustly suffering from the wrongness of their plight. In other words, it is thought to misrepresent reality by encouraging an evasion of the evils that cry out for action. In the hands of the powerful and comfortable, the love of beauty is a luxury that screens out the world's victims, muffles the howl of those who know little or no beauty. Or, from the other side, beauty dulls the oppressed to the injustice of their predicament—an opiate of the people. "Sing your spirituals of heaven," the slave owners urged, as they tightened the chains for the night. This suspicion of beauty has become a shrill cry in our time. Striving for beauty in art becomes nothing less than a moral crime, equivalent to being shown photos of 9/11 and remarking on what lovely weather it was that day. Artists, it is said, are best to be done with beauty's attendant immorality, deny its supposed ties with goodness, and devote their energies to keeping society ethically vigilant.

These two suspicions we have touched on already. But there is a third and subtler one: beauty is suspected as "harmonizing away" the evilness of evil (thus trivializing it). This suspicion concerns the way beauty is conceptualized. There is a distrust of notions of beauty in which the ideas of balance, symmetry, and equivalence predominate and in some manner incorporate evil accordingly, so that evil's irrational, intrusive quality is suppressed. At worst, evil is included within a closed metaphysics of necessity. Put theologically, it can be suggested that God has eternally desired the history of sin and death as the necessary way of achieving his ends, that evil is an essential component

---

43. It is significant that this cynicism is quickly read back into artists who may not have shared it themselves. A good example is the rush toward "ironic" interpretations of the last movement of Beethoven's Ninth Symphony (e.g., Nicholas Cook, Maynard Solomon). It is supposed that Beethoven could not possibly have been concerned with evoking a sense of joyful triumph after struggle, so we are offered strained readings of Beethoven's joy as supposedly interlaced with a profound hesitation before an "absent God." For a fine discussion of this argument, see Anthony Monti, *A Natural Theology of the Arts: Imprint of the Spirit* (Aldershot, UK: Ashgate, 2003), 148–51.

in the unfolding of history's texture—in short, that beauty is not possible without evil.[44] The consequences for the doctrine of God can be stated very bluntly: either God stands apart from good and evil (and is thus essentially amoral) or to some degree God is evil, perhaps even wholly evil.

Here, all who warm to the metaphysics of German idealism, especially Hegel, or to theologies of creation relying on total systematic consistency need to be acutely wary of the dangers of constructing "aesthetic totality" theodicies. Even John Hick, who is often singled out for succumbing to this, highlights the weaknesses of "the aesthetic theme" in Augustine's theodicy,[45] a critique mounted much more carefully by Balthasar.[46] Anselm's justification of hell in *Cur Deus Homo* has been attacked along similar lines.[47] It is one thing to claim that God can and does bring good out of evil, that sin and death can be taken up to serve God's gracious purpose; it is quite another to imagine that in the eschaton we will look back on some event of mindless cruelty in history and say, "Now, in the total scheme of things, I can see why that had to happen." The classic wrestling with these matters in modern times is to be found in Dostoyevsky's *The Brothers Karamazov*: what aesthetically harmonized final bliss, asks Ivan, could ever justify the torture and death of an eight-year-old child? "I don't want harmony. . . . Too high a price has been placed on harmony. We cannot afford to pay so much for admission. . . . It's not God that I do not accept, Alyosha. I merely most respectfully return him

44. Some have argued that the movie *American Beauty* in effect illustrates "aesthetic total-ity" theodicy as a theistic response to the problem of evil. James S. Spiegel, "The Theological Aesthetic of *American Beauty*," *Journal of Religion and Popular Culture* 4, no. 1 (2003).

45. John Hick, *Evil and the God of Love* (London: Collins, 1977), 88–89. Hick acknowledges the limited usefulness of Augustine's aesthetic model for "natural evil" but has little time for it as applied to Augustine's view of moral evil and its devastating consequences.

46. Hans Urs von Balthasar, *The Glory of the Lord: A Theological Aesthetics*, vol. 2, *Stud-ies in Theological Style: Clerical Styles*, trans. Andrew Louth, Francis McDonagh, and Brian McNeil (Edinburgh: T&T Clark, 1984), 26–129.

47. Frank Burch Brown, "The Beauty of Hell: Anselm on God's Design," *Journal of Reli-gion* 73 (1993): 329–56. See *Cur Deus Homo* 1:15: "And so, though man or evil angel refuse to submit to the divine will and appointment, yet he cannot escape it; for if he wishes to fly from a will that commands, he falls into the power of a will that punishes. And if you ask whither he goes, it is only under the permission of that will; and even this wayward choice or action of his becomes subservient, under infinite wisdom, to the order and beauty of the universe before spoken of. For when it is understood that God brings good out of many forms of evil, then the satisfaction for sin freely given, or if this be not given, the exaction of punishment, hold their own place and orderly beauty in the same universe. For if divine wisdom were not to insist upon things, when wickedness tries to disturb the right appointment, there would be, in the very universe which God ought to control, an unseemliness springing from the violation of the beauty of arrangement, and God would appear to be deficient in his management. And these two things are not only unfitting, but consequently impossible; so that satisfaction or punishment must needs follow every sin."

the ticket."[48] Disentangling beauty from sentimentality is unlikely to be accomplished until it is recognized that evil (as with God's saving grace) cannot be accommodated within systems that seek to make sense of all things within closed cosmological and metaphysical systems.

Admittedly, there are gentler versions of this kind of aesthetic scheme that do not iron out evil's contingency, that do see it as an irrational intrusion, but that nevertheless construe God's salvation (in this life and the next) in terms of the logic or rationality of symmetrical perfection, where atonement and salvation are essentially a matter of "balancing things out," restoring equilibrium. Insofar as they still allow for a genuine contingency in the created order, these accounts definitely mark an advance on "closed system" theologies. However, those who are suspicious of beauty's charms press the question: What in the final "harmony" of the future could ever "match" or compensate for the kind of abysmal sin alluded to by Ivan? And even if one does speak of the possibility of hell, is this best imagined in terms of equivalence, perfectly balancing the good of heaven and thus contributing to the overall "beauty" of God's purposes?[49] The intuition here is that the metaphors of balance, however carefully articulated, are somehow inappropriate to the seriousness of the world's evil and thus to some extent still fall prey to sentimentality.

The Counter-Sentimentality of the Three Days of Easter

Are there, then, ways of construing beauty that avoid the pathologies of sentimentalism? Once again, everything hinges on how determined we are to allow God's reconciling self-revelation in Jesus Christ to form and transform all our prior conceptions of beauty, on whether we are prepared—as Balthasar would put it—to pursue a "theological aesthetics" (shaped by the unique beauty of God's self-disclosure) rather than an "aesthetic theology" (shaped by *a priori* conceptions of beauty).[50] In the previous essay, I outlined something of the contours of a theological account of beauty, oriented to the saving work of

48. Fyodor Dostoyevsky, *The Brothers Karamazov* (Harmondsworth, UK: Penguin, 1958), 287. Significantly, in another place Ivan challenges Alyosha on the question of necessity: "Answer me; imagine it is you yourself who are erecting the edifice of human destiny with the aim of making men happy in the end, of giving them peace and contentment at last, but that to do that is *absolutely necessary*, and indeed quite inevitable, to torture to death only one tiny creature, the little girl who beat her breast with her little fist, and to found the edifice on her unavenged tears—would you consent to be the architect on those conditions? Tell me and do not lie!" Alyosha replies softly: "No, I wouldn't." Dostoyevsky, *Brothers Karamazov*, 287–88 (italics mine).
49. See Burch Brown, "Beauty of Hell."
50. Hans Urs von Balthasar, *The Glory of the Lord: A Theological Aesthetics*, vol. 1, *Seeing the Form*, trans. Erasmo Leivà-Merikakis (Edinburgh: T&T Clark, 1982), 79–117.

the Son and the Spirit and intrinsically related to the being of the Triune God. This now needs to be filled out with particular attention to the Son's journey through crucifixion to resurrection. The dissociation of sentimentality and beauty is only possible inasmuch as we interpret both through the narrative of the church's *Triduum*: Good Friday, Holy Saturday, and Easter Day. Only in this way will the true nature and seriousness of sentimentality be exposed, and only in this way will we begin to understand how it may be countered, indeed, how it has *already* been countered, in the dying and rising of Jesus Christ. In short, Christian sentimentalism arises from a premature grasp for Easter morning, a refusal to follow the three days of Easter as three days in an irreversible sequence of victory over evil. By the same token, a theological account of divine and created beauty can be purged of sentimentality only by appropriate attention to these three days, read as an integrated yet differentiated narrative.

We recall that sentimentality's emotional dynamics are built on a misrepresentation of reality through an evasion or trivialization of evil. A theological counter-sentimentality depends, I suggest, on meeting this with an appropriate construal of the relation between cross and resurrection. The issues here are enormous and much debated, but the core matter for our purposes can be opened up by turning to Alan Lewis's notion of a "stereophonic" reading of the three days of Easter.[51] According to Lewis, the story of Good Friday to Easter can be

> told and heard, believed and interpreted, *two different ways at once*—as a story whose ending is *known*, and as one whose ending is discovered only *as it happens*. The truth is victim when either reading is allowed to drown out the other; the truth emerges only when both readings are audible, the separate sound in each ear creating, as it were, a stereophonic unity.[52]

This is what the New Testament texts themselves offer. We are invited to view the crucifixion in the light of the blaze of Easter; Sunday morning vindicates the Jesus who was crucified, announcing that he was indeed God's chosen one, that the world's sin has been defeated in him. This is to view the

51. Alan E. Lewis, *Between Cross and Resurrection: A Theology of Holy Saturday* (Grand Rapids: Eerdmans, 2001), 32–37.

52. Lewis, *Between Cross and Resurrection*, 33 (italics original). Hence Lewis's insistence that "the multiple meaning of the story will only emerge as we hold in tension what the cross says on its own, what the resurrection says on its own, and what each of them says when interpreted in the light of the other." Lewis goes on to recommend that the second day be seen as the vantage point from which this may be done, for it "serves both to keep the first and third days apart in their separate identities and to unite them in the indivisibility" (33–34).

cross from the outside, as it were, with the synoptic gaze we attain when we know the ending: Good Friday is seen to be a saving initiative, to be "Good." Yet along with this, we are also invited to read the story from the inside, from the perspective of those who live through the shadows of Friday and Saturday *without* knowing the ending, for whom Friday is a catastrophic finale to the would-be Messiah's life, a day devoid of victory, a day of shredded hopes, drained of goodness. Hence the steady, day-by-day rehearsal of the passion story in many of our churches during Holy Week, when we play the events at their original speed.

Why are we given this "inside" story? For no other reason than to impress on us that the healing of the world is achieved in this way and no other. The one whom God vindicates on Easter morning is none other than one numbered with the lowest of the low, naked, ignominious. The resurrection does not erase the memory of Friday: it confirms the cross as the focused place where the weight of the world's evil is borne and borne away. This is how God disarms the principalities and powers and triumphs over them (Col. 2:15); this is how God's idiocy outstrips human wisdom (1 Cor. 1); this is how "it is finished" (John 19:30). The scandal is captured with astonishing power in Rembrandt's etching "The Three Crosses" (1653), where the divine light beam falling from above does nothing to alleviate the horror but rather renders it all the harsher. Easter does of course throw its light on Friday, but not a soothing glow so much as a white light that exposes the rupture between Creator and creature, the depths to which the human creature has sunk, and the depths to which God's love is prepared to reach.

Beauty, Sentimentality, and the Arts

What then can we now say about beauty? And what might this mean for the arts?

As far as divine beauty is concerned, in the previous essay I spoke of God's beauty as the beauty of ecstatic, outgoing love for the other. We can now stress that this outgoing love is nowhere more palpable, nowhere more acutely or sharply defined, than in the "way of the Son of God into the far country";[53] here the intratrinitarian agape "goes out" to that extremity of darkness into which our rebellion leads us, in order to win us back. This is emphatically not to say that the crucifixion as an event of torture and death is really beautiful and not ugly, if only we would change our perspective. That would be gross

---

53. Karl Barth, *Church Dogmatics*, trans. G. W. Bromiley and T. F. Torrance, IV/1 (Edinburgh: T&T Clark, 1974), 157–210.

sentimentality (and, of course, opens the door to sadism or sadomasochism). But it is to say that in and through this particular torture, crucifixion, and death, God's love is displayed at its most potent. The "form" of beauty here is the radiant, splendid form of God's self-giving love. As Cardinal Joseph Ratzinger puts it: "In his Face that is so disfigured, there appears the genuine, extreme beauty: the beauty of love that goes 'to the very end.'"[54] This is what Barth means when he claims that "God's beauty embraces death as well as life, fear as well as joy, what we might call the ugly as well as what we might call the beautiful."[55] He is proposing not that ugliness itself is in fact beautiful or that ugliness belongs in some way to God's own being but rather that God's saving love has graciously stretched out to redeem that which is ugly.[56] Compare Balthasar: "[God's beauty] embraces the most abysmal ugliness of sin and hell by virtue of the condescension of divine love, which has brought even sin and hell into that divine art for which there is no human analogue."[57] In other words, there can be nothing sentimental about God's beauty so understood because it has engaged with the worst and shows itself most vigorously just *as* it does so.[58]

Balthasar's words push us on to consider created beauty (the "divine art"). In chapter 1, I argued that Christ is to be seen as the ultimate measure of created beauty since he is the one in whom creation has reached its eschatological goal. We can now stress that this was achieved only through divine beauty engaging directly with the world's wounded and deformed beauty; in the incarnate Son, crucified, risen, and now exalted, we are given an anticipation

54. Joseph Ratzinger, "The Feeling of Things, the Contemplation of Beauty," www.second spring.co.uk/articles/benedict6.htm.

55. Karl Barth, *Church Dogmatics*, trans. G. W. Bromiley and T. F. Torrance, II/1 (Edinburgh: T&T Clark, 1957), 665. Compare Augustine: "He hung therefore on the cross deformed, but his deformity is our beauty" (Sermon 27.6, in *Patrologia Latina*, ed. Jacques-Paul Migne, 40:89–90).

56. The quote, I should note, is preceded by the words "in this self-declaration"—in other words, in God's self-revealing saving economy.

57. Balthasar, *Glory of the Lord*, 1:124; see also his *The Glory of the Lord: A Theological Aesthetics*, vol. 7, *Theology: The New Covenant*, trans. Brian McNeil (Edinburgh: T&T Clark, 1991), 202–35.

58. This is why we need Nietzsche, because he reminds us of the "ungainliness" of the gospel. "Nietzsche has bequeathed Christian thought a most beautiful gift, a needed anamnesis of itself—of its strangeness: . . . a God who goes about in the dust of exodus for love of a race intransigent in its particularity; who apparels himself in common human nature, in the form of a servant; who brings good news to those who suffer and victory to those who are as nothing; who dies like a slave and outcast without resistance; who penetrates to the very depths of hell in pursuit of those he loves; and who persists even after death not as a hero lifted up to Olympian glories, but in the company of peasants, breaking bread with them and offering them the solace of his wounds. In recalling theology to the ungainliness of the gospel, Nietzsche retrieved the gospel from the soporific complacency of modernity." David Bentley Hart, *The Beauty of the Infinite: The Aesthetics of Christian Truth* (Grand Rapids: Eerdmans, 2003), 126–27.

of God's re-creation of the world's beauty. A constant remembrance of the cross will prevent the pleasure that rightly attends beauty from sliding into sentimentality, for beauty at its richest has been forged through the starkness and desolation of Good Friday: indeed, as the Revelation to Saint John reminds us, the risen Lamb on the throne bears the marks of suffering (Rev. 5:6).

Now we can consider again those three suspicions of beauty I mentioned earlier and offer one or two glimpses of how the arts—insofar as their created beauty comes to terms with the beauty created and re-created in the crucified and risen Jesus Christ—might play a part in fostering a counter-sentimentality today.

There was, first, the suspicion that pursuing beauty fosters a lie, a denial of that heading toward death that marks all the world's phenomena. A Christ-centered response will likely be swift: the ultimate truth about the world is to be found not in this scenario but in the resurrection of the Son of God, whose beauty embodies God's promise for the final destiny of the cosmos. Yet we must now stress that the Son who is risen is the Son who was given up to the corrupting forces of sin and death afflicting creation, and in such a way that creation's beauty is exposed as fatally flawed and broken just *as* its corruptions are met and healed. Similarly, humankind is offered the possibility of being remade in the likeness of the beauty of the risen Son and to enact here and now that beauty in the power of the Spirit. Yet this very truth includes and depends on a direct engagement with and an exposure of the present pathos of the human condition.

Among the most impressive explorations of the world's beauty and pathos was a recent exhibition of works by fifteen North American visual artists, gathered together under the heading "A Broken Beauty" and presented in a book of that title. In the context of a counter-sentimental, "three-days" faith, the project explored beauty in relation to the depiction of the human body, especially in light of attitudes on the body in contemporary society. In this art, as Ted Prestcott puts it, "the bodies speak of a desire for a human image that can carry the weight of complex meanings, where beauty is not a mask and brokenness is not the only reality."[59]

The second suspicion of the quest for beauty was that it distracts us from our moral responsibilities to others in need and distracts the victims of injustice from the wrongness of their predicament. It should be clear by now that the quest for beauty, tempered through the three days of Easter, need not stifle action or deafen us to the cries of the world's wounded. Justice, after all,

59. Theodore L. Prestcott, "The Bodies before Us," in *A Broken Beauty*, ed. Theodore L. Prestcott (Grand Rapids: Eerdmans, 2005), 24.

concerns right relationships, and the same goes for beauty—the beauty God desires for the human community is the proper dynamic ordering of lives in relation to one another. Justice is beautiful.[60]

Some of the most striking Christian art of recent decades has encouraged or has been used to promote an alertness to social injustice and the need for effective action. In this context, we should mention John de Gruchy's profound theological examination of the arts (including Christian art) in apartheid and postapartheid South Africa.[61]

The third suspicion was of the tendency of concepts of beauty to harmonize away the evilness of evil, especially those dominated by notions of balance, symmetry, and equivalence. Matters of considerable controversy swirl around us here, but for our purposes this much at least may be said: The raising of Jesus from the dead vindicates the crucified Christ, not crucifixion; it does not validate or legitimate a view of the world that imagines evil and suffering as necessary to its fulfillment. The three days of Easter do not tell us that the world's pain and agony are required for God to achieve his purposes (still less for God to be God) or that sin is a requisite part of the harmonious fabric of things. They did not happen to confirm some all-pervasive metaphysics of sacrifice within a system of regular balances. God does not bargain with evil but rather shatters its power, overthrowing the principalities and powers; evil is a wholly unnecessary intrusion, an irrational infringement of original goodness. (This area, incidentally, is where musical models of "resolution" in theology need handling with care, insofar as they might suggest that dissonance was written into the cosmic symphony by the Composer.) By the same token, we ought to be wary of schemes of salvation that suggest the divine strategy is, so to speak, primarily to balance things out (as in strictly retributive views of atonement and eschatological justice). The world is not so much balanced as *reconciled*, and reconciled by a God of infinite excess. Through the three days of Easter, evil, sin, and death are defeated by a love that does not simply match what has been hurled at it from rebellious creatures but infinitely goes beyond anything and everything it answers. The fulfillment toward which the resurrection points us and which it anticipates is not a mere restoration of a previous order, a return to the status quo ante of Eden; it is not only a recovery of what is lost but a radical re-creation of all things. Easter is—if I may put it this way—an aesthetic joke, vastly surplus to any

---

60. It is worth recalling that the word "fair" can mean both beautiful and just! For a vigorous defense of beauty against the charge that it encourages injustice, see Elaine Scarry, *On Beauty and Being Just* (Princeton: Princeton University Press, 2001).

61. John W. de Gruchy, *Christianity, Art, and Transformation: Theological Aesthetics in the Struggle for Justice* (Cambridge: Cambridge University Press, 2001).

"requirement" or "compensation," vastly outstripping any expectation and every predictable equilibrium, involving not merely the leveling out but the transformation of creation's brokenness into something of infinitely expanding, superabundant beauty.

By the same token, do we not need to be wary of certain theologies that out of an understandable concern to take suffering seriously actually sentimentalize it by robbing it of its irrationality, its interruptive offense and horror to God? I have in mind here certain forms of "suffering God" theology that in their zeal to affirm divine solidarity with the victims of suffering veer toward imprisoning God in the world's history and hence (albeit inadvertently) come close to eternalizing evil in God (thus, ironically, compromising God's freedom to save or redeem). That more than a hint of sentimentality is at work here is confirmed by the emotional self-indulgence that can quickly creep in: an implicit assumption that God, in order to be worth believing in, *must* answer to our supposed need for a suffering deity.[62] I have in mind also certain British "tragic theologies" that out of a strong fear of metaphysical optimism, of anything that would trivialize evil, can come close to doing just that by appearing to presume a fundamental, perpetual order of violence and strife in creation, a scenario that arguably encourages something more akin to resignation before the magnitude of evil rather than a revulsion stemming from confidence born of resurrection faith.[63]

To close, I cite just two pieces of art, both of which in their own way move against this tendency toward an overharmonized beauty. The first is by the Scottish Roman Catholic composer James MacMillan, who unashamedly relates music's particular powers of tension and resolution to the three days of Easter: "I seem to be going round and round in circles round the same three days in history. The fact is that if history had to be changed—if *we* had to be changed—then God had to interact with us in a severe way."[64] The contours

62. Certain varieties of process theology move strongly in these directions. The work of Jürgen Moltmann is sometimes cited in this connection also, though it should be stressed that he would distance himself sharply from some of the extremes to which his thought has been said to lead. For discussion, see John Thompson, *Modern Trinitarian Perspectives* (Oxford: Oxford University Press, 1994), chap. 3; Kenneth Surin, *Theology and the Problem of Evil* (Oxford: Blackwell, 1986), esp. chap. 4; Paul D. Molnar, *Divine Freedom and the Doctrine of the Immanent Trinity* (London: T&T Clark, 2002), esp. chap. 7.

63. Donald M. MacKinnon, "Atonement and Tragedy," in *The Borderlands of Theology and Other Essays* (London: Lutterworth, 1968), 97–104. See also Daniel W. Hardy, "Theology through Philosophy," in *The Modern Theologians: An Introduction to Christian Theology in the Twentieth Century*, ed. David F. Ford (Oxford: Blackwell, 1997), 252–85, 272–78. For a highly critical treatment, see Hart, *Beauty of the Infinite*, 380–94.

64. James MacMillan, quoted in Jolyon Mitchell, "Sound of Heart," *Third Way* 22, no. 5 (1999): 19.

of MacMillan's outlook find monumental expression in *The Triduum*—three orchestral works relating to the events and liturgies of Maundy Thursday, Good Friday, and the Easter Vigil (respectively, *The World's Ransoming*, the *Cello Concerto*, and *Symphony: Vigil*). In the *Cello Concerto*, the theme is Christ's crucifixion, with the cello soloist shifting between the roles of protagonist, antagonist, and commentator. In the first movement, vulgar dance-hall music evokes Christ's humiliation, and toward the end the players themselves shout the words of the Good Friday Latin plainsong "Crucem tuam adoremus, Domine." In "The Reproaches," MacMillan quotes "Dunblane Cathedral" (a Protestant hymn), a reference to the shooting of sixteen children and their teacher by a lone gunman in Dunblane, Scotland, an atrocity that occurred as MacMillan worked on the piece. The movement climaxes with brutal percussion blows—nails driven mercilessly into Christ's hands and feet. In the Easter work, *Symphony: Vigil*, the music incorporates ecstatic, irregular dance, and its central movement, "Tuba insonet salutaris" ("Sound the trumpet of salvation"—from the *Exsultet*, sung at the Easter Vigil), is described by MacMillan thus:

> The brass quintet, which played unseen at the end of the first movement, now comes into the auditorium and the players position themselves at five different points, representing the trumpets of salvation. The aural perspective takes on new dimensions as music is heard from all angles, and the sounds are bright and startling.[65]

The "resolution" enacted in *Symphony: Vigil* neither effaces the harshness of the memories of the preceding days nor accords them any kind of ultimacy, but through a wide range of carefully controlled musical techniques, transfigures the dissonance into a novel and utterly beguiling beauty. Moreover, its beauty is anything but tidy: the forms overlap; material is scattered, dropped, and picked up again; and we are given a concluding section with (in MacMillan's words) "luminous floating chords on high strings accompanying gently soaring trumpet calls and bright percussion."[66]

The second piece is a poem by Micheal O'Siadhail. After Auschwitz the cry goes up: "Never again." To heed such a cry entails keeping the memory alive; as the years pass, remembrance cannot be allowed to falter or fade.

---

65. James MacMillan, "Composer's Notes," *Boosey & Hawkes*, August 1997, www.boosey .com/pages/cr/catalogue/cat_detail.asp?musicid=771.

66. MacMillan, "Composer's Notes." For further discussion of MacMillan, see Jeremy Begbie, *Resounding Truth: Christian Wisdom in the World of Music* (Grand Rapids: Baker Academic, 2007), chap. 7.

But part of what is needed also are ways of living that refuse to treat the
diabolical forces that led to the Shoa as if they will achieve finality. And that
means knowing how to feast, how to play, how to laugh—how to celebrate
the excessive, anarchic (but never senseless) beauty of the love of God. Of
course, doing this takes us to the very edge of sentimentality—to the verge of
a flagrant evasion and trivialization of evil, an emotional self-indulgence that
avoids responsible action, and to the verge of an empty comedy that does no
more than celebrate life with wide-eyed naïveté. But from the perspective of
the three days of Easter, succumbing to these pitfalls is not inevitable. Part
of any Christian response to evil will be cultivating patterns of life that will
not allow the powers of darkness a foothold, that arise from knowing that in
Jesus Christ a superfluity of love has already exceeded everything that could
be thrown at it, that a resurrection life is available that in its overabundance
will always surpass and outrun "the ruler of this world." Hence the defiance
of Bonhoeffer, who spoke of *hilaritas* as he faced his own execution. Hence
the jazzlike defiance toward which O'Siadhail points us:

> That any poem after Auschwitz is obscene?
> Covenants of silence so broken between us
> Can we still promise or trust what we mean?
>
> Even in the dark of the earth, seeds will swell.
> All the interweavings and fullness of being,
> Nothing less may insure against our hell.
>
> A black sun only shines out of a vacuum.
> Cold narrowing and idols of blood and soil.
> And all the more now, we can't sing dumb!
>
> A conversation so rich it knows it never arrives
> Or forecloses; in a buzz and cross-ruff of polity
> The restless subversive ragtime of what thrives.
>
> Endless dialogues. The criss-cross of flourishings.
> Again and over again our complex yes.
> A raucous glory and the whole jazz of things.
>
> The sudden riff of surprise beyond our ken;
> Out of control, a music's brimming let-go.
> We feast to keep our promise of never again.[67]

---

67. Micheal O'Siadhail, "Never," in *The Gossamer Wall* (Newcastle upon Tyne, UK: Bloodaxe, 2002), 120. Reproduced with permission of Bloodaxe Books. www.bloodaxebooks.com.

3

Faithful Feelings

Music and Emotion in Worship

There can be little doubt that music's emotional power is one of its most celebrated as well as its most controversial features. It has become a lively area of empirical research, and the debate over how music exercises this power continues unabated in philosophical and psychological circles. In this essay, I adopt what has become a fairly broadly supported perspective on the theme and explore what happens when it is set in a theological context, specifically, the trinitarian environment of worship. The result, I hope will be clear, is a striking mutual illumination of music and theology.

The power of music to engage our emotional life is proverbial. David's lyre soothes Saul; "The Star-Spangled Banner" brings a tear to the eye of the patriotic marine; the fifteen-year-old finds solace from a broken heart in a moody ballad. A psychologist observes: "Some sort of emotional experience

This chapter was originally published as Jeremy Begbie, "Faithful Feelings: Music and Emotion in Worship" in *Resonant Witness*, ed. Jeremy Begbie and Steven Guthrie, 323–54 (Grand Rapids: Eerdmans, 2011). I borrow the phrase "faithful feelings" from Matthew Elliott, *Faithful Feelings: Emotion in the New Testament* (Leicester, UK: Inter-Varsity, 2005).

is probably the main reason behind most people's engagement with music."[1] Although this cannot be said of all music worldwide (the functions of music are multiple and highly diverse), it does seem true of a good deal of music in globalized Western society.

And yet music's emotional power is probably its single most controversial feature. Philosophers, psychologists, and music theorists vigorously debate just how it affects our emotions. Many in the Christian church have feared its ability to "get inside" us, not least in worship. Many are anxious that music all too easily turns into a device of manipulation, a tool of moral harm, all the more dangerous because it can work its charms without our being aware of it. Others insist such worries are overplayed, betraying an exaggerated suspicion of anything not amenable to rational control.

In this essay, I ask: What is it about musical sounds and the way they operate such that they become emotionally significant and valuable to us? And what can we learn from this theologically, with regard to music in worship? I first offer some general comments about the nature of emotion and set these in the light of a trinitarian theology of worship. Then I explore the emotional power of musical sounds and go on to situate our findings in the context of this same theology. We will see that certain capacities of music are singularly appropriate for carrying and advancing certain key dimensions of worship. We will also discover that our theology of worship is itself enriched in the process: theology throws light on music, and music throws light on theology.

It should be added that I make no attempt here to offer a comprehensive account of emotion, musical emotion, or musical emotion in worship. But I do highlight what I believe are fruitful possibilities for further exploration and research.

Faithful Feelings

Emotion: Charting the Territory

The literature on emotion is now vast and burgeoning, especially in anthropology, psychology, neuroscience, and philosophy.[2] Here we cannot do

---

1. Patrik N. Juslin and John A. Sloboda, "Music and Emotion: Introduction," in *Music and Emotion: Theory and Research*, ed. Patrik N. Juslin and John A. Sloboda (Oxford: Oxford University Press, 2001), 3–20, here 3.

2. See, e.g., Anthony Kenny, *Action, Emotion and Will* (London: Routledge & Kegan Paul, 1963); Robert C. Solomon, *The Passions* (Garden City, NY: Anchor Press/Doubleday, 1976); Solomon, "The Logic of Emotion," *Noûs* 11 (1977): 41–49; Solomon, "The Philosophy of Emotions," in *Handbook of Emotions*, ed. M. Lewis and J. M. Haviland-Jones, 2nd ed. (New York: Guilford Press, 2004), 3–15; Solomon, *Thinking about Feeling: Contemporary Philosophers on*

justice to the complexity of the field nor to its fervent disputes. But we can at least chart a way through the territory, indicating our reasons for adopting the course we do and referring to supporting literature and alternative positions as we proceed.

It is widely held that some "basic" emotions are universal to all members of the human species.[3] Theorists argue about which these are, but they are usually variants of happiness, sadness, anger, fear, and disgust. The presence of such emotions is usually inferred from three kinds of evidence: reports (what people say they feel), overt behavior (the way people act), and physiological phenomena (the way their bodily systems behave). This has led to a fairly standard way of describing emotional states: as involving an interplay between *conscious experience* (we feel anger, fear, or whatever); *expressive bodily behavior* (if irritated, we may well tense our bodies or press our lips together; if frightened, we might widen our eyes); and *physiological activation* (people who are emotionally agitated will often perspire, their pulse rate increases, blood gets diverted from internal organs to the larger muscles, pupils dilate, and so on).[4]

We need to bear these three components in mind throughout: substantial evidence indicates that our emotional involvement in music involves all

---

Emotions (Oxford: Oxford University Press, 2004); Amelie Rorty, ed., *Explaining Emotions* (Berkeley: University of California Press, 1980); C. E. Izard et al., eds., *Emotions, Cognition, and Behaviour* (Cambridge: Cambridge University Press, 1984); Patricia S. Greenspan, *Emotions and Reasons: An Inquiry into Emotional Justification* (New York: Routledge, 1988); William E. Lyons, *Emotion* (Cambridge: Cambridge University Press, 1993); Antonio R. Damasio, *Descartes' Error: Emotion, Reason, and the Human Brain* (New York: G. P. Putnam, 1994); Damasio, *The Feeling of What Happens: Body and Emotion in the Making of Consciousness* (New York: Harcourt Brace, 1999); Patricia S. Greenspan, *Practical Guilt: Moral Dilemmas, Emotions, and Social Norms* (New York: Oxford University Press, 1995); Michael Stocker and Elizabeth Hegeman, *Valuing Emotions* (Cambridge: Cambridge University Press, 1996); Paul E. Griffiths, *What Emotions Really Are: The Problem of Psychological Categories* (Chicago: University of Chicago Press, 1997); Richard Wollheim, *On the Emotions* (New Haven: Yale University Press, 1999); Nico H. Frijda et al., eds., *Emotions and Beliefs: How Feelings Influence Thoughts* (Cambridge: Cambridge University Press, 2000); Peter Goldie, *The Emotions: A Philosophical Exploration* (Oxford: Clarendon Press, 2000); Goldie, *Understanding Emotions: Mind and Morals* (Aldershot, UK: Ashgate, 2002); Martha C. Nussbaum, *Upheavals of Thought: The Intelligence of Emotions* (Cambridge: Cambridge University Press, 2001); K. T. Strongman, *The Psychology of Emotion* (Chichester, UK: Wiley, 2003); Jenefer Robinson, *Deeper than Reason: Emotion and Its Role in Literature, Music, and Art* (Oxford: Clarendon Press, 2005).

3. Paul Ekman and Richard J. Davidson, *The Nature of Emotion: Fundamental Questions* (New York: Oxford University Press, 1994).

4. David G. Myers, *Psychology* (New York: Worth, 2004), chap. 13. K. R. Scherer calls this the classic "reaction triad." See Scherer, "Neuroscience Projections to Current Debates in Emotion Psychology," *Cognition and Emotion* 7 (1993): 1–41, here 3.

three.[5] Together, they call into question two common tendencies in thinking about emotion. The first is to see emotions as essentially private mental states and the bodily or physiological correlates as quite distinct and contingent. This is clearly mistaken and, in any case, assumes a mind-body dichotomy increasingly recognized as unsupportable.[6] The second tendency is to treat emotions individualistically. Against this approach, theorists urge that emotions, insofar as they are publicly observable bodily states, can profoundly affect, and be affected by, our relations to others: emotions are "intrinsically social."[7] Indeed, as a crucial nonverbal means of relating to others, emotion is to some extent entailed in nearly all social activity.[8] We have evolved highly developed skills for identifying emotion in others and responding accordingly. Not least, emotions can play a major role in establishing and strengthening human unity, in creating and sustaining profound bonds between even the most disparate people—we only need think of how contagious enthusiasm is in a classroom or fear in an airplane.

However, the triadic scheme needs to be supplemented by an element that would seem to play an essential role in occurrent emotional states, namely, cognition. Much recent discussion has surrounded this matter, and it has led to a distinction often made between "noncognitive" and "cognitive" accounts of emotion.

"Noncognitive" labels a family of theories that sees emotion as fundamentally separate from, and even opposed to, the rational and intellectual and, as such, having little if anything to do with the mind's pursuit and grasp of truth. Emotions are basically irrational bodily reactions, transient surges of affect quite unrelated to cognition. Reports of an affective experience can be explained entirely in terms of physiological changes and outward bodily movements. This is sometimes tied to a view of human nature that contrasts the "lower," "animal," bodily nature with the "higher," mental faculties.[9] Many

---

5. John A. Sloboda and Patrik N. Juslin, "Psychological Perspectives on Music and Emotion," in *Music and Emotion: Theory and Research*, ed. Patrik N. Juslin and John A. Sloboda (Oxford: Oxford University Press, 2001), 84–85.

6. Damasio, *Descartes' Error*.

7. Sloboda and Juslin, "Psychological Perspectives on Music and Emotion," 86.

8. Tia DeNora, "Aesthetic Agency and Musical Practice: New Directions in the Sociology of Music and Emotion," in Juslin and Sloboda, *Music and Emotion*, 161–80; Strongman, *Psychology of Emotion*, chap. 10.

9. René Descartes provided one of the first developed accounts of what would today be called a noncognitivist theory of emotion. See Descartes, *The Passions of the Soul* (Indianapolis: Hackett, 1989). For discussion, see Lyons, *Emotion*, 2–8. Modern psychological theory of emotion is widely regarded as initiated by William James, whose views in many ways extend those of Descartes. James claimed that the awareness of physiological changes and bodily movement following the perception of a situation *is* the emotion: "We feel sorry because we cry, angry

thus speak of emotion disdainfully, extolling the curbing power of reason. This outlook commonly links emotions with our "animal nature," as distinct from what makes us human, and some evolutionary accounts of emotion follow this line of thought: emotions are adaptive bodily reactions geared toward survival, both physical and social.[10] Admittedly, not all who hold to a strong distinction between cognition and emotion denigrate the latter. Many encourage emotion in order to "balance out" the rational and intellectual; some feminist theory wants to reinstate our emotional nature against what is seen as a damaging (and typically male) intellectualism,[11] and for the early nineteenth-century Romantics, the presumed irrationality of emotion was generally something to be celebrated (as distinct from scientific rationalism). But underlying these positions, we still find the same dichotomous understanding of reason versus emotion, intellect versus passion.

In discussions of worship, noncognitive approaches to emotion often hold sway. Many are instinctively cautious about sermons that target the emotions, songs that span emotional extremes, exuberant bodily expression. The fear is that we will lose touch with reality, become too preoccupied with the body, open ourselves to unscrupulous manipulation by church leaders. Preaching should be addressed first to the mind and only then (if at all) to the emotions; bodily movement should be kept to a minimum; songs should be concerned with intellectually graspable truth, only secondarily (if at all) with moving us.

In contemporary studies of emotion, however, noncognitivism has fallen on hard times.[12] Among other things there is the problem of satisfactorily dif-

---

because we strike, afraid because we tremble." William James, "What Is an Emotion?," in *The Nature of Emotion*, ed. M. B. Arnold (Harmondsworth, UK: Penguin, 1968), 13. According to the James-Lange theory (so called because the Danish physician and psychologist Carl Lange came to the same conclusion independently), emotions are feelings that occur as a result of bodily processes and behavior, rather than being their cause. Implicit here is a separation of cognition and emotion: "Emotion and cognition seem then parted. . . . Cerebral processes are almost feelingless." William James, "The Emotions," in *The Emotions*, ed. C. G. Lange and W. James (Baltimore: Williams & Wilkins, 1922), 122–23.

10. Classically in Charles Darwin, *The Expression of the Emotions in Man and Animals* (1872; London: HarperCollins, 1998). For an overview of evolutionary approaches, see Strongman, *Psychology of Emotion*, 64–70.

11. See, e.g., Carol Gilligan, *In a Different Voice: Psychological Theory and Women's Development* (Cambridge, MA: Harvard University Press, 1982).

12. See, from the perspective of anthropology, Rom Harré, *The Social Construction of Emotions* (Oxford: Blackwell, 1988); philosophy, John Macmurray, *Reason and Emotion* (London: Faber & Faber, 1935); Ronald De Sousa, *The Rationality of Emotion* (Cambridge, MA: MIT Press, 1987); Martha C. Nussbaum, *Love's Knowledge: Essays on Philosophy and Literature* (New York: Oxford University Press, 1990), 40–43; Nussbaum, *Upheavals of Thought*; M. B. Arnold, "Cognitive Theories of Emotion," in *Encyclopedia of Psychology*, vol. 2, ed. R. J.

ferentiating emotions if they are to be understood solely in terms of bodily changes and movements; of accounting for the way emotions become motives for behavior (we do not say, "I ran away because my heart suddenly beat faster," but "I ran away because I was scared of the mugger with a knife"); and from a neuroscientific perspective, an emotion/cognition dichotomy seems unsupportable.[13]

This takes us to "cognitive" theories of emotion.[14] Common to these is the integral role that cognition is thought to have in emotional experience. There is considerable disagreement, however, about what that role is and what constitutes cognition. The field can be opened up by observing that, generally speaking, what we consider to be fully fledged emotions depend on *beliefs* about the world or oneself. My fear of falling off a two-hundred-foot cliff is dependent on my belief that if I fall, I will die. To say "I am angry with you" implies that I believe you have done or said something that has provoked my anger. Beliefs on which emotions are based may be true or false, rational or irrational, superficial or profound, but without them, it is hard to see how an emotion could arise.

These beliefs in turn form the basis of *evaluation* (or appraisal):[15] "Fear or anger may arouse fight or attack, but they still depend on a realization

Corsini (New York: John Wiley & Sons, 1994); neuroscience, Damasio, *Descartes' Error*. For a summary of critiques, see Matthew Elliott, *Faithful Feelings: Rethinking Emotion in the New Testament* (Grand Rapids: Kregel, 2006), 27–31.

13. Emotional processes are not restricted to subcortical brain regions that are shared with other animals; they recruit parts of the frontal lobes, the largest and latest brain structures to emerge in evolutionary development. Damasio, *Descartes' Error*; Isabelle Peretz, "Listen to the Brain: A Biological Perspective on Musical Emotions," in Juslin and Sloboda, *Music and Emotion*, 105–34, esp. 105–6.

14. It is fair to say, within psychology at least, that the tide has recently turned strongly in favor of such theories (paralleling the ascendancy of cognitive psychology). For a survey of the major theorists, see Strongman, *Psychology of Emotion*, chap. 6.

15. Nussbaum, *Upheavals of Thought*, 28. The distinction Lyons makes between evaluation and appraisal is, I think, questionable (Lyons, *Emotion*, 80); in any case, it is not relevant for us here.

Belief and evaluation are logically distinct (even if in practice intertwined). Lyons, *Emotion*, 35. I believe that the crocodile's teeth are dangerous, but while I may be terrified on seeing a crocodile ten feet away, my friend next to me may be exhilarated: we both believe the teeth are dangerous, but my friend evaluates the danger differently, leading to a different emotion. It is the evaluative component that most accurately specifies and differentiates the emotions, not beliefs. Essentially the same distinction is made by R. S. Lazarus and C. A. Smith when they distinguish between knowledge, consisting of "cognitions about the way things are and how they work," and appraisal, "consisting of evaluations of the significance of this knowledge for well-being." Lazarus and Smith, "Knowledge and Appraisal in the Cognition-Emotion Relationship," *Cognition and Emotion* 2 (1988): 281–300, here 282. Knowledge, in this sense, is a necessary but not sufficient condition for emotion, whereas appraisal, so defined, is both

that something is threatening or annoying, which is an appraisal, however rudimentary."[16] According to William Lyons, "The evaluation central to the concept of emotion is an evaluation of some object, event or situation in the world about me in relation to me, or according to my norms. Thus my emotions reveal whether I see the world or some aspect of it as threatening or welcoming, pleasant or painful, regrettable or a solace, and so on."[17] Because emotion entails evaluation in this sense, different appraisals of the same situation by different people can give rise to different emotions. Indeed, the evaluative factor is probably the best tool for specifying and differentiating emotions: mere physiological changes are insufficient for the task, reports of "feeling" are notoriously hard to assess, and although bodily behavior may provide clues about the emotion, one set of bodily movements can permit a variety of interpretations. We would need to investigate how the subject of an emotion is appraising a situation in order to identify the emotion being experienced with any accuracy.[18]

Even if we hold that belief and evaluation are essential to the very identity of an emotion, this does not mean that emotions are the result of coolly (nonemotionally) entertaining a judgment and then responding accordingly

necessary and sufficient. I would prefer "belief" to "knowledge" in this context, since it allows for the possibility of false belief.

16. Arnold, "Cognitive Theories of Emotion," 259.

17. Lyons, *Emotion*, 58–59.

18. Lyons, *Emotion*, 62–63. For Lyons's response to objections to this view, see *Emotion*, 80–89. Martha Nussbaum mounts a vigorous case for claiming not only that evaluative judgment is a constituent part of emotion but also that emotions are best defined in terms of evaluative judgment *alone*. Emotions *are* evaluative judgments. Nussbaum, *Upheavals of Thought*, esp. 19–88. She argues that "feelings" are not absolutely necessary as definitional elements in any of the emotion types, nor are bodily processes, whether internal (physiological activation) or external (overt bodily behavior).

I have no quarrel with the notion that evaluative judgment plays a constituent and determinative role in emotional experience; it is essential to emotion and a sufficient cause of emotion. And we should certainly resist reducing emotions to irrational, blind instincts. But I am equally unconvinced that the definition of emotion should be confined without remainder to evaluative judgment. See esp. Nussbaum, *Upheavals of Thought*, 44–45, 56–64. Indeed, the components of the "classic triad" ("feeling," bodily behavior, and physiological activation) would also seem to be constitutive of emotion and not themselves reducible to evaluative judgment. Admittedly, in some cases it can be notoriously hard to specify types of feelings, bodily movements, and physiological changes that must be present in every purported instance of an emotional type, such that we will want to include these elements in our definition of that emotional type. But we can say with some confidence that certain feelings, bodily movements, and physiological changes are *frequently* present with a specified emotion. Further, what we normally call "emotion" will include some form of each of these three elements, so to that extent at least, such elements are intrinsic to the identification of an emotion. With respect to physiological activation and bodily movement, Antonio Damasio's study *Descartes' Error* presents substantial neurophysiological evidence to support the claim that bodily states and processes are *intrinsic* to emotion (118, *pace* Nussbaum).

with an emotion. We do not think before every emotion, deliberately and consciously, "I judge this to be a dangerous situation" or whatever. On the other hand, we are not speaking merely of a physiological reflex such as jerking one's hand away from a hot plate. Some might claim that there are "reflex emotions," such as instant embarrassment, the flaring up of jealousy, which seem to include no evaluation. But this is only so if we limit evaluation entirely to deliberate and conscious acts. If we allow a dispositional dimension to evaluations—if we allow that they can be latent and activated instantaneously—the objection is answered. I am afraid of Labradors because some time ago I was bitten by one, and since then I have evaluated them as dangerous. I am afraid of them even though no dog is here in the room now. Were one to enter the room, my fear would be activated, on the basis of a dormant tendency to evaluate Labradors in this way.[19] Jenefer Robinson has recently argued that in an occurrent emotion, there is a two-stage "evaluation": the first is "automatic," and the second is more discriminating, cognitive "monitoring" of the emotion process.[20] But whatever we make of this, the important point here is that, even if we allow that actually occurring emotions may not always arise from a deliberate and conscious act of judgment but can arise from a disposition or tendency to evaluate something in a particular way (formed previously and part of our makeup), and that "automatic" appraisal may be followed by a more discriminating and extended cognitive act of judgment, emotions nonetheless depend on evaluation of *some* sort at *some* stage.

If emotions necessarily entail beliefs and judgments, they will be *oriented to objects*. I am not angry in the abstract but angry *about* something or angry *at* someone. Emotions are *of* or *about* or *at* something—they have "particular

19. See Lyons, *Emotion*, 85–89. Nussbaum speaks of "background" emotion judgments (as opposed to "situational" emotion judgments). I may be angry over time at some persistent wrong, which may shape and pattern many of my actions (I may be generally withdrawn, irritable) yet only be overtly manifest in particular circumstances (when I lash out or lose my temper). Nussbaum, *Upheavals of Thought*, 69–75.

20. Robinson, *Deeper than Reason*, chaps. 1–3. This relates to a lively debate among theorists. R. B. Zajonc and R. S. Lazarus have focused the issues most sharply, the former arguing that emotion precedes cognition and is independent of it, the latter arguing that the cognitive appraisal of meaning underlies all emotional states, even if the thought process of evaluation is instantaneous. See Zajonc, "Feeling and Thinking: Preferences Need No Inferences," *American Psychologist* 35, no. 2 (1980): 151–75; Zajonc, "In the Primacy of Affect," *American Psychologist* 39 (1984): 117–23; Zajonc, "Feeling and Thinking: Closing the Debate over the Independence of Affect," in *Feeling and Thinking: The Role of Affect in Social Cognition*, ed. J. P. Forgas (Cambridge: Cambridge University Press, 2000), 31–58; Lazarus, "Thoughts on the Relation between Emotion and Cognition," *American Psychologist* 37 (1982): 1019–24; Lazarus, "On the Primacy of Cognition," *American Psychologist* 39 (1984): 124–29. To a large extent the debate seems to be about definition (see, e.g., Strongman, *Psychology of Emotion*, 91).

objects."[21] The object-oriented character of emotions is well brought out in a passage from C. S. Lewis's account of grieving at the loss of his wife:

> I think I am beginning to understand why grief feels like suspense. It comes from the frustration of so many impulses that had become habitual. Thought after thought, feeling after feeling, action after action, had H. for their object. Now their target is gone. I keep on through habit fitting an arrow to the string; then I remember and have to lay the bow down. So many roads lead through to H. I set out on one of them. But now there's an impassable frontier-post across it. So many roads once; now so many *culs de sac*.[22]

That emotions are, by their very character, oriented to objects has been challenged by some; it is pointed out that emotions can take vague objects (as when I fear that my plans will come to nothing) and that in some cases there is no object to speak of at all. In depression, a person may be unable to identify the reason for his or her depressed state; there seems to be no particular

21. Lyons proposes that we see these "particular objects" as being of two sorts: "material" objects and "intentional" objects. *Emotion*, 106–9. Material objects are simply actually existing things in the world (although not necessarily composed of physical matter); intentional objects are objects not actually existing in the world but in some manner conceived by the mind. Intentional objects need not be illusory: it makes sense to speak of loving someone who has died—he no longer exists in the world (he is an intentional object), but he is certainly not illusory. (On illusory objects, see Jamie Dow, *Engaging Emotions: The Need for Emotions in the Church* [Cambridge: Grove Books, 2005], 9.) Or, to take another example, I might not believe in the reality of Harry Potter, but I might well respond emotionally to his dysfunctional home situation. What Lyons's distinction does not take into account, of course, are theological realities.

It is perhaps worth alluding to a technical term often used in discussions about emotions and objects and directly linked to what we have said about evaluation. All emotions, it is said, have a "formal object," distinguishable from a particular object. Lyons, *Emotion*, 49–50, 99–104. A formal object is a property implicitly ascribed to a particular object, in virtue of which the emotion can be identified as *this* emotion and not *that*. Faced with a shark, I construe a number of its features (its razor-sharp teeth, its fin above the water) as being frightening, and it is my evaluation of the shark as frightening that makes my emotion fear rather than some other emotion. The formal object in this case is the property or category of "the dangerous": I evaluate the shark as having the property of being dangerous. Without this formal object, the emotion simply makes no sense: emotion depends not just on an object "out there" but on an object evaluated in a certain way. The formal object associated with a given emotion is essential to that emotion and to the concept of that emotion. So with regard to fear, for example, "no description of the concept of fear is correct unless it includes the word 'danger' or some synonym for it." Lyons, *Emotion*, 101. Lyons thinks the term "formal object" is a misnomer, and with good reason since it is not really an object at all but an *evaluative category* employed in the process of appraisal. Even so, understanding the term can help clarify what is involved in the evaluative process we described earlier. (We should note that as an evaluative category, "the dangerous" is in fact a fairly wide one. We might find something "worryingly dangerous" or "excitingly dangerous," for example. But this does not alter the basic point about the necessity of a formal object and distinguishing an emotion with respect to it.)

22. C. S. Lewis, *A Grief Observed* (London: Faber & Faber, 1961), 39.

object or relevant beliefs about an object. In response, two comments are in order. First, in some cases we might well be unable to identify the object or articulate it, but this does not exclude the notion of an object altogether. (This is certainly the case in much depression.) Second, with forms of depression that seem directed to no object and impervious to changes of belief, and with other emotion-like states that seem to lack objects—for example, irritability, equanimity—and that in some cases have no beliefs, I am inclined to agree with those who want to speak here of "moods" or "feelings" rather than emotions, reserving "emotion" for situations with an object or objects and associated beliefs and evaluations.[23] Moods become emotions when they latch on to objects: we might "get up on the wrong side of the bed," waking up in an irritable mood; this mood becomes an emotion of irritation or anger when someone dares to cross our path and say something annoying.[24]

It follows that if emotions have this directional character, arising from beliefs about and evaluations of an object or objects, they can be *appropriate* or *inappropriate*.[25] Emotions can be well founded or ill founded, justified and unjustified, warranted or unwarranted. If a mouse crawls into the room and I jump on the desk screaming wildly, my fear is inappropriate; my evaluation of the situation as dangerous is based on the mistaken belief that the mouse is harmful. But if a masked man runs into the room firing an AK-47 in all directions, extreme fear is appropriate, for my evaluation of the situation as dangerous is based on the quite justified belief that the gunman could kill me.[26] Important to note also is that depending on the context, emotions can

23. See Stephen Davies, "Philosophical Perspectives on Music's Expressiveness," in Juslin and Sloboda, *Music and Emotion*, 23–44, here 27; Nussbaum, *Upheavals of Thought*, 132–34. In practice, the boundary between emotions with a vague object and moods/feelings without an object may not be clear-cut, but the basic distinction still holds and preserves what would seem to be true to the way the word "emotion" is commonly used.

24. I owe this example to my colleague Dona McCullagh.

25. The point was especially well expounded by the Scottish philosopher John Macmurray in his classic, *Reason and Emotion* (London: Faber & Faber, 1935).

26. Incorporated into the well-founded/ill-founded distinction is the distinction between illusory and nonillusory objects. An illusory object of an emotion is one about which I have a false belief or judgment. If I fear a harmless mouse in the room, then the particular object of my fear is illusory because my fear is based on the belief that the mouse can harm me (though of course there is no illusion about the existence of the mouse in the room). If I love my grandfather, believing him to be alive when he is dead, and my love for him depends on him being alive, the object of my love is an illusory object. Emotions based on nonillusory objects are based on correct beliefs about those objects, and emotions based on illusory objects are based on incorrect beliefs about those objects. Strictly speaking, therefore, emotions themselves cannot be illusory. If I am infatuated with someone who I believe is always kind and the person is in fact being cruel to me, the infatuation is not illusory but the object is because of the mistaken belief that the person is always kind and the misevaluation that she is being kind to me. The

be misdirected: for example, when I am elated at passing an exam and express that elation by laughing at someone who has just been injured by a passing car.

If emotions entail beliefs and evaluations about states of affairs beyond our own making and can thus be appropriate and inappropriate, we can conclude (against the noncognitivist) that they are not to be regarded as intrinsically inimical to truthful perception. Indeed, it would seem that they are capable of advancing and assisting our "grasping for the truth"[27] and, as such, are not inherently opposed to reason. This has been argued vigorously on several fronts in recent years.[28] Indeed, it has been stressed that emotions are critical for decision-making: they guide action in contexts where our knowledge is imperfect and we are confronted with multiple, conflicting goals.[29] In making moral choices, the philosopher Martha Nussbaum has insisted on the critical place of emotions: they "are not only not more unreliable than intellectual calculations, but frequently are more reliable, and less deceptively seductive."[30]

emotion is real but not properly founded on a true belief and thus inappropriate. See Lyons, *Emotion*, 109–12.

27. Dow, *Engaging Emotions*, 9.

28. See, e.g., Dylan Evans, *Emotion: The Science of Sentiment* (Oxford: Oxford University Press, 2001); Macmurray, *Reason and Emotion*; Solomon, "Logic of Emotion"; M. P. Morrissey, "Reason and Emotion: Modern and Classical Views on Religious Knowing," *Horizons* 16 (1986): 275–91; Dylan Evans and Pierre Cruse, *Emotion, Evolution, and Rationality* (Oxford: Oxford University Press, 2004); Elliott, *Faithful Feelings*, 36–48.

29. See Dylan Evans, "The Search Hypothesis of Emotion," *British Journal for the Philosophy of Science* 53 (2002): 497–509. Emotions are one of the principal means whereby attention is constrained and directed and decisions thereby structured. First, they define the parameters we take into account in any particular deliberation, and second, in the process of decision-making, they render salient only a small proportion of the possible alternatives and of the conceivably relevant facts.

30. Nussbaum, *Love's Knowledge*, 40. Emotions are "intelligent parts of our ethical agency, responsive to the workings of deliberation and essential to its completion. . . . There will be certain contexts in which the pursuit of intellectual reasoning apart from emotion will actually prevent a full rational judgment—for example by preventing an access to one's grief, one's love, that is necessary for the full understanding of what has taken place when a loved one dies." Nussbaum, *Love's Knowledge*, 41. See also Justin Oakley, *Morality and the Emotions* (London: Routledge, 1992); Elliott, *Faithful Feelings*. One of the most illuminating accounts of the knowledge-bearing character of emotions is provided by the scientist Michael Polanyi. See R. T. Allen, "Polanyi and the Rehabilitation of Emotion," in *Emotion, Reason and Tradition: Essays on the Social, Political and Economic Thought of Michael Polanyi*, ed. R. T. Allen (Aldershot, UK: Ashgate, 2005), 41–54. Against those who habitually regard emotion as entirely passive, irrational, and suspect because of its connection with value, and who recommend an emotion-free attitude in the search for truth, Polanyi insists that emotions are an intelligent response to apprehended realities, that "passion" is a vital component in every act of knowing. Far from inhibiting scientific inquiry and discovery, the passions are indispensable to it. In science the emotions have a threefold function: "selective," "heuristic," and "persuasive." Emotions *enable a scientist to select what is of value*; they indicate that a discovery is intellectually precious, and that it is precious to science. Heuristically,

Finally, because they involve belief and evaluation, emotions are typically *motivators to action.*[31] I act *out* of fear, sadness, or whatever. I evaluate the jellyfish as dangerous and swim away.[32] N. H. Frijda uses the term "action tendencies" to describe the way emotions do not specify the precise action required but provoke types of behavior, *tendencies* to act in this way rather than in that way.[33] We should note that emotions become motives to action when they contain *desire* as part of their occurrent states (whether the desire is conscious or unconscious). If I pity someone in pain, I will want to alleviate that person's suffering; if I take joy in my daughter, I will want to express it to her in some way.

Emotion and Faithful Worship

I have offered a brief sketch of a cognitive account of emotions. How might this be situated within a theology of Christian worship?

By "worship" here, I mean those regular occasions when the church is gathered by the Triune God to receive and celebrate its corporate identity in a focused, concentrated way. More succinctly, in worship we are reoriented by God to God. If sin is a rejection of our calling to honor the Creator, a refusal to praise God, in worship we are redirected (reconciled) to the One worthy of all praise and reoriented in love to one another and thus built up as the people of God. And as we are built up as God's people, we are redirected to God's world in mission. The indwelling agent of this reorientation is the Holy Spirit, and its mediator is Jesus Christ.[34]

---

emotions *sustain the process of discovery* by intimating particular discoveries that have yet to be made and sustaining the ongoing pursuit of them. As for their persuasive function, emotions *enable the scientist to communicate convincingly* his or her discoveries to others; in the case of a great or significant discovery, this can never be a completely formal and mechanical process, for the formal systems we already have at our disposal will likely be inadequate. Michael Polanyi, *Personal Knowledge: Towards a Post-Critical Philosophy* (New York: Harper & Row, 1964), chaps. 6 and 7, esp. 132–60. Polanyi also speaks of another emotional dimension of science: the permanent intellectual *satisfaction* that comes from having made a discovery. *Personal Knowledge*, 173.

31. Lyons, *Emotion*, chap. 11, esp. 168–69.

32. The same emotion, it should be noted, can motivate different actions. A mugger with a knife comes running toward me in an alleyway; I may run in the opposite direction, I might try to disarm him with my newly learned self-defense skills, or I might jump out of the way.

33. Nico H. Frijda, *The Emotions* (Cambridge: Cambridge University Press, 1986), 69–94.

34. For fuller treatments of the trinitarian character of worship, see James Torrance, *Worship, Community and the Triune God of Grace* (Carlisle, UK: Paternoster Press, 1996); Thomas A. Smail, *The Giving Gift: The Holy Spirit in Person* (London: Hodder & Stoughton, 1988); Robin Parry, *Worshipping Trinity: Coming Back to the Heart of Worship* (Carlisle, UK: Paternoster, 2005); Christopher J. Cocksworth, *Holy, Holy, Holy: Worshipping the Trinitarian God* (London: Darton Longman & Todd, 1997).

Worship so understood will be *faithful*. We can expand on this with regard to the emotions. First, worship is faithful in the sense that it is *properly oriented*—primarily to God and, in the power of the Spirit, to others with whom we worship and to the world we represent and to which we are sent. Emotion, therefore, will be rightly directed. Thus oriented, faithful worship will also be appropriate—to God, others, and the world. As far as emotion in worship is concerned, the greatest danger lies not in emotion per se but in emotion that is not properly directed and/or inappropriate. So, for example, if we are more enthralled by the sound of the choir than by the God it praises, the emotion is misdirected; if someone spends an entire service trembling and cringing with fear before God, the emotion is inappropriate.[35]

Second, faithful worship is *with and through Christ*, for Christ guarantees its proper orientation (in the Spirit, to God the Father, other worshipers, and the wider world), and he ensures it will be appropriate (true to God's character and purpose and thus to other worshipers and the wider world).

Crucial here is the "vicarious humanity of Christ."[36] Christ, as fully human, embodies and enables faithful worship. He is faithful, full of faith in the Father, not only in his earthly life of loving and obedient self-offering to the Father, culminating in crucifixion, but also in his continuing risen life—Christ is now the human High Priest who, on the ground of his atoning work, leads us in our worship (Heb. 2:12; 4:14; cf. Rom. 8:34). In him, our humanity has been taken and through the Holy Spirit re-formed, returned to God, so that now with him we can know his "Abba, Father" as our Abba, Father. In this way the church's worship is united with the one perfect response of the incarnate Son, with his once-for-all offering of worship on the cross, and with his ongoing worship of the Father in our midst as High Priest. And this is possible through the same Spirit who enabled and undergirded Christ's own earthly self-offering. Worship, in short, is a sharing by the Spirit in the Son's communion with the Father by the Spirit.

Understood in this way, worship is an invitation to be rehumanized as we grow in the likeness of Christ. The axiom of Gregory Nazianzen pertains here: "What is not assumed is not saved." Christ assumed the whole of

35. Indeed, in this latter case, the fear is ill founded, for it is based on a false belief about God, namely, that God is essentially threatening or destructive. See Dow, *Engaging Emotions*, 9.
36. See T. F. Torrance, "The Mind of Christ in Worship: The Problem of Apollinarianism in the Liturgy," in T. F. Torrance, *Theology in Reconciliation: Essays towards Evangelical and Catholic Unity in East and West* (Eugene, OR: Wipf & Stock, 1996), 139–214; Graham Redding, *Prayer and the Priesthood of Christ in the Reformed Tradition* (London: T&T Clark, 2003); Christian D. Kettler, *The God Who Believes: Faith, Doubt and the Vicarious Humanity of Christ* (Eugene, OR: Cascade Books, 2005).

our humanness in order to redeem us. Included in this redemption are our emotions, likewise our renewal in his image. Emotions are not intrinsically fallen or incidental to our humanness but rather part of what God desires to transform, not least in worship. At its best, then, worship is a school of the emotions. Whether confessing with heavy Lenten hearts or shouting Easter acclamations, we learn to become emotionally mature, to become (so to speak) a little less adolescent.

Third, faithful worship is a *truthful activity*. We have noted that our emotions can play a key part in truthful perception. In worship, when we discover through the Spirit and with Christ a new dimension of the Father's love for us, or the hidden need of the person in the pew next to us, or some new dimension of evil in a terrorist atrocity, our emotions, far from hindering our grasp of truth, enable a clearer discernment of it.

Fourth, faithful worship is a *uniting activity*. To be redirected to the Father through the Son by the Spirit is to discover the love that is eternally given and received between Father and Son, the love with which we can be bound together (John 17:21). All worship in the Spirit builds up the body of Christ and encourages unity (1 Cor. 14:5, 12, 26). Emotions can, of course, rupture relations, but as we have noted, they can also be instrumental in generating and sustaining powerful bonds between people and as such serve the Spirit's work of bringing about the reconciled unity made possible through the death of Christ.

Fifth and finally, faithful worship is an *ex-centric activity*: to be caught up in the life of the Triune God entails being propelled out into the world as agents of transformation. In Miroslav Volf's words, worship happens in the rhythm of "adoration and action."[37] If emotions typically generate "action tendencies," they will likely have a key place in provoking the desire to do God's will, in energizing God's people for mission.

Music and Emotion

If our argument has been along the right lines, inasmuch as music is implicated in our emotional involvement in worship, it should promote the features of worship just described. We could speak at length about each feature, but our focus in this essay is fairly specific: What is it about musical sounds and the way they operate that makes them emotionally significant and valuable

37. Miroslav Volf, "Worship as Adoration and Action: Reflections on a Christian Way of Being-in-the-World," in *Worship: Adoration and Action*, ed. D. A. Carson (Grand Rapids: Baker, 1993), 203–11.

to us? And what can we learn from this theologically, with regard to music in worship?[38]

Objects?

A difficulty presents itself immediately. We have spoken of emotion being oriented to objects. Gentle music in a restaurant might create a "mood" or "proto-emotion," but to be fully fledged, we have said, an emotion requires an object of some kind (together with beliefs about and evaluation of the object). However, musical sounds do not in any clear or consistent way represent, denote, or convey objects for us to be emotional about (except in the relatively rare cases when extramusical phenomena are simulated). How, then, can we speak of the experience of genuine emotion in and through musical experience when no objects are attached to the musical sounds?[39]

38. Sloboda and Juslin make a distinction between "intrinsic" and "extrinsic" sources of emotion in musical experience, the former being features of the musical sounds themselves, and the latter being factors that belong "outside" the music but by virtue of which an emotional response occurs. Sloboda and Juslin, "Psychological Perspectives on Music and Emotion," 91–96. Here I am concerned with "intrinsic" sources. This is not to deny that a wide range of emotionally significant extrinsic factors may be operative whenever we make and hear music. But it is nonetheless quite legitimate to ask, what might be emotionally potent about the sounds themselves and the way they operate?

Therefore, I am not considering the role of emotionally loaded associations that music may stimulate ("they're playing our tune, darling") or cases where musical sounds simulate an object that elicits an emotional response in us (e.g., the thumping of an elephant charging toward us).

And I am not considering highly dubious theories that posit a *necessary* link between musical sounds and a person's occurrent emotion. For example, some locate the emotional content of music in *persons*—which usually means either the creator of music ("expressivist" theories) or the hearer/listener ("arousal" or "evocation" theories). For extensive criticisms of the former, see Stephen Davies, *Musical Meaning and Expression* (Ithaca, NY: Cornell University Press, 1994), 170–84; A. H. Goldman, "Emotions in Music (a Postscript)," *Journal of Aesthetics and Art Criticism* 53 (1995): 59–69; Roger Scruton, *The Aesthetics of Music* (Oxford: Clarendon Press, 1997), 144–45. For critique of arousal theories, see Scruton, *Aesthetics of Music*, 145–48; Davies, *Musical Meaning and Expression*, 184–99. Problematic also are "representational" theories, where music's expressiveness is said to depend on it representing emotion. This notion implies that to be moved by music we must be able to perceive, along with the sounds, some extramusical "emotion" to which the music in some manner directs us. Music may simulate an object that arouses an emotion in us, but in this case it "represents" the object, not the emotion. For discussion, see Scruton, *Aesthetics of Music*, chap. 5.

39. This problem was famously highlighted by the philosopher Eduard Hanslick (1825–1904), who claimed that music (and he is thinking of instrumental music without words) is unable to arouse or represent basic emotion (joy, melancholy, anger, fear, etc.) in an artistically relevant way. Eduard Hanslick, *The Beautiful in Music: A Contribution to the Revisal of Musical Aesthetics* (New York: Da Capo Press, 1974). In support, he argued that music itself is not capable of providing the materials necessary for emotional arousal: beliefs appropriate to the experiencing of an emotion and objects of emotion (something to be emotional about). Hanslick was not denying that the experience of music can occasion deep feelings. (He believed this could happen

The answer, I believe, lies in recognizing that music is heard never on its own but as part of a perceptual complex that includes a range of nonmusical phenomena, for example, the physical setting in which we hear the music, memories of people associated with it, artificial images (as in the case of film and video), words (the lyrics of a song, program notes, the title of a piece, what someone said about the piece on the radio), and so on. As Nicholas Cook puts it, "Pure music . . . is an aesthetician's (and music theorist's) fiction."[40] Music is perceived in a manifold environment. And this generates a fund of material for us to be emotional "about." Music swims in a sea of potential objects. The problem of how genuine emotion can be felt through music without objects only arises if we posit a sealed-off world of pure music. No such world exists.

So, for example, we go to a film. We hear music along with images and words. The music's emotional properties get "hooked onto" those word and images, drawing us deeper emotionally into the drama. Sometimes the music's general emotional properties are nuanced (focused, made more precise) by words and images. More commonly, the words and images supply the general emotional properties, and the music nuances them. For example, toward the end of the film *The Mission*, the main theme music returns as the South American mission station is pictured being burned to the ground along with its converts. The images and words provide the emotional objects; the music's emotional properties nuance the emotions evoked by them. In this way, we are pulled into the story all the more profoundly: we feel more intensely the heartrending poignancy of this tragedy, one especially devastating given that the mission station was founded by the priest who played this music's melody on a pipe.[41]

---

through "personal associations," or through emotionally unstable people being triggered by particular features of music quite arbitrarily.) But he denied that such feelings were relevant to the artistic nature and purpose of music. The expressiveness of music, for Hanslick, lies rather in its play of forms, its own interior logic arising from the patterning of sounds.

40. Nicholas Cook, *Analysing Musical Multimedia* (Oxford: Clarendon Press, 1998), 92. Cook makes this point against Peter Kivy and Stephen Davies, who want to distinguish between emotions that require an object and those that do not, and who claim that music can represent the appearance of the latter but not the former (because music cannot convey or represent objects). As Cook rightly points out, doing this is to treat music as if it were heard in a vacuum (86–92).

41. In response to the initial challenge about music and objects, it might well be argued that the aesthetic configuration of the music constitutes the emotional object. We are moved directly by the qualities of the sounds, their interplay, arrangements, and syntactical structure. I hear a chord sequence, a guitar riff, an intricate elaboration, the shape of a song, the form of a sonata, and I find that its patterning, arrangement, and internal "sense" generate emotion—a feeling of wonder, perhaps, or amazement. Even with melancholy music, we will be moved by how beautifully melancholy it is. Sloboda and Juslin point out that psychological research has "embarrassingly little to say" about this kind of aesthetic response. See Sloboda and Juslin,

Bodily Behavior

However, even bearing in mind this context of potential objects, it is quite legitimate to ask what the musical sounds themselves might be bringing to the emotional experience. To be more specific: How is it that certain types of musical sound come to be given emotive descriptions ("cheerful," "heartrending," etc.)? It has often been shown that a wide variety of listeners can reach a large measure of agreement about the emotional character of musical stimuli, likewise composers about the kind of music that will generally be considered appropriate for, say, a scene in a film.[42] What grounds this agreement? Can particular sounds themselves possess features that give them emotional potency?

This field is immensely complex, and the answers to these questions have to be somewhat tentative and provisional. But we can make a start by considering the notion of a "perceived property," as developed by the philosopher Peter Kivy.[43] When I hear joy in the last movement of Beethoven's Seventh Symphony, argues Kivy, I am hearing it not representatively (in the way I see a mountain in a mountain picture) but rather in the way I see the greenness of a leaf, as a quality perceived. Kivy contends that there are distinct (if complex)[44] emotive properties of music, perceived not as representing something else but as properties of the music itself, and on the basis of which we describe the music as "mournful," "ebullient," or whatever.

What grounds might we have for claiming that music can have such properties? For many, the most promising way to begin answering this question is through "contour theory." Associated in particular with Kivy and Stephen

---

"Psychological Perspectives on Music and Emotion," 81. This response may well be a component in the perception of some music, especially in situations where some kind of "aesthetic contemplation" is most easily practiced—in a concert hall, perhaps. But in culture at large and worldwide, by far the majority of situations where we hear music will not conform to this pattern.

42. See, e.g., Martyn Evans, *Listening to Music* (Basingstoke, UK: Macmillan, 1990), 62; A. Gabrielsson and P. Juslin, "Emotional Expression in Music Performance," *Psychology of Music* 24 (1996): 68–91; Sloboda and Juslin, "Psychological Perspectives on Music and Emotion," 94. See the extensive discussion of this matter in Davies, *Musical Meaning and Expression*, 243–52.

43. See Peter Kivy, *Introduction to a Philosophy of Music* (Oxford: Clarendon Press, 2002), 31–36.

44. Emotive properties are not simple and uniform. When we ascribe an emotive property like mournfulness to a piece of music, we do so because of a number of features that together lead us to ascribe the quality "mournful" to it. If I call my car red, there is nothing I can point to in order to persuade you it really is red except the one color of the red car. I do not say, "It's red because of this or that"; redness is a simple property. But if I say, "This piece of music is mournful," you might ask, "What's mournful about it?" and I would then have to point to several features of the music that would back up the claim: slow tempo, minor key, subdued dynamics, falling melodies, or whatever. Nonetheless, even if complex, its mournfulness is a quality in its own right (an "emergent" quality), distinct from the many qualities that generate it.

Davies,[45] this theory holds that music can bear a structural similarity to the heard and seen manifestations of human emotive expression, and that it is this similarity that leads us to ascribe emotive properties to it. A number of emotions have behavioral expressions that are constitutive of their nature, and these expressions have distinctive "physiognomies." The contour theory holds that musical sounds correspond in various ways to bodily expressions characteristic of emotive states. It is not so much that music embodies emotion as that music embodies bodily behavior characteristic of emotion. (This highlights the importance of the second element in the "classic triad" of emotion.)

The two forms of bodily expression that are marked out as most relevant are *vocalization* and *gesture*. It has long been recognized that nonverbal vocalization—rhythmic and melodic utterances without words—is a major medium of human emotional communication. Humans have an innate ability to produce and perceive certain rhythms, contours, and timbres that encapsulate an emotional state; indeed, some vocal sounds, in the emotional states they express, are fundamental and invariant across cultures (and even across species). This ability is taken into the practice of speech—we can quickly recognize emotion in a speaker by the sound of his or her voice, even if the words are emotionally neutral. Certain musical patterns are heard as emotionally expressive, it is argued, because of this capacity. So, for example, cheerful people tend to speak quickly, often in bright and loud tones, and in a high vocal register. Music we call "cheerful" will likewise often tend to be fast, loud, and use upper registers; phrases will tend to rise in pitch more than they fall (e.g., the "Et resurrexit" from Bach's *Mass in B Minor*). Melancholy or grief-ridden people tend to speak softly, slowly, and haltingly; their voices tend to sink at the end of sentences, and they use the lower part of their vocal register. The same often goes for melancholy melodies (e.g., Chopin's "Funeral March"). The empirical evidence supporting the link between vocal and musical expression of emotion is now substantial.[46]

45. Peter Kivy, *Sound Sentiment: An Essay on the Musical Emotions, including the Complete Text of the Corded Shell* (Philadelphia: Temple University Press, 1989), esp. chaps. 2–8; Davies, *Musical Meaning and Expression*, 228–77; Davies, "Philosophical Perspectives on Music's Expressiveness," 34–37; Kivy, *Introduction to a Philosophy of Music*, chaps. 3–7. For critique, see Goldman, "Emotions in Music (a Postscript)"; Geoffrey Madell, *Philosophy, Music and Emotion* (Edinburgh: Edinburgh University Press, 2002), chap. 1.

46. Charles Darwin noted that "when the voice is used under any strong emotion, it tends to assume . . . a musical character." Darwin, *Expression of the Emotions*, 92. Some scholars, such as Stephen Davies, are doubtful that vocalization is crucial for the recognition of music as emotionally significant; Davies, "Philosophical Perspectives on Music's Expressiveness," 35n7. But this is to set aside a considerable body of research: see, e.g., A. Kappas et al., "Voice and

It has been shown that gesture associated with emotional states also corresponds in striking ways to the dynamic features of music. According to Davies, music presents "emotion characteristics in appearances";[47] a piece of music sounds sad in the way that a weeping willow looks sad, not because it is sad but because it "presents the outward features of sadness."[48] And by far the most important human appearances in this regard are bodily movements, especially gait, bearing, or carriage. Sad people typically walk in a slow, halting way, with drooping bodies. Music we call "sad" tends to be slow and halting, with falling, faltering melodies. By embodying bodily motion, music embodies emotion.

This receives some corroboration from psychological and neuropsychological research. The links between emotion and bodily behavior are very close, something confirmed by the phenomenon known as "proprioceptive feedback," that "going through the motions" of an emotion can, at least to some extent, generate a similar mood.[49] Singing happy music may well, in the right conditions, engender a happy mood, which when directed to certain objects may well become a full-fledged emotion.[50] Particularly important here is rhythm. Heard rhythm and bodily movement are closely related in humans—we are able to synchronize auditory beats and bodily motion with

Emotion," in *Fundamentals of Nonverbal Behavior: Studies in Emotion and Social Interaction*, ed. R. S. Feldman and B. Rime (Cambridge: Cambridge University Press, 1991), 200–238; K. R. Scherer, "Expression of Emotion in Voice and Music," *Journal of Voice* 9 (1995): 235–48; J. Panksepp and G. Bernatsky, "Emotional Sounds and the Brain: The Neuro-Affective Foundations of Musical Appreciation," *Behavioural Processes* 60 (2002); P. N. Juslin and P. Laukka, "Communication of Emotions in Vocal Expression and Music Performance: Different Channels, Same Code?," *Psychological Bulletin* 129 (2003): 770–814; P. N. Juslin and P. Laukka, "Emotional Expression in Speech and Music: Evidence of Cross-Modal Similarities," in *Emotions Inside Out: 130 Years after Darwin's "The Expression of the Emotions in Man and Animals,"* ed. P. Ekman et al. (New York: New York Academy of Sciences, 2003), 279–82; Iain Morley, "The Evolutionary Origins and Archaeology of Music" (PhD diss., University of Cambridge, 2006), 162–73, 177–81; M. M. Lavy, "Emotion and the Experience of Listening to Music: A Framework for Empirical Research" (PhD diss., University of Cambridge, 2001), 39–47. Lavy writes: "Humans have a remarkable ability to communicate and detect emotion in the contours and timbres of vocal utterances; this ability is not suddenly lost during a musical listening experience." "Emotion and the Experience," v.

47. Davies, *Musical Meaning and Expression*, 221–28.

48. Davies, *Musical Meaning and Expression*, 239. See also Olga McDonald Meidner, "Motion and E-motion in Music," *British Journal of Aesthetics* 25 (1985): 349–56; Lavy, "Emotion and the Experience," 54–57.

49. Iain Morley, "Evolutionary Origins and Archaeology of Music," 173–77.

50. Psychologist David Myers asks: "If assuming an emotional expression triggers a feeling, then would imitating others' expressions help us feel what they are feeling? . . . The laboratory evidence is supportive. . . . Acting as another helps us feel what another feels." Myers, *Psychology*, 476.

great precision.[51] It is thus not surprising to find that rhythm often plays a part in our ascribing emotional qualities to music, given that musical rhythm can evoke qualities of bodily movement characteristic of certain emotions (e.g., joyful music tends to be fast, like the movements of joyful people). But especially crucial to note here is the power of rhythm to *bind people together* through synchronization; it has long been known that one of the most powerful ways to unite a group is through rhythmic music. And given rhythm's connections with emotion, it is one of the quickest ways in which emotion is spread and shared. As we join in the movements of others, through "feedback" a mood is easily generated.[52] This is especially so if the bodily gestures are visible to members of the group: visual, auditory, and motor cues combine to create a potent and mutually reinforcing mix and can lead to fervent emotion when directed toward various objects. We only need think of a protest march with chanting—combining musical rhythm, vocalization, and gesture (marching and pounding fists)—or the rock concert, where it is almost impossible not to join with the emotionally charged stamping, swaying, and clapping we see and hear all around us.

This links up with those who want to describe our emotional participation in music as a kind of dance. Roger Scruton writes of a "sympathetic response" to music in which we find emotional meaning in the sounds and respond accordingly with movements of our own—whether overt or internal, voluntary or involuntary. We "dance with" or "move with" the sounds.[53]

We have spoken mainly of melody and rhythm. But what of harmony?[54] Take, for example, chords such as major, minor, and diminished, which are widely held to have a particular affective quality (e.g., minor chords are routinely regarded as expressive of negative emotion, such as sadness and sorrow). How might they gain this emotional character, and how does this square with contour theory?

---

51. According to Aniruddh Patel, "there is not a single report of an animal [apart from humans] being trained to tap, peck, or move in synchrony with an auditory beat." Patel, *Music, Language, and the Brain* (Oxford: Oxford University Press, 2008), 409. See M. Molinari, M. G. Leggio, M. De Martin, A. Cerasa, and M. Thaut, "Neurobiology of Rhythmic Motor Entrainment," *Annals of the New York Academy of Science: The Neurosciences and Music* 999 (2003): 313–20.

52. "Rhythm turns listeners into participants, makes listening active and motoric, and synchronizes the brains and minds (and, since emotion is always intertwined with music [and with the body, we would add], the 'hearts') of all who participate." Oliver W. Sacks, *Musicophilia: Tales of Music and the Brain* (New York: Alfred A. Knopf, 2007), 244–45.

53. Scruton, *Aesthetics of Music*, 354–64.

54. Against contour theorists, Geoffrey Madell insists that "in introducing the element of harmony we introduce something which really does not have any parallel to human behaviour." Madell, *Philosophy, Music and Emotion*, 13. This is too sweeping, but Kivy acknowledges this weakness and confesses he cannot address it satisfactorily. Kivy, *Introduction to a Philosophy of Music*, 43–45.

In part, it seems, these acquire their emotional character through their relation to other chords (or implied chords). In real-world music, chords appear not in isolation but alongside others, and in Western music they relate to one another through patterns of tension and resolution. In its small-, medium-, and large-scale dimensions, at many different levels, and (potentially) engaging every parameter (including melody, dynamics, texture, meter, and timbre), music consists of movements from rest to instability, followed at some stage by a return to rest. One of the most important ways in which this is played out is through harmony: music is heard according to the "gravitational pull" or "attraction" of a target, the "tonic" chord (the "home" key). Chords other than the tonic are heard as drawn toward it in varying degrees depending on their "distance" from the tonic, and a sense of musical motion is generated by the push and pull away from the tonic. Indeed, an extremely common structure is the progression from rest (home key), toward a "distant" place (foreign key), back to rest (home key): home-away-home again.[55]

Many theorists have related this tension-resolution pattern to music's expressiveness.[56] Indeed, "tension" and "resolution" are terms frequently used in speaking of emotions: my anger "resolves" into acceptance, my anxiety into peace of mind, and so on. And we should note that the emotional character of the resolution is given a distinctive hue by virtue of its position: it is the resolution *of a tension*. So, for example, the "joy" of a major chord resolving minor music is commonly perceived not simply as possessing joy but "joy-as-resolution."[57]

55. See Joseph Peter Swain, *Musical Languages* (New York: Norton, 1997), chap. 2. I explicate this more fully in Jeremy Begbie, *Theology, Music and Time* (Cambridge: Cambridge University Press, 2000), chap. 2. For the most thorough treatment of the notion of "distance" in tonal music, see Fred Lerdahl, *Tonal Pitch Space* (New York: Oxford University Press, 2001).

56. For a short survey of some of the relevant literature, see Lerdahl, *Tonal Pitch Space*, 188–92. Stephen Davies speaks of the tensions and resolutions typical of music at some length but sees their significance for contour theory only in their suggestion of order and purposiveness: "musical movement invites attention to expressiveness because, like human action and behavior . . . it displays order and purposiveness." Davies, *Musical Meaning and Expression*, 229. That is, musical movement is invested with human expressiveness because it possesses a logic akin to human action (rather than to random or fully determined movement). But according to numerous writers, it is not simply the overall dynamic of purposiveness that gives musical movement its emotional power but (much more) its *internal configurations of tension and resolution*, the way in which we are moved from stability to instability, "toward" and "away from" centers of rest.

57. It would seem that a particular form of the tension-resolution scheme plays a large part in the emotional intensity of Western music: the generation and confirmation/violation of expectations. The first scholar who sought to demonstrate this at length was Leonard Meyer, who contended that we experience music in the context of stylistic norms that have their roots in our habitual tendency to resolve ambiguity. Leonard B. Meyer, *Emotion and Meaning in Music* (Chicago: University of Chicago Press, 1956). In his early work, Meyer held that emotions are

How might these findings relate to contour theory? Further research is doubtless needed. But if music recruits the same emotional circuits as other activities associated with emotion, it is hardly fanciful to suggest that correlations will be made between, on the one hand, the tensions and resolutions of chord sequences and, on the other, the tensions and resolutions of bodily behavior that accompany various emotional states. After all, the terms "tension" and "rest" are clearly applicable to some forms of bodily process characteristic of emotion—apprehension frequently comes with restlessness, emotional calm with a restful posture, and so forth—and similar things could be said of the move from equilibrium to tension and tension to resolution. Indeed, the very words "tension" and "resolution" (or "relaxation") can describe bodily states connected to emotion.

But this still leaves us with the questions: Why should particular chords be seen as more or less dissonant and consonant, more or less "resolved" in the first place? Is this entirely a matter of sociocultural contingency? And how might the emotive correlations of this be accounted for by contour theory, that is, in terms of bodily behavior? In response, some might say that the crying of a baby or the howl of a person in distress (emotional vocalizations) are normally highly dissonant, and that our reaction to extreme dissonance is often to cringe or frown. Maybe, but a more direct physiological explanation is probably more plausible. Simply put, dissonance provokes a less pleasant sensation than consonance. The widely reported experience of a disagreeable "roughness" between tones regarded as dissonant could be cited in this

---

experienced due to violations of expectancy. As we are taken through a piece of music, we find its patterns converge with and diverge from basic stylistic templates. Deviations from a musical stylistic norm arouse strong affect (surprise, frustration, and so forth). "Emotion or affect is aroused when a tendency to respond is arrested or inhibited." Meyer, *Emotion and Meaning in Music*, 14. In his later work, in what would seem to be an effort to give his theories a more objective leaning, Meyer shifts significantly away from the notion of "creating expectations" to that of "implication": a musical event is said to imply another by rendering it more or less probable. See Meyer, *Explaining Music: Essays and Explorations* (Chicago: University of Chicago Press, 1978). Although some of his contentions have been widely challenged, Meyer's work spawned a large body of writing that fruitfully follows the lines that he opened up. His stress on the emotional potential of musical expectation (or implication) has been substantially confirmed and carried forward by psychological research. See, e.g., J. J. Bharucha, "Melodic Anchoring," *Music Perception* 13 (1996): 383–400; T. Eerola and A. C. North, "Expectancy-Based Model of Melodic Complexity," in *Proceedings of the Sixth International Conference on Music Perception and Cognition*, ed. C. Woods et al. (Keele, UK: Keele University Department of Psychology, 2000), 1177–83; Sloboda and Juslin, "Psychological Perspectives on Music and Emotion," 91–92; John A. Sloboda, "Empirical Studies of Emotional Response to Music," in *Exploring the Musical Mind*, ed. John A. Sloboda (Oxford: Oxford University Press, 2005), 203–14, esp. 209–13; David Huron, *Sweet Anticipation: Music and the Psychology of Expectation* (Cambridge, MA: MIT Press, 2006).

connection,[58] and there is evidence that our description of major chords as emotionally more positive than minor is bound up with similar factors.[59]

Contour theory has considerable advantages over its rivals; perhaps the most important is its focus on emotion's links to the body. But three main qualifications are in order. First, even if there is a correspondence between behaviors and musical sounds, we should avoid implying that being moved by music entails a mental act whereby we spot the resemblance between a musical stimulus and a (remembered) bodily expression of emotion. It would seem rather that emotionally significant musical sounds and vocalizations/gestures that express emotions are dealt with by the same neurological systems; they relate at the level of brain processing, not at the level of two objects being perceived as similar. Second, the contour theory may well be too restrictive. To explain musical expressiveness solely in terms of its links with public bodily behavior (as in Stephen Davies's version) seems too narrow. For one thing, it would appear that emotional gesture and vocalization are virtually inseparable.[60] Moreover, as I have just suggested, in some cases it seems reasonable to believe that music is described in emotional terms chiefly because of its direct physiological effects, rather than because its contours are associated with emotional behavior.

The third qualification concerns expression and arousal. One of the strengths and driving forces of contour theory is that it seeks to avoid positing any necessary link between musical sounds and a person's occurrent emotion—whether composer, performer, or listener. It purports to show how music can have emotionally expressive properties without that being tied to the producer's or the hearer's emotions. To use Kivy's analogy, the Great Saint Bernard dog looks sad but as far as we know is no sadder than any other dog and will not necessarily make us sad. Music can be expressive of an emotion without expressing or arousing that emotion.[61] Nevertheless, in

58. On this, see Lerdahl, *Tonal Pitch Space*, 80–82; Donald Hall, *Musical Acoustics* (Pacific Grove, CA: Brooks/Cole, 2002), 393, 439–43.

59. A. J. Blood et al., "Emotional Responses to Pleasant and Unpleasant Music Correlate with Activity in Paralimbic Brain Regions," *Nature Neuroscience* 2 (1999): 382–87; Lerdahl, *Tonal Pitch Space*, 80–81.

60. Morley, "Evolutionary Origins and Archaeology of Music," 177–83. For example, as Morley puts it: "A down-turned mouth, slackness of posture, lower voice and reduced pitch contour in vocalisation . . . are all part of a gamut of physiological responses associated with sadness and/or depression" (218).

61. See note 38 above. "The sadness is to the music rather like the redness to the apple, than it is like the burp to the cider." O. K. Bouwsma, "The Expression Theory of Art," in *Philosophical Analysis: A Collection of Essays*, ed. Max Black (Englewood Cliffs, NJ: Prentice-Hall, 1950), 71–96, here 94. Contour theory also avoids the key drawback of representational/referring theories, for it does not claim that the music's emotional power depends on hearing musical

real-world situations, a composer or performer may express emotion through music. And with respect to arousal, music frequently does (and is frequently intended to) arouse emotions (or at least moods) in ways that are at least to some extent fairly predictable: given certain conditions, there will be a strong tendency for particular musical sound patterns to engender this or that mood or emotion. (No film composer would be in business otherwise.)

To summarize: although conclusions in this field must be somewhat provisional, I am suggesting that when we ascribe emotional properties to music we are doing so because of correspondences between the musical sounds and the physical expressions of emotional states or, to be more accurate, because musical sounds are processed by the same neurological systems as bodily behavior characteristic of emotions. And, it would seem, the most relevant bodily behaviors in this respect are vocalization and gesture. (However, in some cases there may be a more direct link through immediate physiological effect.) I have also stressed that we cannot assume a necessary link between this or that music and a corresponding affect in the music maker or the music hearer, but music may nonetheless be used to express emotion, and we can frequently speak of the tendency of particular musical sound patterns to spawn moods and emotions of particular types.

Representative Concentration

The question still remains, however: Why do we *value* the emotional expressiveness of music? What benefit do we gain?

We would be foolish to insist on there being only one benefit; again, any response must be provisional. But a large part of the answer, I suggest, lies in the notion of *concentration*. Typically, our emotional lives are messy. Emotions are often confused and transient; they are tangled, come and go, jump out at us at odd times. Likewise the bodily movements characteristic of them: If I am angry, I might throw my arms all over the place, stamp my feet, shout things I only half mean, grit my teeth, or mutter intermittently.

Suppose, however, a dancer wants to display anger. She will likely deploy particular movements—a glare perhaps, a clenched fist, a thrust of the head. Such movements are concentrated in at least three senses. First, and most basic, they will be purified, free from irrelevance and off-putting distractions, distilled, pared down. Second, they might also compress a range of gestures into one, for instance, condensing complex angry states into a single sweep of

---

sounds as representative of / referring to melancholy and cheerfulness, any more than seeing a green bus as green depends on seeing it as representative of / referring to greenness. We hear sadness and cheerfulness not as referents but as properties of the musical sounds.

the arm. Third, they might specify one type of emotion rather than another, *this* emotion rather than *that* emotion.

Something similar applies to music. (And the dancer analogy is especially fitting, given what we have said about bodily behavior.)[62] Insofar as bodily behavior is embodied in music, it is not the inchoate vocalizations and gestures characteristic of our emotional life but bodily behavior translated into the formalities of music: particular melodic shapes, appoggiaturas, suspensions, falling chromatic lines, and so forth. The last movement of Tchaikovsky's *Pathétique* Symphony is not expressive of grief as we normally experience it; rather, it offers concentrated "grief in music." Through carefully structured and ordered devices, the piece is pared down, shorn of irrelevance. In some passages, we might speak of grief emotions compressed and in others of a particular grief—Tchaikovsky knows how to differentiate reflective grief from despairing grief, for example.[63] When we appropriate these concentrated expressive qualities of music in relation to objects about which we can be emotional, just because the qualities are "concentrated" they have the capacity to transform our emotional involvement ("purifying," "compressing," and "specifying" our emotions); in short, *they enable a more concentrated emotional engagement with the object or objects with which we are dealing.*

Latent here, I suggest, is a dynamic of *representation*. Consider Samuel Barber's "Adagio for Strings" when performed at the funeral of President John F. Kennedy. By embodying concentrated emotional qualities, music could give voice to, or "speak for," thousands. The mourners could be emotionally represented by the music; they could identify with it and be pulled into its concentrated expressiveness and thus grieve more deeply, perhaps more appropriately.[64] Not long ago, a friend of mine led a funeral service for a young mother who had taken her own life, leaving an only son. Immediately after the formalities at the graveside, her son lifted a set of bagpipes and played a lament for his mother. My friend said that it was as if he had summed up for everyone what they really wanted to say, "deep down." At that funeral, they were emotionally represented by music. This may be why people who grieve

62. On the very close relation between music and dance with respect to emotion, see Morley, "Evolutionary Origins and Archaeology of Music," 173–77. Also C. L. Krumhansl and D. L. Schenck, "Can Dance Reflect the Structural and Expressive Qualities of Music? A Perceptual Experiment on Balanchine's Choreography of Mozart's Divertimento no.15," *Musicae Scientiae* 1 (1997): 63–85.

63. This is perhaps the sort of thing Mendelssohn had in mind when he said that music is not *less* but *more* precise than words. Quoted in Nussbaum, *Upheavals of Thought*, 251.

64. Of course, music is not some kind of person who represents people; rather, because of its emotional qualities, it can *serve* to represent people as it is taken up and used in particular situations.

often do not want cheerful music or something that merely plays the chaos of their grief back to them, but instead something that can both connect with their grief as it is and help them find new forms and depths of emotion, perhaps forms that help place their sorrow in a larger, more hopeful emotional context and in this way begin to re-form them.

Clearly, then, through music we can be emotionally educated, for we can be introduced to types of emotion previously unknown to us. Just as unfamiliar muscles are toned in a workout, music can give us an emotional workout ("I never knew I had those muscles there"; "I never knew I could feel that way"). In a Pentecostal service of praise, for example, we may well feel not only a joy in God that we have previously felt but a new depth or type of joy. Music can help us discover something that we could feel, that we have not felt before.[65] And we might add, we can also be educated emotionally: we might discover what we should feel in particular situations, in the presence of particular objects.

This discussion is certainly not intended to be a complete account of the emotional benefit we gain from music. But I suggest that "representative concentration" may often belong to the heart of the matter: that in relation to objects of emotion, music can concentrate our emotional engagement (through purification, compression, or specification); and that this dynamic is one of representation, in which music "speaks for us," on our behalf.[66] And just because it involves this process of concentration, music can be a means of emotional education.

Music, Emotion, and Worship

We have asked, what is it about musical sounds and the way they operate that makes them become emotionally significant and valuable to us? And we have answered, at least in part, they become emotionally significant because they possess qualities corresponding to bodily behavior characteristic of emotion. Music can be emotionally valuable because (among other things no doubt) it embodies emotional qualities in a concentrated way and is thus capable of concentrating our emotional engagement with objects, in a representative way. Further, in the process, we can be emotionally educated.

65. The central weakness of theories that suggest music merely resembles, reflects, mirrors, copies, and so on our emotions is that they invariably fail to come to terms with the emotionally *transformative* effect of music.

66. Some will object that other art forms are capable of operating in similar ways. Indeed they are, but as my argument so far would indicate, music's distinctive contribution is its translation of emotional bodily movement into sound. This makes it neither superior nor inferior to other forms of art, but it does make it distinctive.

It is time to return to worship and explore the resonances between our findings and the theology of worship outlined earlier. What can we learn from these findings theologically? The first thing to say relates to bodily behavior. That music's emotional capacities are so closely linked with the body need not be underplayed. Quite the opposite, for bodily renewal is part of God's intention for humanity—the physical body of Jesus is not only the vehicle of salvation but the very site of God's promise for our own physical transformation: it is subject to judgment and death and raised from the dead as a pledge of the resurrection of our own bodies (1 Cor. 15:35–58). Even now, life is given to our mortal bodies by the Spirit of the Father who raised Jesus from the dead (Rom. 8:11), in anticipation of the Spirit-filled life of the age to come. Worship in the Spirit, through Christ, will by its very nature be caught up in this body-transforming momentum.

But we have said that in music, emotionally significant bodily movements are embodied in a concentrated (musical) form, in such a way that the music can represent us and concentrate us emotionally as we are drawn into its life. Here the dynamics of musical emotion and the dynamics of emotion in trinitarian worship come together in a remarkable way, especially when we recall what we said earlier about the vicarious humanity of Christ. In the life of Jesus, emotional "concentration" becomes *redemptive*. As one of us, Jesus lives a life of sinless and perfectly concentrated emotion in the midst of our emotional confusion. In him, we witness emotion shorn of all sinful distraction and confusion. In his anger at Chorazin, Bethsaida, and Capernaum (Luke 10:13–15), we see anger purified of corrupt motives, driven only by an opposition to all that stands against God's love. In his joy when praying to the Father (Luke 10:21), we see joy as it is meant to be, an elation completely centered on the one who sent him and able to meet the worst the world can thrust at him. In his grief at the tomb of Lazarus (John 11:35), we see grief as it could and should be: stinging to the depths and utterly free of sentimentality. And on other occasions we find variegated emotion compressed, generalized emotion nuanced and focused, and both made specific—all in the service of his mission. Here in this human being emotion is concentrated; here we are emotionally represented.

Now, by the Spirit, as our risen, human representative, Christ can concentrate our emotional life in the likeness of his—and not least in worship. He is the High Priest, tempted yet without sin, sympathizing with our weaknesses, unashamed to call us his brothers and sisters, and alive to intercede for us, appearing in God's presence on our behalf. We are not required to perfect our offering for it to be accepted but can rely on the one who takes our cries before the Father more truly and authentically than we ever could ourselves. Doing so will mean purging, compressing, and specifying our emotions, whether directly in relation to God or in relation to all the other emotional objects relevant to worship: other worshipers perhaps, or a reference in the creed, a sick friend we pray for, a difficult decision at work.

It seems, then, that a striking correspondence exists between the dynamics of musical emotion and the dynamics of worship. The upshot for our purposes is twofold. First, it seems that music is particularly well suited for being a vehicle of emotional renewal in worship, an extraordinary instrument through which the Holy Spirit can begin to remake and transform us in the likeness of Christ, the one true Worshiper.

Of course, music's power is open to abuse. If the orientation is askew or the emotion inappropriate, then manipulation, sentimentality, and emotional self-indulgence are among the ever-present dangers. So, for example, an upbeat mood engendered by jubilant music, instead of growing into an emotion by being turned appropriately to God or one another, may never be directed anywhere and never grow into an emotion proper. (When people speak about the danger of music "whipping up the emotions," this is usually what they mean.) Or we may find emotion is misdirected—as when the musical tenderness of a love song to Jesus is used by a teenager to feed his infatuation for the girl in the next pew (or, indeed, his infatuation with the girl is simply transferred to Jesus via the music). Or an emotion may be specified inappropriately—as when a hymn on the cost of the cross is set to consistently ebullient music. Perhaps the most worrying tendency today is the use of music with a very limited range of emotionally significant qualities or music that cannot specify anything but the broadest and most basic emotions—in short, music that can never help to educate congregations as to the enormous range of emotion to be found, for instance, in Scripture.

But emotional abuse should not lead us into a stultifying "anti-emotionism." To "grow up" into Christ is to grow up emotionally as much as anything else, and carefully chosen music in worship may have a larger part to play than we have yet imagined.

Second, we have seen, I think, that not only does theology illuminate music, but music illuminates and enriches our theology, in this case the theology of worship. Indeed, the dynamic of representative concentration that has emerged in our study of music brings to the fore and helps us understand more deeply not just something crucial to worship's emotional character but something crucial to all worship. Just as ambassadors on foreign trips carry the needs of their country with them, concentrating their people's concerns and speaking as they would speak if they could, so Christ takes our muddled and often half-meant worship and concentrates it in the presence of "Abba,

Father." In prayer "through Jesus Christ our Lord," our own prayer (so often feeble and confused, with sighs too deep for words) is purged, compressed, and specified, and we are educated in the process, discovering not only what we already knew we wanted to say but also what we could or perhaps should say. Even our "crumpled 'Amens'"[67] are shaped into things of beauty. In saying our creeds, half understood and muttered half-heartedly, we can be confident that Christ will take and perfect what we say and mean and is at work to purge, compress, and specify our belief so that in due course we can discover more of what we could and should affirm ("Lord, I believe; help my unbelief," Mark 9:24). Such is the liberating momentum at the heart of every gathering of God's people: we have a High Priest who worships in our midst.

67. Murray Rae, "Grace and Its Expectations: Offering Up Our Crumpled Amen," *Refresh* 5, no.1 (2005): 11–13.

4

Openness and Specificity

A Conversation with David Brown on Theology and Classical Music

One of the prominent voices in the theology and arts arena currently is David Brown, emeritus professor at the University of St. Andrews. Along with countless others, I have learned much from Brown's formidable and encyclopedic knowledge and from his frustration at the way theologians typically ignore large tracts of cultural activity as unworthy of their attention. Here I respond to his treatment of classical music, where despite the undoubted gains of his approach, I believe much more attention needs to be given to the normative criteria that govern the theological enterprise. An engagement with Brown will throw into relief some of the most fundamental matters concerning how we respond to the arts with theologically attuned eyes and ears. I conclude with some comments on the implications of my critique for a theological reading of the music of J. S. Bach (with some overlap with chap. 1).

It is hard to think of anyone who would not benefit from David Brown's exploration of classical music as it appears in *God and Grace of Body*.[1] As

An earlier version of this chapter appears in Jeremy Begbie, "Room of One's Own? Music, Space, and Freedom," in *Music, Modernity, and God: Essays in Listening*, 141–75 (Oxford: Oxford University Press, 2013). Used by permission of Oxford University Press.

1. David Brown, *God and Grace of Body: Sacrament in Ordinary* (Oxford: Oxford University Press, 2007), chap. 5.

with everything that he writes, it is informed by an extraordinary breadth of reading and an eagerness to open up what might for some be an unfamiliar field in an accessible and compelling way. It becomes quickly evident, however, that Brown approaches music with distinctive questions and interests in view, and these are shaped to a large extent by strong and particular theological concerns, set out principally in *Tradition and Imagination* and *Discipleship and Imagination*.[2] In reflecting on Brown's theological reading of classical music, therefore, I would like to begin by venturing a sketch in very broad terms of some of the key guiding theological passions that energize and inform what he describes as a form of "natural religion,"[3] together with what I take to be the negative side of those passions, the kind of assumptions and attitudes he would eschew when engaging music theologically.

Guiding Passions

Brown has, first of all, a fervent concern to discern and do justice to the generous presence of God in areas of human endeavor where God is not overtly recognized or acknowledged as present. In three densely packed volumes,[4] he invites us to explore the theme of "religious experience" through culture, those mediations of a God "whose generous activity extends well beyond the Church."[5] This understanding of graced reality, needless to say, includes artistic activity: "If God is really our Creator, then the urge to deepen contact with him is likely to permeate human creativity in whatever form it is found."[6]

The underside of this understanding is an irritation, expressed many times, with what Brown regards as a blinkered vision and lamentable failure of nerve among his theological colleagues. He urges that the range of what is to count as religiously significant for academic study is far wider than theologians have typically assumed, certainly extending well beyond the well-worn loci of worship, ethics, and politics. It includes large tracts of "ordinary" human

2. David Brown, *Tradition and Imagination: Revelation and Change* (Oxford: Oxford University Press, 1999); Brown, *Discipleship and Imagination: Christian Tradition and Truth* (Oxford: Oxford University Press, 2000).

3. David Brown, *God and Enchantment of Place: Reclaiming Human Experience* (Oxford: Oxford University Press, 2004), 9.

4. Brown, *God and Enchantment of Place*; Brown, *God and Grace of Body*; Brown, *God and Mystery in Words: Experience through Metaphor and Drama* (Oxford: Oxford University Press, 2008).

5. Brown, *God and Grace of Body*, 237.

6. Brown, *God and Grace of Body*, 222.

experience that were once widely regarded as redolent of the divine.[7] Thus in Brown's project, we find a notable abundance of metaphors suggestive of exploration, venturing out beyond safe boundaries, beyond ecclesiastical ghettoes, and so forth. He certainly exemplifies this width of vision himself. In the case of music, he must be virtually the only distinguished academic theologian to engage with, for example, the music of Gustav Mahler and Anton Bruckner, and the only one to risk so full and sustained an engagement with popular music.[8]

Second, we find a repeated stress on the importance of what might best be described as a generous attentiveness on the part of the theologian, of journeying into cultural arenas with eyes alert and ears attuned. This is pivotal to "creative dialogue." The underside of this is a frustration with those who operate with fixed pre-understandings that, as Brown would have it, foreclose the possibility of fresh theological discovery from those with unfamiliar or different perspectives; "theological discussion of the arts," he believes, "is more often than not plagued by prior presuppositions, as though theologians knew themselves to be already in possession of criteria for judging the arts rather than having first to enter into creative dialogue with them."[9] So in the course of his discussion of classical music, when he urges that we hear music from non-Christian faith traditions, he recommends hearing it "from within," commenting, "The temptation is to suppose that uniqueness is best defended for one's own faith by refusing dialogue. That seems to me quite the wrong sort of response."[10]

Third, congruent with this belief, we find a passion for respecting the integrity and particularity of cultural endeavor, in the arts as much as anywhere else. The arts should be allowed to do their own work in their own ways, given space to be themselves. Attention to the particularities and context of the art in question is to be seen as intrinsic to theological interpretation. So, for example, Brown comments that "Haydn and Bruckner . . . were both devout Christians, but we shall gain little of the experience they sought to transmit,

---

7. In a recent paper, he writes: "Theology has retreated from areas of human activity that would once have been thought also to be major areas for its concern." David Brown, "In the Beginning Was the Image: Why the Arts Matter to Theology" (paper presented at the Society for the Study of Theology, University of Manchester, April 12–15, 2010), 4. "I do want to resist the tendency of so many of my fellow-Christians to impose over-simplistic or narrowly specific criteria for what may or may not communicate the divine." Brown, *God and Grace of Body*, 220.

8. See, e.g., Brown, *God and Grace of Body*, chap. 6.

9. Brown, "In the Beginning Was the Image," 5–6.

10. Brown, *God and Grace of Body*, 245.

unless we work first at understanding their contrasting methodologies."[11] The underside of this is a strong aversion to any form of instrumental rationality, the tendency to gauge value solely in terms of utility—something Brown detects in many theologians. He is especially critical of those who assess the arts according to the extent to which a clear, verbally expressible theological "point" or "programme" can be distilled from them. He complains that "so deep does instrumental rationality run in our culture that the practice of theology also often reflects that same approach, valuing the arts not in their own right but only in so far as they 'preach the gospel.'"[12] His opposition to artistic instrumentalism is especially acute when it is applied to Scripture; we should strongly resist the temptation to see "the arts as only appropriate when illustrative of truths already known through Scripture and instead carefully explore meanings first and with the expectation that the arts too can operate as independent vehicles of truth."[13] Moreover, the arts do not have to be seen as bringing about some theologically sanctioned moral or aesthetic benefit to be judged as of theological worth. They "must first be heard in their own right before any critical assessment is offered"[14] and, above all, heard as potential mediators of the divine.

This notion relates to a fourth passion, and it concerns theological criteria, something expounded most fully in *Tradition and Imagination*. Here we find Brown insisting with considerable force that Scripture should be acknowledged as belonging to a continuum of culturally embedded tradition, as emerging from and contributing to a process. The underside is that Scripture must not be privileged as occupying a normative criteriological role "over" or "above" extrascriptural tradition. The attempt to treat Scripture as if it could be extracted from historical and cultural contingencies is common among those eager to defend its authority, but it is a deeply flawed strategy because Scripture is so obviously inextricably intertwined with and shaped by such particularities. Especially notable here is the elevated place Brown grants to the imagination and the arts in the historically and culturally grounded practices of tradition formation.

> So used are theologians to engaging with the written word that it is all too easy for them to forget that for most of Christian history, with the great mass of the population illiterate, most Christians' primary experience of their faith will have been visual and, though probably to a lesser degree, aural. The drama of the liturgy, hymns and sermons, re-enactments of the biblical stories in mystery

11. Brown, *God and Grace of Body*, 244.
12. Brown, *God and Enchantment of Place*, 22.
13. Brown, "In the Beginning Was the Image," 6.
14. Brown, *God and Enchantment of Place*, 23.

plays, and the visual imagery present throughout the church building would have been what inspired and directed their faith.[15]

It is not only theologians and ecclesiastical councils who lead the way in doctrinal development, he argues, but also storytellers and painters—their artifacts are integral and indispensable to the tradition-forming process. These products of artistic creativity are not self-contained or static but emerge through interaction with their surrounding cultures and (sometimes) other religious traditions. Just because Scripture does not stand apart from the ceaseless making of tradition, the arts can in some cases serve to improve and correct biblical texts.[16]

Such are some of the main passions that I have found to inform Brown's ambitious undertaking. As far as music is concerned, it is perhaps not surprising, then, to find him wanting to speak of its "sacramental role":[17] music is a finite reality through which "God's presence in our midst [can] once more be made known."[18] (He speaks of music's combination of the "ethereal and material.")[19] In the case of classical music, he leads us on a fascinating and lavishly footnoted tour of various musicians, pointing to implicit and explicit religious or quasi-religious dimensions of their lives and work, ranging widely across the spectrum from composition to reception: Bach, Beethoven, Schubert, Mahler, and Bruckner are all considered, as are some major figures of twentieth-century music almost wholly ignored by mainstream academic theology (Schoenberg, Stravinsky, Poulenc, Messiaen). Wisely, he is careful not to overstate or overinterpret the textual evidence for any composer's belief or intentions or the theological freight of the texts they set. He makes passing mention of the theological potential of musical processes—harmony, rhythm, and so forth. Music has its own distinctive powers, even when allied with texts, something to which even Scripture bears witness.[20] Quite properly, he steers a course between the positions he calls "subjectivism" and "objectivism": music achieves its effects neither entirely by virtue of its grounding in universal properties of the physical world, nor entirely by virtue of variable individual, social, and cultural idiosyncrasies, but through a combination of both.

15. Brown, *Tradition and Imagination*, 322.
16. Brown, *Tradition and Imagination*, chap. 7, and "Conclusion."
17. Brown, *God and Grace of Body*, 246. Brown's interest in sacrament is long-standing; see, e.g., David Brown and Ann Loades, eds., *The Sense of the Sacramental: Movement and Measure in Art and Music, Place and Time* (London: SPCK, 1995); David Brown and David Fuller, *Signs of Grace: Sacraments in Poetry and Prose* (Ridgefield, CT: Morehouse, 1996).
18. Brown, *God and Grace of Body*, 247.
19. Brown, *God and Grace of Body*, 219–22.
20. Brown, *God and Grace of Body*, 224, 230.

Misgivings

Reading these reflections on music, however, especially when set in their wider philosophical and theological context, leaves me with some serious questions. Put succinctly, I am not convinced that a project of this scope, range, and ambition can advance much further without a greater degree of theological specificity than is evident here, and this, I believe, affects engaging with music as much as any other cultural activity. Such a comment, of course, runs the risk of sounding constricting and deadening, as if I were recommending something amounting to an intellectual and cultural retreat, a narrowing down of conversation, a refusal to believe that anything positive and fruitful can be learned from beyond the walls of the *ecclesia*. In fact, I believe the opposite is the case. Perhaps the best way to understand why is to backtrack over the four passions I have outlined above and offer some theological comments on each. I take them in reverse order.

First is the matter of Scripture and tradition. Undoubtedly, the temptation to drive a wedge between biblical texts and subsequent tradition and treat the former as wholly exempt from the dynamics of tradition formation has frequently caused much harm. But what are we to say about the church's repeated return to these texts as normative for Christian wisdom and understanding, something that the church does not claim for any other textual tradition? As Kathryn Tanner has observed in a review of *Tradition and Imagination*, "Rather than signalling a loss of normativity, the fact that Christians constantly add their own images and narratives to scripture indicates its abiding central significance for their lives."[21] Brown presumably believes that the church has simply been wrong to consider Scripture as normative in this way; the scriptural canon as he regards it, even if in one sense "closed," is in effect reconfigured in every age, exemplifying the ongoing and ceaseless process of tradition making. But this hardly explains why postscriptural readings of scriptural texts have been treated as just that, *readings*, construals, and not as substitutes for the texts—what the church has "made" of and with the texts has not buried the texts themselves.[22] Need there be anything intrinsically contradictory about holding to the epistemic and existential primacy of Scripture for the life of the church *while at the same time* endorsing the church's need for postbiblical tradition, the need to allow extrabiblical sources to correct construals of Scripture, and the need to resist regarding Scripture

---

21. Kathryn Tanner, "Review of David Brown, *Tradition and Imagination: Revelation and Change*," *International Journal of Systematic Theology* 3 (2001): 120.
22. Tanner, "Review of David Brown," 120–21.

as a self-contained deposit of fixed meaning (the matters that so concern Brown)?[23]

Brown's stance on the normativity of Scripture, of course, provokes the central question of criteria. He tells us he does not yet want to burden his project with detailed criteriological stipulations, in part because, as he puts it, "Criteria set in advance can all too easily read like alien impositions that have failed to grapple sufficiently with the way the world is."[24] So toward the end of *Discipleship and Imagination*, even though he lists the criteria that have been implicit in his foregoing argument, he eschews any strong (let alone "absolute") prioritizing of any of them.

Admittedly, there does appear to be a fairly strong christological thrust at the heart of Brown's project (and there is certainly no antitrinitarianism).[25] He undoubtedly wants to affirm that the person and figure of Christ is in-eradicably vital to the Christian faith. And especially pivotal, it seems, is the incarnation—the "primordial sacrament"[26]—not least because of its witness to God's endorsement of the inherent goodness and value of the material world and of the human body as divinely graced. The incarnation undergirds his view of revelation through tradition: "God's kenotic embroilment"[27] dem-onstrates the way God operates within the processes of change, accommodates himself to the chances and changes of our mortal lives. And this "embroil-ment" is hardly trivial when it comes to the arts and music, for such a reading of the incarnation underwrites the very structure and dynamic of human creativity—or, more accurately, of God's involvement in human creativity, and that includes musical creativity as much as any other.

An insistence on the centrality of the incarnation is hardly problematic in itself. Indeed, many scholars (including me) would contend that it is here above all that Scripture finds its concrete focus of divine authority—the Christ attested therein is the Word become Word-User; the one who is internal to God's being, the Logos, becomes the bearer of *logoi*, and thereby generates fresh speech acts among his followers that become formative of God's renewed people. Out of this word-generating momentum, certain texts, eventually gath-ered as canonical, emerge. There have been several recent accounts of biblical

23. See the highly nuanced and carefully judged essay by Kevin J. Vanhoozer, "Scripture and Tradition," in *The Cambridge Companion to Postmodern Theology*, ed. Kevin J. Vanhoozer (Cambridge: Cambridge University Press, 2003), esp. 166–69.

24. Brown, *God and Enchantment of Place*, 3.

25. Something noted by Rowan Williams in his review of *Tradition and Imagination*; Rowan Williams, "Review of David Brown, *Tradition and Imagination: Revelation and Change*, OUP, 1999," *Theology* 104 (2001): 453.

26. Brown, *God and Enchantment of Place*, 6.

27. Brown, "In the Beginning Was the Image," 10.

authority along these lines, many of them highly sophisticated, in which the Bible is regarded neither as a closed repository of timeless, indubitable truths, nor simply as one patch of textual color in an unbroken continuum of historical tradition, but rather as a testimony centered on the incarnate Son and thus caught up in the dynamic of God's action of reconciling self-communication and now divinely appropriated as normative for reshaping the church and its participation in the drama of redemption.[28]

In Brown's scheme, of course, the incarnation does not function in this way with respect to biblical authority but rather demonstrates the way God characteristically operates in the formation of revelatory tradition, of which Scripture is one instance. What is puzzling in Brown's account is *why* the incarnation should be accorded any normative centrality at all, for even if it is to be deemed pivotal to the New Testament's testimony, this very testimony (it seems) always stands under the judgment of externally derived criteria that are de facto regarded as ultimately superior. Could not this core testimony, then, be regarded as in principle dispensable? Brown seems to believe that "incarnation" refers to a phenomenon that is ontologically distinct from the biblical tradition about it,[29] but if that is the case, would this not suggest that this tradition should be accorded some kind of epistemic and methodological priority over subsequent tradition?

What might we say about Brown's passion to do justice to the integrity and particularity of cultural endeavor, in this case, music? If I understand Brown correctly, the fundamental enemy here is theological instrumentalism, when preset and fixed theological criteria and agendas are allowed to determine our reading of the arts, music included. This is especially dangerous, Brown believes, when allied with the belief that a piece of music can be reduced to a clearly articulable message and indeed *must* be so reducible if it is to be regarded as meaningful, or to the belief that music must support a theologically approved moral or aesthetic goal to be considered of any worth. This inevitably means riding roughshod over the distinctive ways in which music operates and ignoring the integrity of any particular piece of music—the intentions behind it, its cultural determinants, its social context, its history of

28. See, e.g., Kevin J. Vanhoozer, *Remythologizing Theology: Divine Action, Passion, and Authorship* (Cambridge: Cambridge University Press, 2010); James K. A. Smith, *Speech and Theology: Language and the Logic of Incarnation* (London: Routledge, 2002).

29. Brown writes: "What God in effect did in the incarnation was commit himself to a developing tradition. Not only did he expose himself to the vagaries of being human, he also submitted himself to the uncertainties of human comprehension in abandoning himself to humanity's most characteristic way of thinking: gradual perception through creative retelling of the story of his identification with us in Jesus. Even the incarnation could only be made known as part of a developing tradition." *Tradition and Imagination*, 278–79.

reception, and so forth. Most seriously, we effectively exclude the possibility that music can offer a sacramental mediation of God's presence in its own right or afford fresh divine truth not known in advance. To be clear, then, Brown is not opposing instrumentality per se, despite the heavy anti-instrumentalist pleading. After all, the invitation to sense the divine through music is *itself* an invitation to employ music as an instrument toward an end, namely, as a (potential) vehicle of divine presence.[30] The key enemy, it seems, is interpreting art with predetermined theological ends of an all too narrow range.

Brown's concern to respect the distinctive modi operandi of music; to respect the integrity of music with all its associated contextual particularities; to avoid the linguistic imperialism that insists all meaningful activity be capable of reduction to declarative assertions (scriptural, doctrinal, or otherwise); and to avoid suggesting that music must serve an immanent moral or aesthetic end to be accorded religious value—these are all surely well placed. But when it comes to his comments on theological prejudgments, I am much less convinced. That some theological convictions can distort our perception of reality is hardly a controversial view. However, Brown's way of expressing this truism raises acute questions. As we have noted already, he insists that "criteria set in advance can all too easily read like alien impositions that have failed to grapple sufficiently with the way the world is." But from what point of view are we to determine accurately "the way the world is"? To be asked, indeed urged, to adopt a distinctive (and highly generalized)[31] theological vision of the world's sacramentality of the sort Brown advocates is itself to be urged to adopt a theological prejudgment that—presumably—is believed *not* to distort our perception of "the way the world is." This perspective, we are being told, will give us a better view of the way things are than others. (Even if we grant that criteria will always need to be adapted to the reality in hand, this can hardly mean that we could ever operate in an environment *without* criteria.) The issue, then, concerns not whether criteria "set in advance" are operating but *which* criteria are operating—and, to repeat, here Brown is less than clear.

30. As Nicholas Wolterstorff and many others have maintained, all pieces of art are instruments and objects of action, caught up in complex webs of human intention and practice. Nicholas Wolterstorff, *Art in Action: Toward a Christian Aesthetic* (Grand Rapids: Eerdmans, 1980).

31. In the course of a review of two of Brown's books, Clive Marsh writes: "He can too often, too easily, refer to 'the transcendent,' 'the sacramental,' 'the spiritual' or 'spiritual values' as if these can be uniformly identified within or behind whatever he examines. I can hear the postliberals sharpening their quills already." Marsh, "Review of David Brown, *God and Grace of Body: Sacrament in Ordinary*, Oxford: Oxford University Press, 2007, and David Brown, *God and Mystery in Words: Experience through Metaphor and Drama*, Oxford: Oxford University Press, 2008," *International Journal of Systematic Theology* 13, no. 1 (2011): 106.

This is perhaps the best point for me to comment on Brown's remarks about my own work. He criticizes (gently) my book *Theology, Music and Time* as being "essentially illustrative rather than a learning exercise," in that "music is used to expound or develop biblical insights" and these "insights" are never challenged by "how God is found to act elsewhere."[32] In fact, as even a glance at the book will show, I range far beyond biblical texts and include a large section on the dynamics of postscriptural tradition. And the book as a whole is designed to resist treating music as illustrative gloss to the work of theology, as if it bore no distinguishing theological capabilities of its own. In any case, the critical divergence between us does not lie at this level. Rather it is exposed when Brown writes that the biblically oriented insights I develop are never challenged by "how God is found to act elsewhere." I can only respond: "And which God might this be? Presumably, following Brown, a God about whom claims of presence and activity are to be judged according to criteria independent of and superior to those attested by Scripture." But again we are left unclear about what these nonnegotiable criteria might be and, no less importantly, what reason or reasons we might have for embracing them.

Similar comments could be made about the posture of generous and dialogical attentiveness that Brown recommends. Early on in *God and Enchantment of Place*, he complains that "what one finds in Balthasar no less than in Barth is that it is the Christian revelation that constantly sets the criteria of assessment. So there is little sense of learning or of discovery, and more a feeling of the imposition of predetermined judgements."[33] Leaving aside the question of the fairness of this assessment of Balthasar and Barth (I think they and many others would be surprised to learn that there is little sense of learning and discovery in their writings), what is especially striking, remarkable in fact, is the assumption that "the Christian revelation" will of necessity distort one's ability to listen and learn, that to adopt a position oriented to the self-disclosure of God in Jesus Christ inevitably diminishes the possibilities of discovery. On what grounds should this be accepted?

None of what I have said is intended to deny or weaken the importance of the first passion I noted in Brown: to recognize the width of divine presence in the world at large and the possibilities of divine encounter that it affords. Admittedly, rather than invest quite so much in the language and ontology of "presence," I would prefer to interpret these "rumours of transcendence" in terms of God's graceful, reconciling action, linked to a far more overt and developed doctrine of the Holy Spirit. But this does not gainsay the force

---

32. Brown, *God and Grace of Body*, 245.
33. Brown, *God and Enchantment of Place*, 7.

of Brown's key concern here. For almost twenty years, in conversation and practical involvement with countless musicians of little or no overt religious affiliation, in academic music departments as much as concert halls, with "popular" musicians as well as "classical," I have frequently been startled by unexpected signals and gestures of the Creator's ways with the world.

J. S. Bach—Fresh Perspectives

In the last part of this essay, I want to return to music and indicate very briefly how a greater theological specificity might actually advance rather than impede Brown's desire to explore music's ability to offer what he calls "experience of the divine."[34] And I do this by reference to the work of Johann Sebastian Bach (1685–1750), with whom Brown opens his survey of composers.

Quite properly, Brown wants to argue that Bach's instrumental music can be heard as carrying theological freight in its own right, and this would have been in keeping with Bach's own convictions, in particular his views about cosmic order. Bach was almost certainly committed to the notion that music should be grounded in and reflect a divinely ordered, harmonious universe. Brown contends that Bach was not an enemy of "reason and natural religion" or a supporter of any strict sacred-secular divide; rather, for Bach all music "was . . . seen as a reflection of the divine."[35] He concludes: "[Bach] was in a sense engaging in a natural theology of music, whatever he wrote,"[36] and goes on to suggest (if I understand him correctly) that like certain versions of natural theology, Bach's music is capable of non-Christian as well as Christian interpretations of the deity evoked. Leaving aside what many would regard as a rather loose use of the term "natural theology," the impression given is, I think, blander than it needs to be. It is not so much that these observations on Bach are untrue or ill founded, but that they do not go nearly far enough. Here, I would submit, is an area where distinctions and greater philosophical and theological precision can significantly deepen and widen a theological exploration of this remarkable musician.

The notion that music making and music hearing are ultimately rooted in the structures of the cosmos at large is ancient and persistent (as Brown notes); it runs from the Pythagoreans through the church fathers, through Luther, many Lutherans, and numerous Enlightenment theorists. And in one form or another, it still has its proponents today. However, the way in which this

34. Brown, *God and Grace of Body*, 248.
35. Brown, *God and Grace of Body*, 254.
36. Brown, *God and Grace of Body*, 254.

order or harmonious universe is conceived, and the manner in which music
is understood to be embedded in it, can vary quite considerably, as can the
ways in which this musical-cosmic order is thought to find its origin in the
Creator. As a considerable body of research has demonstrated, Bach's music
does not always sit well with at least some prominent models of aesthetic
harmony. We need to keep this in mind when commentators draw attention to
the mathematical elements in Bach's music, to those occasions, for instance,
when numerical quasi codes seem to be incorporated into the musical texture (threes for the Trinity and so forth), or where the large-scale structural
determinants of a piece are capable of mathematical expression. Even at his
most mathematical, Bach will typically include material that is anything but
mathematically "closed" in any strict sense. To cite one instance: although
there is ample evidence in the *Goldberg Variations* of mathematically regular
sequence and symmetry, they are interlaced with striking and unharmoniz-
able irregularity.[37] As a number of scholars have argued, although Bach was
undoubtedly influenced by some leading Enlightenment theorists, especially
in his later years, he was quite capable of working against many emphases
typical of Enlightenment thinking. There is an immediately attractive and
beguiling quality about much of Bach's output, an interplay between the
predictable and the unpredictable, the foreseen and the unforeseeable, which
many notions of aesthetic order will struggle hard to accommodate.

A related feature of Bach's music that has received a good deal of attention
in recent scholarship is his approach to time and temporality. In his recent
substantial study, *Bach's Dialogue with Modernity*,[38] John Butt of Glasgow
University takes issue with a fellow Bach scholar, Karol Berger, who contends
that Bach displays an overriding commitment to closed, cyclic temporality—
evinced very clearly, he believes, in the opening movement of the *St Matthew
Passion*—and that it was not until the late eighteenth century that composers
begin to show a deep interest in directional time, the irreversible movement
from past to future.[39] Butt concedes that in the course of the late eighteenth
and nineteenth centuries, the temporal order of musical events became far
more crucial than it was for Bach. Nonetheless, Butt views Bach as standing
"on the cusp of musical modernity,"[40] combining repetitive, symmetrical com-

---

37. Peter F. Williams, *Bach: The Goldberg Variations* (Cambridge: Cambridge University
Press, 2001), 46.

38. John Butt, *Bach's Dialogue with Modernity: Perspectives on the Passions* (Cambridge:
Cambridge University Press, 2010).

39. Karol Berger, *Bach's Cycle, Mozart's Arrow: An Essay on the Origins of Musical Modernity* (Berkeley: University of California Press, 2007).

40. Butt, *Bach's Dialogue with Modernity*, 109.

ponents with directionality (albeit to different degrees in different pieces), thus mingling premodern and modern sensibilities. With regard to the *St Matthew Passion*, while acknowledging its symmetries, Butt claims that the sense of "linear, passing time" is vivid and striking. There is an "overwhelming sense of change"[41] and of the uniqueness of its critical events, many of which are portrayed as effecting subsequent change. Butt underlines the opening movement's heterogeny and discontinuities and argues that its ritornello is strikingly open-ended both tonally and melodically.[42] Indeed, the entire *Passion* is "lacking tonal closure"; "the work somehow craves completion beyond its own span."[43] Even in the more symmetry-laden *St John Passion*, Bach balances "repetitively ordered (or symmetrical) elements with a sense of musical direction."[44] In a similar vein, speaking of sections of the *Mass in B Minor*, Butt comments:

> Bach has given us a sense of symmetrical circular time simultaneously with a linear or progressive quality. The Bachian sense of time demands progress within stability, a dynamic approach to cyclic time that evokes something of the energy of a spiral.[45]

It should be evident that these musical dynamics, read theologically, press us far beyond the somewhat plain vision that Brown evokes. If Bach's music is to be heard as evocative of a deity's presence—heeding Brown's urging—we are pushed toward imagining a presence that is redolent with the lively generation of novelty, of the sort the church has traditionally associated especially with the Holy Spirit, a contingent dynamic operating within the world that yet also reaches beyond the world, improvising, we might say, on the givenness of the particularity of Christ. We could well be encouraged toward a rich view of God's engagement with time that points us beyond the rather tired polarity of circular versus linear conceptions. The features Butt highlights—consistency interlaced with directionality, unique interruptions that issue in fruitful subsequent change, an irreducible open-endedness that resists complete closure—are hardly unfamiliar to an informed scholar of the biblical narratives, for example, and quite congruent with a vision of human history as being drawn toward a fulfillment by the God of Jesus Christ (a God

41. Butt, *Bach's Dialogue with Modernity*, 107.
42. Butt, *Bach's Dialogue with Modernity*, 66–67, 101–2.
43. Butt, *Bach's Dialogue with Modernity*, 100.
44. Butt, *Bach's Dialogue with Modernity*, 109.
45. Butt, *Bach's Dialogue with Modernity*, 110. Of the *Goldberg Variations*, Butt notes "a sense of recurrence that could go on *ad infinitum*, but it is one in which things are somehow different at each recurrence." Butt, *Bach's Dialogue with Modernity*, 109.

both committed to and respectful of the world's order), a fulfillment that this world cannot of itself generate.

None of these observations *proves* this or that theological vision of reality. There can be no musical "natural theology" in that sense. The point is rather that if, as Brown wishes, we are to seek signs of the Creator's presence in music, the question of the specific character and ways of this Creator cannot be set aside and deserves to be considered with a detail and depth that does justice, in this case, to the Christian tradition's normative documents.

It is striking that the scholars who are pointing to these dynamics in Bach most strongly are frequently not the theologians but the Bach specialists. It would be regrettable and ironic indeed if Christian theologians at this point were reluctant to meet such scholars with the richness of a well-grounded Christian vision, just when the lineaments of such a vision are being evoked from outside the church. To be sure, there is a type of specificity that closes down conversation, but there is another that does just the opposite.

5

Confidence and Anxiety
in Elgar's *The Dream of Gerontius*

Edward Elgar's setting of John Henry Newman's epic poem *The Dream of Gerontius* stands as one of the undisputed musical masterpieces of the nineteenth century. With palpable and passionate conviction, it carries the listener on a momentous journey from death to purgatory. Despite its obvious allegiance to an elaborate Roman Catholic eschatology, I explore what a number of scholars have recognized is a profound ambivalence surrounding this masterpiece—one that is musical, certainly, but intertwined with this, also cultural and psychological. In this essay, I argue that a biblical-theological perspective opens up the deepest levels and significance of this ambivalence.

It is hardly surprising that Elgar's *The Dream of Gerontius* (1900), considered by many to be the finest Victorian music ever written, has been characterized as a work of consolation and comfort, borne along by broad currents of affirmation, confidence, and hopefulness. It traces the epic journey of an

This chapter was originally published as Jeremy Begbie, "Confidence and Anxiety in Elgar's *Dream of Gerontius*," in *Music and Theology in Nineteenth-Century Britain*, ed. Martin Clarke, 197–241 (Aldershot: Ashgate, 2012). I am most grateful to the Reverend Dr. Jeremy Morris and Dr. J. P. E. Harper-Scott for their valuable comments on an earlier version of this chapter.

elderly Christian believer, an ordinary sinner ("a man like us," Elgar insisted)[1] who faces the terrors of death and judgment and is faithfully conveyed by his Guardian Angel through the afterlife to purgatory. Gerontius approaches purgatory serenely, anticipating the eventual joy of intimacy with God, with the Angel singing softly and gently as Gerontius's Soul is laid in the purifying waters. Elgar draws the Angel's song together with Psalm 90 ("Lord, thou hast been our refuge") and with reminiscences of the earlier paean "Praise to the Holiest" in an immensely satisfying synthesis. With the strings rising heavenward, Elgar finally resolves the disturbed D minor tonality, which opened the work: an unambiguous D major "Amen" brings the oratorio to a secure and assured close.

A glance at the context of the piece seems to support a positive reading of this sort. Though his faith waned considerably in later years, at the turn of the century Elgar was a "publicly faithful" Roman Catholic in a largely Protestant environment, declaring himself as such in interviews and attending Mass regularly.[2] He had been well educated in the basics of Catholic theology. He dedicates the work: "A.M.D.G." (Ad Majorem Dei Gloriam, "To the greater glory of God"). All this suggests that *Gerontius* was provoked by a theological conviction that went much deeper than mere cultural conformity. And on a wider front, at this time Elgar had every reason to be confident about his abilities; in particular, the rapturous reception of his *Variations on an Original Theme* (1899) had made him a national figure in music and helped secure the beginnings of an international reputation. Moreover, although *Gerontius* was written in 1900, for many its musical language breathes the spirit of the nineteenth century, seemingly having far more in common with the expansive optimism of British colonialism than with the kind of ambivalences and disillusionment characteristic of modern music of the prewar and postwar years.

And yet, as much scholarship shows, a closer and more careful exploration of *Gerontius* reveals a rather more subtle and complex picture, with

1. "I imagined Gerontius to be a man like us, not a Priest or a Saint, but a sinner, a repentant one of course but still no end of a worldly man in his life, & now brought to book." Letter of August 28, 1900, quoted in Howard Smither, *A History of the Oratorio*, vol. 4 (Chapel Hill: University of North Carolina Press, 2000), 368.

2. Charles Edward McGuire, "Measure of a Man: Catechizing Elgar's Catholic Avatars," in *Edward Elgar and His World*, ed. Byron Adams (Princeton: Princeton University Press, 2007), 21–23. Leon Botstein writes: "Though his traditional faith in God may have waned in later years, theology mattered to Elgar, even if indirectly through its consequences in the politics of culture." Botstein, "Transcending the Enigmas of Biography: The Cultural Context of Sir Edward Elgar's Career," in *Edward Elgar and His World*, ed. Byron Adams (Princeton: Princeton University Press, 2007), 372.

darker colors streaking across the late Victorian glow. Especially notable is an ambivalence that seems to pervade the work, generated through what might best be described as an unresolved oscillation between confidence and anxiety, striving and shrinking, reaching forth and holding back. It can be discerned in different forms across a wide range of Elgar's music. Its presence is confirmed in what Matthew Riley has called the "double-edged emotional vocabulary" that emerges among those who encounter Elgar's music—"heroic melancholy" (W. B. Yeats), "crippled grandeur" (Peter Pirie).[3] My purpose in this essay is to examine this ambivalence in some detail but from a specifically theological perspective, indeed, as embodying a distinctive theological stance or attitude; the focus will be on *The Dream of Gerontius*, a work in which, despite initial appearances, the theological character of the ambivalence is especially clear.

Textual Perspectives

Elgar drew his libretto from an epic poem by John Henry Newman (1801–1890). The most prominent English Roman Catholic of his age (beatified in 2010) and a convert from Anglicanism, Newman penned "The Dream of Gerontius" in 1865, amid an expanding Victorian fascination with eschatology (the "last things"). It became one of the best-known literary pieces on death and the future life in nineteenth-century England, offering an imaginary vision of the physical and metaphysical journey into and through the afterlife, presented in the nondidactic "poetry of dogma."[4]

Elgar abridged Newman's text considerably. We spend proportionately far longer with Gerontius's last hours on earth than we do in the original poem, and Elgar is generally more intensely focused than Newman on the physical, emotional, and spiritual experience of Gerontius himself—Gerontius is the Everyman with whose fallen and frail humanity we are invited to identify. Especially notable in part 2 is the way in which the questioning and inner struggles of Gerontius's Soul figure far more prominently than any descriptions of his surroundings: Elgar slices out sizable sections of metaphysical geography from Newman's text.

3. Matthew Riley, "Heroic Melancholy: Elgar's Inflected Diatonicism," in *Elgar Studies*, ed. Julian Rushton and J. P. E. Harper-Scott (Cambridge: Cambridge University Press, 2007), 284–307, here 284.

4. See Robert Carballo, "Newman as Librettist: Towards a Non-Didactic Poetry of Dogma," in *The Best of Me: A Gerontius Centenary Companion*, ed. Geoffrey Hodgkins (Rickmansworth, UK: Elgar Editions, 1999), 56–64.

Part 1, which Geoffrey Rowell describes as "Newman's picture of an ideal Christian death,"[5] presents us with a tumultuous struggle. Any assurance felt by Gerontius seems to be repeatedly under threat. To be sure, Gerontius's fear is strikingly contrasted with the power of Christ, who has trod this fierce path ahead of him (a recurring theme throughout the work), and of Mary the mediator. And his creedal recital ("Sanctus fortis") carries a clear affirmative tone. But the presentation could hardly be described as categorically positive or hopeful, not at this stage at least. The confidence is constantly dragged back by "that sense of ruin, which is worse than pain." And though hell may not be explicitly named as such, its lurking presence as a real possibility for Gerontius and all like him is pervasively present.[6]

Perhaps we should not read too much into this. After all, we are being deliberately led into Gerontius's writhing so that we might fully identify with it: there is hope for all who struggle like this. In any case, here (and in part 2) the ever-present and supportive communion of saints plays a key role, and the authoritative tones of the church's liturgy deliver unambiguous reassurance "from beyond." After his death, the Priest's "Proficiscere . . ." ushers in words whose blazing strength Elgar renders with unforgettable force: "Go forth upon thy journey, Christian soul."

It is when we come to part 2, however, which takes us into the next world, that we encounter what would seem to be a rather more deep-seated ambivalence regarding the Soul's confidence before God. In his refreshed state of "inexpressive lightness," he is greeted by his Guardian Angel, who from now on accompanies him, instructing and encouraging him on his complex and eventful journey. The Soul is eventually led to the House of Judgement, where he is granted a momentary and terrifying glimpse of the Judge, only

5. Geoffrey Rowell, *Hell and the Victorians: A Study of the Nineteenth Century Theological Controversies concerning Eternal Punishment and the Future Life* (Oxford: Clarendon Press, 1974), 159.
6. The Assistants pray:
 From the nethermost fire;
 From all that is evil;
 From power of the devil;
 Thy servant deliver,
 For once and for ever.
 By Thy birth, and by Thy Cross,
 Rescue him from endless loss;
 By Thy death and burial,
 Save him from a final fall;
 By Thy rising from the tomb,
 By Thy mounting up above,
 By the Spirit's gracious love
 Save him in the day of doom.

to shrink back and plead to the Angel to take him to the "penal waters." The Angel grants him his wish, and there the work closes. Like the poem, Elgar's oratorio leads us not to heaven with the Soul in full intimacy with God (even though the Soul's joy is said to be an anticipation of heaven)[7] but to purgatory.

The doctrine of purgatory, not explicitly developed in any biblical texts, came into full flower in the West in the twelfth and thirteenth centuries, though its roots lie much further back. Although sometimes embellished in highly intricate (and often controversial) ways, in its essential or basic form it speaks of a temporary "place" (or state) that one enters at death, en route to heaven. It is a preparation for heaven, not a lesser hell. Those in purgatory are heaven bound, their positive future assured—hence early in part 2 the Soul's Angel can sing: "Alleluia, / And saved is he."

The development of this teaching seems to have had a number of interlinked motivations,[8] but among them was the church's strong sense that despite baptism and its regenerative power, we carry on sinning and are duly compromised by sin's burden and effects. The *medicamenta poenitentia*, or "medicines of penance," were designed to deal with such obstacles to communion with God. But what if a person dies in a state of impurity? They will not be prepared for the kind of direct encounter with the Creator that awaits them, even if they have been baptized and claimed as God's own. This is the background to one of the most celebrated moments in *Gerontius*—the Soul's lightning-brief encounter with God, from which he instantly recoils. "Take me away," he cries. Agonizingly aware of his own uncleanness, his sheer unreadiness for God, he begs the Angel to lead him to the "lowest deep" of purgatory, where he can sing of his "absent Lord."[9]

In the church, therefore, purgatory came to be seen as a kind of extension to the earthly practice of penance, a purification (purgation), a moral preparation prior to eternal closeness with God, and one in which the believer can be assisted by the prayers (especially the masses) of the church militant on earth. As far as Newman's view of purgatory is concerned, which reaches its mature form with "Gerontius," it seems that unlike some of his continental colleagues, he wanted to distance himself from the punitive dimensions

7. The words of the Angel to Gerontius:
   That calm and joy uprising in thy soul
   Is first-fruit to thee of thy recompense,
   And heaven begun.

8. For a very clear overview, see Paul J. Griffiths, "Purgatory," in *The Oxford Handbook of Eschatology*, ed. Jerry L. Walls (Oxford: Oxford University Press, 2008), 427–45; also Jan N. Bremmer, *The Rise and Fall of the Afterlife* (London: Routledge, 2002).

9. There is, then, in Newman's words (not Elgar's), "The Longing for Him, when thou seest Him not; / The shame of self at thought of seeing Him."

(including physical pain) that had been attached to the doctrine of purgatory in some of its versions, stressing instead its purifying role. It was also likely that he was especially impressed by a particular poem of Ettore Vernazza, a disciple of Saint Catherine of Genoa (1447–1510). Like Catherine, Newman spoke of purgatory as a prison (the phrase "golden prison" appears in "Gerontius") and of purgatory beginning in this life—purgation beyond death is seen as a continuation of what begins here.[10]

The theological ambivalence of the text's ending arises not simply because of its "temporal" irresolution—its ending in purgatory rather than heaven—but because of the distancing from God that purgatory necessarily entails. The still-sinful believer consigned to purgatory is unready for direct intimacy with the divine, an unreadiness that cannot simply be ignored or instantly eradicated but must rather be dealt with appropriately. The fact that we end where we do in "Gerontius" reminds us of this very fact: our alienation from God can be extended after death. Juan Velez comments on Newman's outlook:

> A pure soul is attracted to God, while a sinful soul shuns the presence of God, whose sight would cause it greater pain than hell itself. Catherine [of Siena] thought that each soul goes voluntarily to its own place. She taught that hell is the proper place for a soul in mortal sin; otherwise it would be in a "still greater hell." Newman wrote that, even if a soul in mortal sin were able to go to heaven, it would find it horrible.[11]

Elgar seems to have understood purgatory's remoteness from God well. Indeed, he was anxious that this dimension might be weakened were he to use highly dramatic music for the Soul's momentary encounter with the Judge. In extended correspondence with his friend Jaeger on the matter, he wrote:

> Please remember that none of the "action" takes place in the *presence* of God: I would not have tried *that* neither did Newman. The Soul says: "I go before my God," but *we* don't. We stand outside—I've thrown over all the 'machinery' the celestial music, harps etc.[12]

10. For clear treatments of Newman's conception of purgatory, see Michael Wheeler, *Death and the Future Life in Victorian Literature and Theology* (Cambridge: Cambridge University Press, 1990), 308–24; Juan R. Velez, "Newman's Theology in the *Dream of Gerontius*," *New Blackfriars* 82, no. 967 (2001): 387–98; Rowell, *Hell and the Victorians*, 157–63.

11. Velez, "Newman's Theology," 392.

12. Quoted in Percy M. Young, *Elgar, Newman and The Dream of Gerontius: In the Tradition of English Catholicism* (Aldershot, UK: Scholar Press, 1995), 117 (italics original).

And, of course, even the Soul can only bear a painfully brief glimpse of the divine.

Tonal Ambivalence: Musicological Perspectives

The Soul's notorious shrinking before God raises some pointed questions to which we shall return in due course. For the moment, we simply note the way in which it resonates with the ambivalence present throughout the portrayal of our emblematic believer: a man who is both desperate to cast himself upon God and yet at the same time intensely aware (heightened through immediate divine encounter) that his condition and God's ways with sinful souls make this very act intensely problematical.

This note of faith radically restrained by acute anxiety finds its counterparts, many would argue, in some of Elgar's specifically musical techniques. In a recent and important book, J. P. E. Harper-Scott has argued that, contrary to many popular readings, Elgar can be interpreted as a subtle and important harbinger of twentieth-century modernism. Eschewing biographical and Romantic interpretations, focusing resolutely on the "works themselves," and drawing on a heady mixture of modified Schenkerian analysis and Heideggerian philosophy, Harper-Scott contends that many of Elgar's characteristic strategies point ahead to the strident contradictions and negative, undermining forces that are typical of later modern music.

Harper-Scott pays considerable attention to what he calls Elgar's "immuring-immured" tonal structure: where an opening and closing key (a quasi-tonic) contains, or immures, another more "viable" key that Elgar nevertheless ultimately spurns. Elgar's First Symphony (1908) famously begins and ends with a striking "motto" theme in A flat major. Held within this tonality, however, we find the immured tonality of D. This tritonal tension opens rifts and instabilities, creating a "tonal malaise" that is never satisfactorily resolved. The much-delayed closure of the symphony is not convincing, Harper-Scott believes—at least not if we are looking for a fully integrated comprehensive teleology, of the sort associated with Beethoven's "heroic" style, for example, where oppositions are absorbed into a final apotheosis. "The immuring tonic has the last word, but can we be certain that it does not ring hollow?"[13]

There is no final victory, but only a "massive hope." Elgar's quest ends, like Tolkien's *The Lord of the Rings*, with the hero (if there is one at all) scarred and

---

13. J. P. E. Harper-Scott, *Edward Elgar, Modernist* (Cambridge: Cambridge University Press, 2006), 106. See chap. 3 and 184–99.

enfeebled by his travails; superficially happy, but deeply unsettled at heart. . . .
The symbolic implications of Elgar's structural technique are, then, antiheroic
and thoroughly modern.[14]

Although he regards Elgar's mature modernist phase as running from
1904 to 1913, Harper-Scott believes the immuring-immured structure first
appears in the "neo-Romantic" *Gerontius*.[15] He reads part 1 as the enclosure
of one tonal area (E♭/ B♭—from the first "Kyrie" to "Sanctus fortis") by "two
solid walls" of D. In part 2, we move from a double-tonic complex (C/E♭,
attained after an extended preface beginning in F major), to a final closure
in D. We thus find there are two immuring-immured structures at work
here:

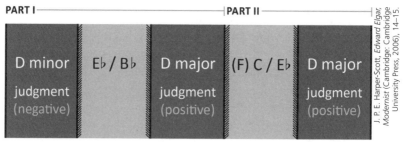

Figure 5.1 Immuring-immured tonal structures in *The Dream of Gerontius*,
according to J. P. E. Harper-Scott.

Elgar could never have concluded the piece with a "simplistically positive
outcome" since purgatory is only a temporary transit.[16] So we close in D
major. D is the key of judgment in this work—D minor for judgment viewed
negatively (as at the opening), and D major for judgment viewed positively
(as at the end of part 1 and at the close of the work). For his ending, Elgar
could hardly use the key associated with orientation to God (E♭) since the
drama, as we have seen, does not conclude in God's presence:

> Being-towards-God, the E♭/ B♭ movement in Part I ("Kyrie" to "Sanctus fortis"),
> or the pairing of Part II (Angels joining in a vast hymn of praise), remains locked

---

14. Harper-Scott, *Edward Elgar, Modernist*, 195, 196. The reference to "massive hope"
alludes to Elgar's own comments about the symphony, that there is "no programme beyond a
wide experience of human life with a great charity (love) and a *massive* hope in the future."
Letter to Walford Davies, November 13, 1908, in *Edward Elgar: Letters of a Lifetime*, ed. Jerrold
Northrop Moore (Oxford: Clarendon Press, 1990), 205.

15. Harper-Scott, *Edward Elgar, Modernist*, 14–15.

16. Harper-Scott, *Edward Elgar, Modernist*, 14.

away between the iron walls of the Judgement that prevents the human soul from reaching its destiny within the confines of the work.[17]

Harper-Scott continues:

> *The Dream of Gerontius* is the high point of Elgar's neo-Romantic phase (the later biblical oratorios make no significant stylistic advances), and in it he sets himself on a course that would lead into the critique of human and musical history that constitutes his modernist phase. For although the work ends with hope—Purgatory is not Hell, after all—the hope is not certain to be fulfilled. Nothing in the immuring-immured structure absolutely compels an ultimately optimistic interpretation: we cannot be *certain* that The Soul will end up with God, however likely it seems.[18]

Not dissimilar perspectives are opened up by Matthew Riley. In an article titled "Heroic Melancholy: Elgar's Inflected Diatonicism,"[19] he notes that diatonicism (using only notes in the chosen scale) and chromaticism (using notes outside the scale) are often played off against each other by Elgar in the course of a piece. In the oratorios, diatonicism is used "to represent states of spiritual peace or grace,"[20] while chromaticism is commonly used to frame diatonic passages or as symbolic of hostile forces that are finally overcome. Such conflicts and dualities do not form the whole story, however, for Riley points to passages in which diatonicism includes the distinctive use of a particular interval between two notes, known as the augmented fourth. This interval creates "a wrinkle in the diatonic system," one that is distinctively Elgarian, giving, for example, his "noble" music an unmistakable yearning, melancholic quality.

On one level, *Gerontius* appears to display nothing but a straightforward opposition between diatonicism and chromaticism, with the former winning through:

> Part I charts an overall course from agonized chromaticism to radiant diatonicism as the anxious prayers of the dying man and the assistants are replaced by the magisterial intervention of the Priest, banishing the feverish bedside atmosphere in a blaze of pure D major. As for Part II, the music of the rapt opening section, representing the experience of the newly disembodied Soul,

17. Harper-Scott, *Edward Elgar, Modernist*, 14.
18. Harper-Scott, *Edward Elgar, Modernist*, 14–15 (italics original). The point is overplayed; in Catholic orthodoxy, no one can exit purgatory to hell but only to heaven. See Griffiths, "Purgatory," 428–29.
19. Riley, "Heroic Melancholy."
20. Riley, "Heroic Melancholy," 285.

does not introduce an accidental [a note foreign to the scale] until its eighteenth
bar, whereas in the Demons' Chorus, the Angel of the Agony's solo and the
chords at and immediately prior to the moment of judgement, chromaticism
is rampant. From this perspective, the oppositions of good and evil, peace and
turbulence, fear and consolation, could hardly be more starkly etched.[21]

However, things are not this simple. Riley notes that as the oratorio pro-
ceeds, "inflected diatonicism" becomes more frequent, and he relates its melancholic ambivalence to the theological trajectories we have noted—we are
not given an account of a journey from agony to ecstasy but from one agony
(before death) to another (the spiritual agony of a particular judgment) and
thence to purgatory for purifying judgment.

In part 2, he observes that inflected diatonicism "is reserved for the music of
beings that possess a clear philosophical understanding of the Soul's destiny—
in other words, the music of angels."[22] They above all know what is really going
on. Riley points to the series of paradoxes that attend the Angel's description
of the effect of glimpsing God: being gladdened yet pierced, transformed yet
burned, and so forth.

The sight of God does not effect anything so obvious as a redemption
from sin or a triumph over evil but instead raises the Soul's consciousness of
its own imperfection to a new level, so that it willingly accepts its destiny.[23]

Future Ambivalence: The Wider Musical-Cultural Context

We have already mentioned Harper-Scott's reading of Elgar as an early modernist. His book is one of several attempts to situate Elgar in the musical context of
late nineteenth-century tonality as (in some sense) a "progressive."[24] We cannot

21. Riley, "Heroic Melancholy," 300.
22. Riley, "Heroic Melancholy," 302. Significant also is that "the most sustained use of
diatonic tritones in the angels" music occurs when the theologically most significant verses
of the chorus are reached, namely, in the passage between the two strong statements of the
"Praise to the Holiest" refrain, containing a hushed setting of Newman's words that center
on Gethsemane (302).
23. Riley, "Heroic Melancholy," 301.
24. See, e.g., James A. Hepokoski, "Elgar," in *The Nineteenth-Century Symphony*, ed.
D. Kern Holoman (New York: Schirmer, 1997); Julian Rushton and Daniel M. Grimley, "Introduction," in *The Cambridge Companion to Elgar*, ed. Daniel M. Grimley and Julian Rushton
(Cambridge: Cambridge University Press, 2004), 1–14; Charles Edward McGuire, "Edward
Elgar: 'Modern' or 'Modernist?' Construction of an Aesthetic Identity in the British Music
Press, 1895–1934," *Musical Quarterly* 91, no. 1/2 (2008): 8–38. From rather a different perspec-
tive, see Hans Keller, "Elgar the Progressive," in *Elgar: An Anniversary Portrait*, ed. Nicholas
Kenyon et al. (London: Continuum, 2007), 104–11.

explore in any detail what has become a highly complex and somewhat contentious matter, but we can at least signal the latent theological dimensions of the discussion. This is especially pertinent with regard to the perceived presence (or otherwise) of hope in Elgar's music as it relates to particular currents in the late nineteenth- and early twentieth-century British context in which he finds himself. Arguably, the severe interrogation of the notion of hope that in myriad ways became so much a part of European society in the early years of the twentieth century can be read as implicitly theological—concerning the extent to which a purely immanent hope, generated out of the intrinsic possibilities of human resourcefulness alone, can sustain Western culture in the face of humankind's capacity for destructiveness and, in particular, in the face of death's apparent negation of all constructive human endeavor. Harper-Scott comments:

> The broad gesture of [Elgar's] tonal structures do not point to the kind of absolute truths, attractive to the nineteenth-century mind, that can be found in the thought of Hegel, Marx or Freud, or the music of Beethoven's heroic style. Certainly Elgar's structures point onwards, but it is not entirely clear which direction they are going, or whether any larger force is guiding them.[25]

In an essay on Elgar's theater music, the same author comments:

> Elgar's music always seems aware of humankind's inbuilt capacity for self-destruction and does not write heroic narratives. He consistently stresses human impotence, yet even in his blinding realisation in *Gerontius*, The Soul confines himself only to Purgatory, not Hell: humankind cannot achieve, but can still hope.[26]

Yet as Harper-Scott goes on to show, the way in which Elgar's later music develops would suggest this hope is distinctly frail and tenuous. Elgar's mature modernist output exhibits the "idea" of "the ironic, pessimistic deconstruction of the heroic *per aspera ad astra* [through hardships to the stars] narrative."[27] The orientation is contrasted with Beethoven:

> On Beethoven Hero's account . . . authentic choices may be made and may lead ultimately to fulfilment for the individual and, which follows from that, true

---

25. Harper-Scott, *Edward Elgar, Modernist*, 15. Harper-Scott speaks of ambivalence and ambiguity in Elgar in his neo-Romantic phase, evident in *Caractacus*, where apparent imperialist sentiments are undercut by musical settings that move in a very different direction. Harper-Scott goes on to argue that despite the postcolonialist reading of Elgar, his imperialism was in fact "only tweed-deep" (18; see the whole section, 15–19).

26. J. P. E. Harper-Scott, "Elgar's Unwumbling: The Theatre Music," in Grimley and Rushton, *Cambridge Companion to Elgar*, 183.

27. Harper-Scott, *Edward Elgar, Modernist*, 223.

community among all human beings. But on Elgar's account human beings are either too scared to make self-defining choices or else get so bound up with the needs and demands of individual others or the expectations of society as a whole that they fail to break free and find themselves.[28]

On this account, Elgar's music embodies an "understanding of human existence, which was as much informed by his view of the march of human and musical history as by his own personal existential struggles" according to which "there really seems to be little hope for a positive outcome."[29]

Inner Ambivalence: Psychological Perspectives

The reference to "personal existential struggles" is significant, for, not surprisingly, many have linked the unresolved musical ambivalences in Elgar's output to aspects of his own personality. Recent biographers make much of the turmoil and inner contradictions of the composer, his proneness to searing self-doubt and fierce despondency. The conductor Mark Elder writes of Elgar's "strange quirky mixture . . . of inner self-belief" and "a huge neurosis about nobody understanding his music."[30] Another writer expresses it thus:

Elgar's moods were capricious and contradictory; he may have struggled with manic depression. Within this turbulent inner environment warred a series of competing binaries: belief in God jousted with a Victorian belief in progress; high art opposed popular success; and dreams of nostalgic chivalry alternated with an enduring fascination with modern technology. While anyone who approaches a study of Elgar must beware of the biographical fallacy that offers a facile conflation of man and work, how can any scholar examining this volatile life not believe that Elgar's infamous mood swings are not reflected in his work on the deepest possible level?[31]

One of the most interesting treatments of this dimension of Elgar's work comes from Byron Adams, who wants to trace close associations between

28. Harper-Scott, *Edward Elgar, Modernist*, 229. Daniel M. Grimley speaks of "the heroic masculine subject of Elgar's chamber music whose authority is continually denied, refused, or undermined" as part of his "confrontation with a new modernist subjectivity." Grimley, "'A Smiling with a Sigh': The Chamber Music and Works for Strings," in Grimley and Rushton, *Cambridge Companion to Elgar*, 138.

29. Harper-Scott, *Edward Elgar, Modernist*, 230.

30. Mark Elder, "Conducting Elgar," in *Elgar: An Anniversary Portrait*, ed. Nicholas Kenyon (London: Continuum, 2007), 133.

31. McGuire, "Edward Elgar," 29.

what he calls Elgar's "tortured personality" and his first oratorio.[32] Those allergic to any form of musical psychobiography will shrink at this kind of treatment, but whatever details may be disputed, the overall case can hardly be ignored. Adams reads *Gerontius* in the context of a waning *fin de siècle* "decadence," in which a deep attraction to Roman Catholicism is mingled with an aesthetic "in which failure and decay are regarded as seductive, mystical or beautiful."[33] It seems that late nineteenth-century Catholicism provided an environment in which the erotic, together with intense experiences of shame and suffering (bodily and spiritual), could be explored in depth, with Wagner invoked as the paradigmatic composer in this respect. *Gerontius* is replete with "decadent signifiers," argues Adams; very early in the work's reception, the strong echoes of *Parsifal* (its "unsettling aura of decadence") were noted, and later commentators could speak critically of its "erotic religiosity,"[34] its lack of emotional restraint bordering on the hysterical. E. A. Baughan in 1909 described *Gerontius* as "almost grovelling in its anguish of remorse," commenting, "I detect the hysterical prostration of the confessional. It is too much a repentance of nerves."[35] Such critical reactions were linked to a fear of erotic excess, not least homoeroticism. Adams raises the possibility that this dimension might explain in part why Oscar Wilde saw Newman as a precursor of the decadents. "Passages of Newman's poetry and prose express a delicately sublimated homoeroticism as refracted through the doctrinal prism of his unwavering Catholicism,"[36] something evident, for example, in the relationship between the Soul and his Angel. Intertwined with this is an exploration of the aesthetic and erotic power of shame, which reaches its "most spectacular expression" in the climactic "take me away" of *Gerontius*. Elgar's own immersion in shame—over, for example, his lack of formal musical education, his Catholic identity in an intensely Protestant environment, his lower-middle-class origins—is integral, Adams argues, to the portrayal of Gerontius; rather than expressing it directly, Elgar projects himself into the personality of this elderly dying Catholic. Elgar's torment was not allayed, however, for the somewhat chaotic first performance of *Gerontius* provoked an intense outburst of anger: "I always said God was against art. . . . I have allowed my heart to open once—it is now shut against every religious feeling &

32. Byron Adams, "Elgar's Later Oratorios: Roman Catholicism, Decadence and the Wagnerian Dialectic of Shame and Grace," in *Edward Elgar and His World*, ed. Byron Adams (Princeton: Princeton University Press, 2007).

33. The quotation is from Ellis Hanson, *Decadence and Catholicism* (Cambridge, MA: Harvard University Press, 1997), 3.

34. Adams, "Elgar's Later Oratorios," 87, 88.

35. Quoted in Hanson, *Decadence and Catholicism*, 89.

36. Adams, "Elgar's Later Oratorios," 89.

every soft, gentle impulse *for ever*."[37] Even if this remark was perhaps not wholly genuine at the time, in later years Elgar expressed the grievance by distancing himself from all things religious.

> Elgar may have felt that God had condemned him, like Judas, to be an eternal "outsider of outsiders." Even the imprisoned [Oscar] Wilde believed that he had been granted grace; Elgar, however, locked in the prison of his wounded psyche, was so enmeshed in his self-loathing that he was unable to partake of such consolation. Lacking Wagner's heroic egotism, the chronically self-doubting Elgar may have felt there was no surcease for his frequent depressions, no balm to assuage his gnawing anxiety, and no grace to mitigate his shame. Instead he lashed out at God and humanity, repudiating some of his most radiant music— the vessel that brought grace to repentant sinners—as a mere "penalty" of his "English environment."[38]

As the last quotation shows, for all that Adams belongs to an academic guild that would be keen to eschew moral (let alone religious) value judgments, there can be little doubt that he views Elgar's shame-ridden "decadence" to a significant extent as pathological.[39] Even if he does overstate his case somewhat, his claims are congruent in many respects with our observations about Elgar's music and about the wider contemporary social and cultural currents that seem to have affected him.

Pressing the Theological Questions

In this section we turn more directly to theology and ask whether there are irreducibly theological factors in play in what we have observed. (In fact, we have already touched on them.) Of course, for some the very presence of any serious belief in God will itself be regarded as pathological and thus as compromising Elgar's mental stability, even if it is conceded that it might have helped him produce some glorious music. Others more attuned to the Christian tradition in its different manifestations will be more inclined to ask whether it is only a particular strand (or strands) of belief that is problematic. I suggest that Elgar's oscillation between confidence and anxiety, exemplified in *Gerontius* but evident elsewhere, at its deepest level concerns a theological ambivalence

---

37. Jerrold Northrop Moore, *Edward Elgar: A Creative Life* (Oxford: Oxford University Press, 1984), 334 (italics original).
38. Adams, "Elgar's Later Oratorios," 105.
39. Edmund Gurney's suggestive phrase about Wagner comes to mind, that it betrays "a faint flower of disease, something overripe in its lusciousness and febrile passion." Quoted in Hanson, *Decadence and Catholicism*, 36.

with respect to a distinctive view of the status of the Christian in relation to God, an ambivalence that is thoroughly consistent with and clearly exposed in Newman's vision of purgatory. I am not claiming that this particular version of purgatorial doctrine constitutes a simple or singular cause of his anxieties, religious or otherwise. I am contending, however, that it throws into relief aspects of Christian theology and piety (by no means confined to the Roman Catholic Church) that can foster and encourage something of the ambivalent malaise in Elgar's output that we have been tracing. Moreover, if, as I have suggested, Elgar was to some degree caught up in the questioning of certain forms of social hope in the late nineteenth and early twentieth centuries, a theological perspective might well provide deeper insight into what was at stake in these turbulent and complex interrogations.

Considerable caution is required here since unthinking Protestant overreactions to the idea of purgatory have been all too common and often display an insensitivity to the intentions behind the doctrine's emergence and to the distinction between its basic form and its various (often overspeculative and widely criticized) improvisations. Even today, half-remembered and ill-informed prejudices continue to dog discussions, especially when the identity of this or that group (usually Protestant or Catholic) is felt to be at stake. Nonetheless, one does not need to be a tetchy Protestant to ask questions about the propriety of the doctrine and some of its satellite ideas. Here we concentrate on purgatory as evoked and imagined in *Gerontius* and what it implies about the attitudes of confidence and anxiety that have been central to our concerns in this essay.

In Newman's poem, the following lines are given to the Guardian Angel:

> And these two pains, so counter and so keen,—
> The longing for Him, when thou seest Him not;
> The shame of self at thought of seeing Him,—
> Will be thy veriest, sharpest purgatory.[40]

In fact, Elgar did not include these words, but their spirit encapsulates perfectly the oscillation between reaching out and shrinking back that is so persistent in *Gerontius*. A sensitive reader will not fail to notice the sharp contrast with the way the New Testament envisions the believer's postmortem encounter with God (even acknowledging the heavily poetic and metaphorical character of Newman's text). It is hard to believe that the apostle Paul, for example—or indeed any writer of the New Testament—would imagine

---

40. Rowell comments that these couplets "contain the essence of Newman's understanding of purgatory." Rowell, *Hell and the Victorians*, 160.

approaching God after death with the plea "take me away." The reason, I suggest, is twofold. First, the process of cleansing from sin is understood as taking place through the direct action of God, more precisely, through Jesus Christ in the power of his Spirit. Purgation cannot happen in some "place" of its own at a distance from God (a gap mediated by the angels and saints) where the believer has awareness only of an "absent Lord." The notion of a Christian's continuing alienation from God or longing for God after death is thus hard to justify in New Testament terms; indeed, the biblical texts give no hint that Christ will be with the "saints," while the purgatorial "souls" will be in another "place" or state. (Undoubtedly part of the trouble here is the tendency in some Catholic traditions to develop a punitive dimension to purgatory that it is understood extrinsically and unrelationally, that is, in abstraction from the direct action of the God who is committed to reconciling and restoring the believer.) Second, for the apostle Paul, Christ's death brings to an end the propensity to sin and the effects of sin. Bodily death marks the cessation of the person qua sinner (Rom. 6:6–7; Col. 2:11–14): for those "in Christ" there is (and will be) "no condemnation" (Rom. 8:1). Thus, even leaving aside for the moment the issue about the extent to which it is appropriate to envisage something akin to a "time line" beyond death, it is hard to find evidence in the New Testament for any belief in a cleansing of believers after death, pending the final resurrection.[41]

Basic to both these positions is a solidity of assurance that is arguably compromised by the notion of a postmortem extended cleansing. In relation to the first, there is the assurance not only that Christ has already gone ahead of us as the human forerunner of our own cleansing, the one whose own life, death, and resurrection are the basis (and embodiment) of the purgation of human nature (a repeated refrain in Newman's poem, as in "A second Adam to the fight / And to the rescue came" from "Praise to the Holiest"), but also that the agent of cleansing is *Christ himself*, that our purging is driven and *directly* effected by the reconciling love of God in action (something much less evident in the Newman text). In relation to the second point, there is the assurance that, for the believer, to experience physical death with Christ means that the reign of sin will end for that person; it will not have to be experienced in any form in the next life. The final encounter, therefore, cannot include the continuation of shame, for shame has already been taken care of. Nor for those "in Christ" will there be punishment for sin, for again, that has already

41. There have been some highly strained attempts to read some New Testament texts this way (e.g., 1 Cor. 3), but these are not widely accepted. See N. T. Wright, *For All the Saints? Remembering the Christian Departed* (London: SPCK, 2003), 28–36.

been dealt with at the crucifixion.[42] In the biblical texts, none of this seems to weaken a sense that shame is highly appropriate in this life, that humanly devised evil is hazardous, and that a genuine battle of immense consequence is being waged—complacency and sentimentality are repeatedly shunned. But even here, sin and shame are constantly set in the infinitely wider context of what has already been achieved in Christ, which both exposes and forgives human wickedness in the same gracious act, an act whose full effects will be wholly revealed after death.[43]

Thus with attention in the New Testament focused on the one who alone has secured and now secures our purgation, the note of assurance is of a radically different register than that suggested by Elgar's oratorio. Even if one does posit an "intermediate state" of some sort (between death and final resurrection), in the biblical texts a believer's life beyond death is never characterized by the kind of introverted and crippling sense of shame so graphically and effectively rendered by Newman and Elgar but rather by an outwardly directed, "eccentric" joy in God through (and because of) Christ.

It is telling that the former pope, Benedict XVI, sought to mitigate the very difficulties we are noting here.[44] In an important book on eschatology from 1977, the then-Cardinal Ratzinger urges that the purgatorial fire is none other than Jesus himself, working in the believer the transformation required for heaven: "the inwardly necessary process of transformation in which a person becomes capable of Christ, capable of God and thus capable of unity with the whole community of saints."[45] This cannot be understood as taking place according to the time of created things but is better seen as "existential time" (*Existenzzeit*). As such, it marks entry into our final, fulfilled destiny.[46]

---

42. This is not necessarily to deny a so-called intermediate state between death and final resurrection nor the appropriateness (or otherwise) of prayers for the dead. Though these notions have undoubtedly "nurtured purgatorial thinking" (Griffiths, "Purgatory," 431), many hold to them who do not subscribe to the basic or traditional concept of purgatory.

43. Some believe that the traditional doctrine of purgatory is the result of projecting the (necessary) process of moral cleansing in this life into the next life. See, e.g., N. T. Wright, *Surprised by Hope: Rethinking Heaven, the Resurrection, and the Mission of the Church* (New York: HarperOne, 2008), 183.

44. Joseph Ratzinger, *Eschatology, Death and Eternal Life* (Washington, DC: Catholic University of America Press, 2007).

45. Ratzinger, *Eschatology, Death and Eternal Life*, 230.

46. "Purgatory is understood in a properly Christian way when it is grasped christologically, in terms of the Lord himself as the judging fire which transforms us and conforms us to his own glorified body. . . . The purification involved does not happen through some thing, but through the transforming power of the Lord himself, whose burning flame cuts free our closed-off heart, melting it, and pouring it into a new mold to make it fit for the living organism of the body." Ratzinger goes on to say that the judgment after death and the judgment on the last day are in fact "indistinguishable. A person's entry into the realm of manifest reality is an entry into his

Ratzinger thus questions any necessary link between the intermediate state and purgatory. More than this, the notion that purgation could happen at some kind of alienated distance from God is unambiguously rejected; speaking of the final transformation of our sinful human nature, Ratzinger states bluntly: "Encounter with the Lord *is* this transformation."[47] The Soul's "take me away" would, we conclude, be hugely misleading on this account.

We have been working largely at the individual and psychological level, but the relevance of these theological comments to the wider sociocultural matters we raised earlier will be quickly apparent. Since the stark phenomena of human destructiveness and death (on every level from the human to the cosmic) radically call into question the viability of any firm confidence that a "better future" of stability or permanence can be generated from within the world's own resources, the matter of whether hope for this world can ever be grounded in anything that comes *to* the world as unachievable *gift* is unavoidable. Put differently: Is the Elgarian fluctuation between hopefulness and anxiety to be regarded as a purely immanent and, in principle, endless, irresolvable struggle? The root difficulty with the Newmanian purgatorial scheme in this connection is not that it is devoid of all hope (purgatory is, after all, a temporary condition with an assured positive outcome) but rather its implicit distancing from the direct grounding of hope in the presence and actions of God; its hopefulness is thus severely weakened (at least in New Testament terms) and the way opened rather too easily for the kind of introverted, hyperanxious, and overly self-conscious posture of Gerontius's Soul.

definitive destiny and thus an immersion in eschatological fire. The transforming 'moment' of this encounter cannot be quantified by the measurements of earthly time. . . . The 'temporal measure' of this encounter lies in the unsoundable depths of existence, in a passing-over where we are burned ere we are transformed." Ratzinger, *Eschatology, Death and Eternal Life*, 229, 230. Ratzinger reiterates and expands on these convictions in his 2007 encyclical, *Spe Salvi*:

> Some recent theologians are of the opinion that the fire which both burns and saves is Christ himself, the Judge and Saviour. The encounter with him is the decisive act of judgement. Before his gaze all falsehood melts away. This encounter with him, as it burns us, transforms and frees us, allowing us to become truly ourselves. All that we build during our lives can prove to be mere straw, pure bluster, and it collapses. Yet in the pain of this encounter, when the impurity and sickness of our lives become evident to us, there lies salvation. His gaze, the touch of his heart heals us through an undeniably painful transformation "as through fire." But it is a blessed pain, in which the holy power of his love sears through us like a flame, enabling us to become totally ourselves and thus totally of God. . . . It is clear that we cannot calculate the "duration" of this transforming burning in terms of the chronological measurements of this world. The transforming "moment" of this encounter eludes earthly time-reckoning—it is the heart's time, it is the time of "passage" to communion with God in the Body of Christ. (*Spe Salvi*, para. 47, http://www.vatican.va/holy_father/benedict_xvi/encyclicals/documents/hf_ben-xvi_enc_20071130_spe-salvi_en.html)

47. Ratzinger, *Eschatology, Death and Eternal Life*, 231 (italics original).

I have tried to show that the deepest problems concerning purgatory are not about eschatological geography or temporality but about the orientation and character of human hope, and this inevitably entails considering theological or quasi-theological questions. Doubtless, many musicologists and music theorists, even when faced with Elgar's sacred works, will hesitate to venture into this kind of territory, for academic protocol hardly encourages expeditions into the imposing issues of theology. Yet the very nature of a work like *Gerontius* seems to press for it, and it is hard to deny that every manifestation we have discerned (textual and musical) of Elgar's poignant and irresolvable alternation between confidence and anxiety at root concerns the foundational question about what or who can be ultimately trusted and how that trust shapes hope. It would be ironic indeed if musicologists critical of Elgar were at this point to succumb to another version of the composer's own ambivalence—tempering a proper intellectual boldness with a misplaced academic anxiety.

6

The Holy Spirit at Work in the Arts

Learning from George Herbert

If we want to see a profoundly theological sensibility at work in and through poetic form, few can match the output of poet, orator, and Anglican minister George Herbert (1593–1633). In this essay, through a reading of one his best-known poems, I attempt to draw on his wisdom with regard to the special link many have discerned between the arts and the Holy Spirit.

For many, it seems entirely natural to assume a close link between the arts and a divine spirit. The connection has a long and distinguished history, and it appears regularly in the current theology and the arts conversation. At the popular level, many will speak quite naturally of an artist being "inspired," of music as affording a peculiarly "spiritual" experience, of artistic creativity and "spirituality" as close cousins.

At some stage, however, we may well want to ask questions not only about what is being assumed about the arts here but also—our main concern in

This chapter was originally published as Jeremy Begbie, "The Holy Spirit at Work in the Arts: Learning from George Herbert," *Interpretation* 66, no. 1 (2012): 41–54. I am immensely grateful to Dr. Malcolm Guite for his many insights into Herbert's "Ephes. 4. 30" and for his helpful comments on an earlier draft of this essay. It was written before I could benefit from John Drury's excellent *Music at Midnight: The Life and Poetry of George Herbert* (Chicago: University of Chicago Press, 2014), a book it would be hard to praise too highly.

this essay—about the identity of the "spirit" so readily invoked.[1] As far as Christians are concerned, the reasons for wanting to loosen the ties between God's Spirit and the particularities of Christian faith when engaging with the arts are understandable; among them is the desire to do justice to God's activity beyond the confines of the church, to take seriously what many see as a close association of the arts with the broad category of "religious experience." The singer Sting once said: "I think music is the one spiritual force in our lives that we have access to, really. There are so many other spiritual avenues that are closed off to us, and music still has that, is still important, is important for me. It saved my life. It saved my sanity."[2] Nonetheless, there are obvious dangers in too eagerly identifying this or that overwhelming artistic experience with an experience of the one named as Holy Spirit in the New Testament. The specificity of the latter sits awkwardly with at least some of the "Spirit-talk" that pervades our culture at large.

Of course, artists often suspect theologians of cramping the arts in a zeal for doctrinal correctness, and not without good reason. If we want some clarity about the relation of the arts to the Holy Spirit of the Christian faith, it is wise to let the arts themselves have as much say as possible, to give them proper space to operate theologically. In this essay, I propose to allow a remarkable poem of George Herbert (1593–1633) to do just this. "Ephes. 4. 30," from Herbert's collection *The Temple*, does not lay out for us anything like "a doctrine of the Holy Spirit" or an account of literary creativity; in any case, as David Jasper has put it, "Herbert does not *tell* you, he *shows* you."[3] But the poem is replete with signals that, taken along with material from some of his other poems, give us a fair sense of what Herbert would have assumed about the relation of the arts to the Third Person of the Trinity, and in a way that is especially enlightening for the theology-arts conversation today.

Ephes. 4. 30

Grieve not the Holy Spirit, &c.
And art thou grieved, sweet and sacred Dove,
    When I am sowre,
    And crosse thy love?

1. For an excellent treatment of these matters, see Steven R. Guthrie, *Creator Spirit: The Holy Spirit and the Art of Becoming Human* (Grand Rapids: Baker Academic, 2011).

2. Quoted in Albert L. Blackwell, *The Sacred in Music* (Cambridge: Lutterworth Press, 1999), 168.

3. David Jasper, "'Something Understood': From Poetry to Theology in the Writings of George Herbert," in *George Herbert's Pastoral: New Essays on the Poet and Priest of Bemerton* (Newark: University of Delaware Press, 2010), 273–87, here 279 (italics original).

Grieved for me? the God of strength and power
  Griev'd for a worm, which when I tread,
  I passe away and leave it dead?

Then weep mine eyes, the God of love doth grieve:
  Weep foolish heart,
  And weeping live:
For death is drie as dust. Yet if ye part,
  End as the night, whose sable hue
  Your sinnes expresse; melt into dew.

When sawcie mirth shall knock or call at doore,
  Cry out, Get hence,
  Or cry no more.
Almightie God doth grieve, he puts on sense:
  I sinne not to my grief alone,
  But to my Gods too; he doth grone.

Oh take thy lute, and tune it to a strain,
  Which may with thee
  All day complain.
There can no discord but in ceasing be.
  Marbles can weep; and surely strings
  More bowels have, then such hard things.

Lord, I adjudge my self to tears and grief,
  Ev'n endlesse tears
  Without relief.
If a cleare spring for me no time forbears,
  But runnes, although I be not drie;
  I am no Crystall, what shall I?

Yet if I wail not still, since still to wail
  Nature denies;
  And flesh would fail,
If my deserts were masters of mine eyes:
  Lord, pardon, for thy sonne makes good
  My want of tears with store of bloud.[4]
    (From *The Temple* [1633], by George Herbert)

The poem presses us to ponder questions in four main areas: first, concerning the identity of the Spirit; second, concerning the relation of the Spirit to

---

4. I use here the text as it appears in Helen Wilcox, ed., *The English Poems of George Herbert*
(Cambridge: Cambridge University Press, 2007), 172–73.

Scripture; third, concerning the poet and poetry as media of the Spirit; and fourth, concerning the role of music in relation to the Spirit.

What/Whose "Spirit"?

"And art thou grieved . . . ?" We are introduced abruptly to Herbert's sudden realization of what the Ephesians verse implies. In the second main section of Ephesians 4, the apostle Paul contrasts two forms of life, the old humanity and the new humanity in Christ, and at verse 25 starts to present detailed exhortations to promote the latter. Out of the blue, he introduces a command quite unique in the New Testament: "And do not grieve the Holy Spirit of God, with whom you were sealed for the day of redemption."[5] That sin should lead to our own grieving is to be expected, but what doubles the pain for Herbert and provokes his "ejaculation of astonishment"[6] is the awareness that sin grieves God's Spirit: "I sinne not to my grief alone, / But to my Gods too; he doth grone."[7] (In Herbert, the "sowre" or bitter [line 2] typically stands for the state of sinfulness, contrasting with the "sweetness" of God's goodness conveyed by the Spirit, or as here, the sweetness of the Spirit himself: "sweet and sacred Dove.") God's deep care for the speaker—a "worm" (Job 25:6; Ps. 22:6)—is set against our characteristic contempt for worms, which we tread on and kill without so much as a second thought.

Paul's audience was corporate. Herbert, though by no means intending to rule out that dimension, is eager that the sting of the verse is not dispelled and thus focuses the verse on the individual—himself and all who identify with him. "Grieved for *me*?" The only appropriate response is grief and tears:

> Then weep mine eyes, the God of love doth grieve:
> Weep foolish heart

A well-established tradition of "literature of tears" was in place by this time, but here Herbert's perspective is quite distinctive. How many tears could ever

5. Echoing Isa. 63:10: "But they rebelled and grieved his holy spirit."

6. Elizabeth Clarke, *Theory and Theology in George Herbert's Poetry: "Divinitie, and Poesie, Met"* (New York: Oxford University Press, 1997), 118.

7. That God could experience grief was hardly an uncontroversial view at the time. Herbert's contemporary, the Puritan Richard Sibbes (1577–1635), for example, asserted that "the Holy Ghost cannot properly be grieved in his own person, because grief implies a defect of happiness in suffering that we wish removed." Sibbes, "A Fountain Sealed," *Works V* (Edinburgh, 1863), 414–15.

be adequate to the grief engendered, sufficient as a response to God's love? The speaker has sentenced himself to ceaseless weeping.

> Lord, I adjudge my self to tears and grief,
>   Ev'n endlesse tears
>   Without relief.

If he were to cry all he should, his "flesh would fail." No amount of weeping can repair the breach our sin has created. Only death will bring an end to the weeping.

The speaker knows he *must* weep but cannot conceivably weep *enough*.[8] That is his agony. Recalling the Spirit (in the fifth stanza) does nothing to alleviate the intensity of his predicament.

> If a cleare spring for me no time forbears,
>   But runnes, although I be not drie;
>   I am no Crystall, what shall I?

The "cleare spring" here is most likely the Holy Spirit, poured out by Christ ("The water that I will give will become in them a spring of water gushing up to eternal life").[9] In fact, the theme of running fluid is implicit throughout the poem, with its ubiquitous weeping and flowing tears. We find a vivid contrast between the speaker's tears, which are never fresh, never pure or clear, and the stream, which is ever fresh, pouring from Christ, who is perfectly pure—represented by "Crystall," a pun appropriately capitalized—and who, like a crystal but unlike the speaker, will never die. But at this stage, this knowledge hardly helps. For the speaker is poignantly aware that he is "no Crystall."

In this compressed impasse, we notice that the speaker has turned from addressing God to addressing himself, unable to disentangle his knowledge of God from a simultaneous awareness of the potentially never-ending and imprisoning effects of his own sin. Only in the last lines is he released from his interiority and turned outward; he now addresses the "Lord" (i.e., the Father):

> Lord, pardon, for thy sonne makes good
> My want of tears with store of bloud.

8. Herbert points us to "both the necessity and the impotence of human penitence." Richard Strier, *Love Known: Theology and Experience in George Herbert's Poetry* (Chicago: University of Chicago Press, 1983), 9.

9. John 4:14. Compare John 7:37–38.

Now our attention is relocated from our heavy obligations to what has
already been done on our behalf—the Son's death that secures our "pardon."
(Note that two verses after Ephesians 4:30, Paul writes: "Be kind to one
another, tenderhearted, forgiving one another, as God in Christ has forgiven
you.") Again the theme of flowing liquid appears, but this time it is the blood
of Christ. His "store of bloud" has provided what our tears could never provide; his is the penitence, the repentance we could never offer.

In all this, the poem's trinitarian geography should not elude us. It begins
by addressing the Spirit and closes by addressing the Father about the Son—an
address that, in New Testament terms, is only possible through the Spirit. The
Spirit has rendered the speaker "ecstatic," uncurling him from his paralyzing
condition. The pattern is deeply reminiscent of Calvin, for whom assurance
came not by inward scrutiny but by an ex-centric movement of the Spirit
within us toward Christ. Only in this way is what Calvin called "evangelical
repentance" possible.[10]

Consistent with this belief, there is no suggestion here or elsewhere in
Herbert that the divine love so revealed is a transient or nonessential dimension of God's character, activated to satisfy the consequences of human law
breaking. By so clearly pointing us at the start to sin as a spurning of love, to
the grieving of the "God of love," to the fact that "he doth grone" (evoking
Rom. 8:22–27), sin is revealed from the outset as a personal offense against
a God whose inner heart is love. The divine grief is that of wounded love,
the sorrow of a God whose unconditional dedication—shown supremely at
the cross—has been rebuffed. The pun on "crosse" as early as the third line
presses the point—Golgotha enacts the epitome of love. Richard Strier observes that "Herbert's most characteristic way of describing God is in terms
of 'power and love'—absolute power in the service of absolute love."[11] In this
poem, notably, God's "strength and power" are redefined through a love that
can grieve and die for us.

We have not spoken of the arts yet, but as far as the Spirit is concerned,
Herbert's poem is clearly opening up a fertile theological landscape in which
the Spirit is being portrayed, at least partly Calvinist in character[12] and redolent with a characteristically Protestant stress on *sola gratia*—by grace alone
Christ has accomplished what we could not, and by grace alone humans are

10. Calvin, *Institutes* III:3, 4.
11. Strier, *Love Known*, 5.
12. Elizabeth Clarke argues that Herbert, in the context of the early Stuart church, is best
considered a "conformist Calvinist" (though not exclusively or narrowly so): conformist in
matters of order and ecclesiastical authority and "unambiguously Calvinist in his doctrine and
spirituality." Clarke, *Theory and Theology*, 10.

justified and adopted by the Spirit into God's company in Christ, all contributing merit being thereby excluded.[13] The categories are relational through
and through (even the form of the poem is conversational, like so much of
Herbert's poetry) and trinitarian in shape.

Spirit and Scripture

Just because his approach to the Spirit is inextricable from this trinitarian and
christological matrix, the link between the Spirit and Scripture (the supreme
written attestation to the trinitarian God and through which this God speaks)
is close and unbreakable in Herbert. Insofar as he is a poet "in the Spirit,"
he is a poet of Scripture.

"Ephes. 4. 30" is one of five poems in *The Temple* with a biblical title. The
opening "And" tellingly links the poem's questioning directly to the Pauline
verse. It "has the effect of placing us, for a moment, with Herbert in the act
of reading Scripture."[14] And that is just where Herbert wants to place us.

By far the most important source of all of Herbert's work is the Bible, the
"book of starres" that lights the route to "eternall blisse,"[15] in whose words he
was profoundly immersed both in private devotion and through the Church of
England's liturgy. Indeed, the vast majority of his poems are, in effect, inventive
yet textually disciplined interactions with the Old and the New Testaments.
To read Herbert, writes Jasper, "is to become wholly one with the scriptures
that inhabit not only almost every image and metaphor, but every word of
his verse."[16] What is striking is the way in which neither faithfulness to the
text nor poetic artifice seem to be sacrificed in the process: one commentator
points to Herbert's ability to write "poems of such astonishing freshness"
despite being "so deeply indebted to traditional materials."[17]

Herbert was fully aware of movements in his own day that would attempt to
pull the Spirit and human words (in particular the words of Scripture) apart,
those on the radical "left" of the Reformation, for example, who claimed inspiration apart from or even in judgment over the Bible. In this regard he also
found himself in tension with the views of the eminent Roman Catholic Juan
de Valdés (ca. 1500–1541). Although he warmed to Valdés in other respects,

13. For the argument that "justification by faith" lies at the heart of Herbert's work, see
Strier, *Love Known*.
14. Chana Bloch, *Spelling the Word: George Herbert and the Bible* (Berkeley: University of
California Press, 1985), 33.
15. "The H. Scriptures. II," line 14, in Wilcox, *English Poems of George Herbert*, 210.
16. Jasper, "'Something Understood,'" 284.
17. Bloch, *Spelling the Word*, 112.

Herbert reproached the Spanish reformer for his tendency to exalt personal illumination and oppose "the teaching of the spirit to the teaching of the scripture,"[18] and not because Herbert believed that without biblically informed discernment, the Spirit's movements within us could easily be confused with those inner urgings generated merely by our sinful natures.

For Herbert, it is through Scripture that the Spirit will speak most pointedly, involving our deepest passions in a life-transforming process. The Spirit bears witness to the truth of the gospel, "revealing and applying the generall promises to every one in particular" with "syncerity and efficacy."[19] Though many of the poems do lead us into the internal wrestlings of a particular individual, the reader is not to be left unmoved: "The dividing line between the self and the reader is not a wall but a semipermeable membrane."[20] In "Ephes. 4. 30," we are to read ourselves in or into Herbert's (and Paul's) text; hence what one writer calls the "didactic impulse" evident in *The Temple*— meaning not simply the impulse to transmit information but, more widely, to re-form the reader.[21]

Poet, Poetry, and the Spirit

Within circles of a broadly Reformed viewpoint, the relation of Spirit and Word would hardly have been a controversial matter. More contentious was the issue of the vocation of the poet. It is easy to forget that in Herbert's milieu some considered the very business of writing devotional poetry a highly dubious enterprise. Many, not least Calvinists, were skeptical of the possibility of the Spirit operating through the oblique and potentially confusing devices of the poetic imagination.

It seems that Herbert saw himself as a Christian lyric poet (as distinct from the secular love poet) for whom the forms of secular writing could be adapted for devotional ends: "Brought . . . to Church well drest and clad."[22] Certainly, he displays exceptional literary skill: there is an extraordinary precision and exactitude, an intense concentration and economy of terms combined with an abundance of meaning, ingenious punning and conceits, semantic dislocations and ironies. Yet Herbert himself seems to have been ambivalent about

18. Quoted in F. E. Hutchinson, ed., *The Works of George Herbert* (Oxford: Clarendon Press, 1945), 317.

19. Quoted in Strier, *Love Known*, 145.

20. Bloch, *Spelling the Word*, 171.

21. See Chauncey Wood, "Herbert's Biblically-Titled Poems," *George Herbert Journal* 26, no. 1/2 (2002–2003): 35–45; Bloch, *Spelling the Word*, chap. 4.

22. "The Forerunners," line 17, in Wilcox, *English Poems of George Herbert*, 612.

his own skills in fusing the poetical and theological; among other things, he was keenly aware of the hazard of obscuring truth through excessive literary artifice, as he puts it, "Curling with metaphors a plain intention."[23] And throughout there is a deep concern for the need to curb the distorting effects of human sin.

In order to understand Herbert's struggles and achievement, it is helpful to recall the convergence of seventeenth-century Reformation theology and the Renaissance rhetorical tradition in literature out of which his work emerges, a convergence that raised serious issues about the capacity of poetry to act as a mode of divine communication. Elizabeth Clarke maintains that Herbert was likely influenced by contemporary discussions of authorship, one of the key places where literary theory and theology intersected.[24] Medieval writers had commonly accounted for authorship by employing the terms of scholastic accounts of causality: God is seen as the Prime Mover in a succession of causally related movements, resulting eventually in human authorship and, in due course, in "moving" the reader. A God-given intermediary principle of grace implanted in the author provides the direct cause of his (good) actions. However, the Reformers preferred to speak of the direct presence and impulses of the Holy Spirit within the believer. A vigorous theology of the Spirit's "motions" emerged—impulses within the Christian's inner experience that were thought critical for his or her assurance of salvation. Some also understood motions in a negative sense, as sinful human impulses that needed expunging. Further, literary theory had its own theory of motions, drawing on classical rhetoric, centering on the power of figures of speech to move the hearer. Sir Philip Sidney developed a defense of the poetic (*Apology for Poetry*, 1595) that combined theological and literary strands. Clarke summarizes this vision thus: "Inspired directly by God, or moved by his own love of God, the Christian poet will achieve an *energeia* in his writing which will move his readers to virtue."[25]

Thus, "Herbert was formulating his role as a Christian poet within a nexus of influences whereby assurance of salvation, the inspiration of authorship, the sinful passions of the flesh, and the power of effective rhetoric are all signified by internal impulses, or 'motions.'"[26] In this environment a tension develops between two extremes, one Herbert would know well: at one end, an inflated view of poetic authorship that suggests rhetoric can engender faith, and at the other, a dissolution of human authorship under the overwhelming power

---

23. "Jordan. (II)," line 5, in Wilcox, *English Poems of George Herbert*, 367.
24. Clarke, *Theory and Theology*, 16–25.
25. Clarke, *Theory and Theology*, 21.
26. Clarke, *Theory and Theology*, 23.

of divine inspiration. Herbert appears to choose neither extreme. He senses the potential for the corruption of rhetorical motions on their own—a poetic anxiety suffuses much of his work, the language of "inspiration" seems foreign to him, and he is suspicious of anything that sounds like pleading human merit before God. The restraining motions of the Spirit are constantly needed to counter sin's effects. At the same time, he "operates as if his human rhetoric is sanctioned, and indeed, uses rhetorical strategies which give the impression of validating the poetry."[27] Distinctively literary devices need not be spurned: the Spirit can employ them and with them move the reader or hearer.

Some will appeal to the language of "sacrament" to explicate this. But caution is needed. We are not moving in the ethos of a generalized "sacramentality" or in one where material signs are thought to possess an inherent power of their own to mediate the divine. As Regina Schwartz observes, if there is a sense in which Herbert's poems were designed to operate "sacramentally," we should understand this in the context of something like Calvin's sacramental theology, which is essentially dynamic and trinitarian: by the Spirit's free activity, through engaging physical realities (including language), we are made partakers of the risen and ascended Christ. The physical sign participates in this momentum without ever being identified with or enclosing the realities it mediates. And the Spirit's action is pivotal: "What would make poetry sacramental, according to this logic, would be no less than the agency of the Spirit . . . and the Reformation poets do invoke just such agency."[28]

Informing all this, then, is a subtle understanding of the relation of divine and human agency (the Spirit and the poet) that refuses to set them against each other in a zero-sum scheme. Some have made much of Herbert's sense of the inadequacy of human speech (and with it of the self), even positing the notion of an "extinction" of the author.[29] The territory is complex and contested. Here I make only four observations. First, for Herbert, Scripture itself will likely have been his main model for the fruitful interaction of the Spirit and the poet, the model for the ideal poet probably being David the psalmist (the indebtedness of "Ephes. 4. 30" to the Psalms is obvious).[30]

27. Clarke, Theory and Theology, 274.

28. Regina M. Schwartz, Sacramental Poetics at the Dawn of Secularism: When God Left the World (Stanford, CA: Stanford University Press, 2008), 122.

29. Perhaps most pointedly in Stanley E. Fish, Self-Consuming Artifacts: The Experience of Seventeenth-Century Literature (Berkeley: University of California Press, 1972), chap. 3. See also Jasper, "'Something Understood,'" 273–87.

30. "It is possibly the example of the Bible that gives Herbert his greatest inspiration. Certainly, the reading of the Scriptures is for Herbert a place where the power of rhetoric and the power of the Spirit meet, and the result is almost literally explosive." Clarke, Theory and Theology, 270.

Second, attentiveness to the biblical testimony means distinguishing two quite distinct matters: on the one hand, the divine-human relation as intended and, on the other, as it has been corrupted through the fall. In the latter case, notions of tension, competition, even the threat of dissolution are apposite; in the former, they are not. From Herbert's viewpoint, the Spirit's sanctification does not entail the diminution of humanness (precisely the opposite) or the dissolving of human finitude in divinity; "the more of God the less of us" is a mentality quite foreign to Herbert, and this applies to the poet as much as to anyone else.[31] Third, a related point can be made about language. Amid the sophisticated treatments of Herbert's poetry and prose, we should not lose sight of the basic distinction between language as finite and language as fallen; Herbert is acutely conscious of the latter and its threat to the Spirit's work, but he seems to believe that finite language need not be treated as *inherently* obstructive, problematic, or distorting. Fourth, and most important, in Herbert's work, specifically poetic devices are seen to have their own aptness for the Spirit's activity. For example, although not present in our poem, Herbert can sometimes use *correctio*—when a statement or expression is immediately qualified by a correcting turn, as if from God. In this way the process of mortification (part of sanctification) is played out in the rhetorical structure of poetic lines.[32] Another example: William Pahlka contends that in Herbert's poems God's presence is indicated by meter, mediating "between the sadly defective expressions of the human will and the perfections of divine will."[33] The order of poetry enacts and (potentially) mediates God's ordering activity.

It seems, then, that implicit in Herbert is a view of the interpenetration of divine and poetic agency (and with this, poetic techniques) that, although rooted in the priority of God's free grace, threatens neither the poet's integrity nor that of the poet's literary palette but enables them to flourish in their particularity.

31. See the remarks about Fish in Bloch, *Spelling the Word*, 35–37. In his review of Clarke, Christopher Hodgkins comments: "Given all of her earlier insistence that Herbert's Calvinism allows for the divine redemption of natural and human means, [Clarke] reverts in the end, like Stanley Fish . . . to treating divine and human creation as locked in a mutually exclusive zero-sum game. Thus divine intervention utterly obliterates poetry, and the holiest poem is mere silence (276–80). Yes, there is much artful silence in Herbert's poetry, yet it is not the silence of resigned defeat or numb absence but of wondering and worshipful presence." Christopher Hodgkins, "Review of *Theory and Theology in George Herbert's Poetry: 'Divinitie, and Poesie, Met'* by Elizabeth Clarke," *Christianity and Literature* 48, no. 3 (Spring 1999): 371–74, here 374.

32. See Strier, *Love Known*, 10–12; Clarke, *Theory and Theology*, 234–36.

33. William H. Pahlka, *Saint Augustine's Meter and George Herbert's Will* (Kent, OH: Kent State University Press, 1987), 177; see Clarke, *Theory and Theology*, 239–40.

Music and the Spirit

In the fourth verse, we are invited to hear the sounds of music.

> Oh take thy lute, and tune it to a strain,
>> Which may with thee
>> All day complain.
> There can no discord but in ceasing be.
>> Marbles can weep; and surely strings
>> More bowels have, then such hard things.

As is well known, Herbert's musical experience was extensive and his sense of music's powers deeply rooted. Evidently he set some of his poems (and sang them) to lute accompaniment, and it is telling that seventeenth-century composers of the stature of John Blow and John Jenkins should write settings of "Ephes. 4. 30."[34] The figure of "wings" in his poem "Church-musick," which appears as we travel in the company of music toward "heaven's doore," indicates that Herbert considered music a potential vehicle of the Spirit, an effective aid to spiritual growth.[35]

Musical imagery abounds in Herbert. In our poem, the speaker exhorts himself to take up the lute and tune it to a melody that articulates his continual penitence ("strain" representing a tune, the speaker's tension, and the tension of the string necessary for good tuning). To lament in this way will never be out of place; "discord" only comes when one stops (there is probably a reference here to the fact that true discords—as distinct from passing dissonances—properly belong only to the end of a piece). The mention of "bowels" plays on the double sense of catgut strings and the biblical notion of the seat of emotion; the lute can more aptly enunciate grief than hard "marbles" (here we find an allusion to marble tombstones and to the fact that dew forms on marble—they "weep" in their own way).

In this poem, music is used metaphorically to advance Herbert's theme of a grief that must find expression. There is no explicit link here between music and the Holy Spirit, but when read alongside some of his other poems, more concerning the Spirit comes to light. In "Employment (I)," the poet prays that God would "extend" him "to some good," that is, employ him usefully.

---

34. The Blow setting can be found in C. A. Patrides, ed., *George Herbert: The Critical Heritage* (London: Routledge & Kegan Paul, 1983), 367–70.

35. See Diane Kelsey McColley, *Poetry and Music in Seventeenth-Century England* (Cambridge: Cambridge University Press, 1997), 147–48; Wilcox, *English Poems of George Herbert*, 240.

> I am no link of thy great chain,
>   But all my companie is a weed.
> Lord place me in thy consort; give one strain
>   To my poore reed.[36]

He rejects the idea that he is merely a link in a static "chain of being"—according to philosophical tradition, a hierarchy of creatureliness stretching up to God—rather he is the one on whom and through whom God acts in specific ways, and in ways that draw on his singular particularity ("my poore reed"). The image is of an ensemble, a consort. Diane Kelsey McColley writes: "In a God-filled world, can a singer of praise really offer anything? Is any of what the poet offers really his?" She continues: "Rather than stating in conventionally Protestant terms that God's grace increases God's glory, Herbert asserts, 'As thou dost impart thy grace, / The greater shall *our* glorie be.'"[37] In a consort we find our part and flourish as we are taken up into the divine purposes. Through music, then, Herbert is subverting the zero-sum mindset we mentioned earlier in connection with divine and human agency. When we hear two or more sounds, we experience a unified aural space in which two audibly distinct sounds can interpenetrate without diminishing each other; indeed, if one string is stimulated to sound by the other through sympathetic resonance, we have an extraordinarily apt aural analogue of the Spirit's work in the poet, just as Herbert appears to conceive it.[38]

Herbert also draws on music with respect to its structure. Some of his poems may have been musically molded from the start such that, for example, musical meter patterned the poetic form.[39] McColley goes further, arguing that Herbert's intricate poetic language is musical through and through.[40] Not only is the music-like sound of his poetry often intrinsic to its force; its meanings are mutually resonant.

> [Herbert] practiced—perhaps invented—a form of language analogous to polyphonic music sung in pure intonation, in which linear arrangements of words form vertical consonances whose overtones, as well as fundamental meanings, are in tune. . . . By many musical means, Herbert's poems create infinitely resounding chords in antiphonally responding souls.[41]

36. "Employment (I)," lines 21–24, in Wilcox, *English Poems of George Herbert*, 205.
37. McColley, *Poetry and Music*, 137 (italics original).
38. For further discussion, see chap. 8 of this volume.
39. See Louise Schleiner, "Jacobean Song and Herbert's Metrics," *Studies in English Literature, 1500–1900* 19, no. 1 (1979): 109–26.
40. McColley, *Poetry and Music*, chap. 4.
41. McColley, *Poetry and Music*, 136–37.

McColley's case builds on the fact that when a person sings a note, what we hear comprises a fundamental tone together with higher frequencies, "overtones," or "partials." Applied to Herbert in "Ephes. 4. 30," thematically related words like "grieve," "weep," "cry," and "tears" together form a consonant "vertical chord," and partials of this chord (puns, etymologies, allusions, and so forth) are also in tune with one another: "Crystall," "runne," "cleare spring," and so forth. Herbert sets off an abundance of intertwining yet coherent meanings and thereby turns his language into a vehicle of disclosure, analogous to the way music was considered in his time to be a means of uncovering the interconnectedness of the cosmos under God. As McColley notes:

> Reading his poems . . . one may feel that his language is not a manipulation of words to express a preconceived idea or control another's thoughts but a way of finding connections, much as music for the music theorists . . . was a way of searching the cosmos and finding relations between mind and matter, or among various kinds of consciousness. . . .
>
> While any art can be manipulated to seduce and deceive, language is the most corruptible. But the more "musical" it is, the less closed-minded it can be and less propaganda it can impose. Although musical proportions may be mathematically expressed, they have no fixed agendas. The purest consonances in music are not without partials, including dissonant ones; but the more the partials in a relationship of pitches are in tune with each other, the "truer" the relation is to the ear. Like pitches, words are complex and mutually responsive. The work of a poem is to unlock perception by finding out at each moment within its form "what key is best." When Herbert's diction finds its key, all the poem's words ring true.[42]

The remarkable vision that opens up here is instructive for us on several levels, especially when we bear in mind that for Herbert the agent of tuning and the enabler of resonance can only be the Holy Spirit. First, we are given a perspective on poetic language that sees it not primarily as a vehicle of self-expression but of discovery, with the potential of penetrating the depths of reality, including theological reality, and not despite but precisely *because* of its technical devices. Such is the way in which the Spirit can and does operate. Second, notable also is the associated belief that by its very nature music is reality disclosing (albeit in a distinctive manner). In Herbert's age, such an idea was still widely held: music could lay bare the numerical associations and proportions of the cosmos and thereby wield moral power. In "Easter,"

---

42. McColley, *Poetry and Music*, 172–73.

Herbert's most famous musical poem, the Spirit is said to "make up our defects with his sweet art," when invited to "bear a part" in the threefold harmony that marks "all musick." Third, in Herbert's case it would appear that the experience of music, and the imagery that music generates, has facilitated this Spirit-borne, reality-disclosing capacity of poetry to flower. A nonverbal art form has informed a verbal art form and enabled it to flourish.

Conclusion

Near the beginning of this essay, I noted the current tendency, when speaking theologically about the arts, to allow "spirit" language to free-float theologically. Not everyone, of course, will warm to Herbert's theological perspectives, but for any engagement with the arts that wants to call itself Christian and attend to the Holy Spirit in particular, he displays a disciplined theological imagination at once winsome and informative. And what is perhaps most valuable is that he offers this as a *poet*, a weaver of exquisitely pointed yet multiply resonant verse.

For Herbert, to state the obvious, the Spirit is not that of an undifferentiated transcendence, inert infinitude, or nameless "presence," but the Spirit of the covenanting God whose internal dynamic is a life of love. The christological concentration is evident throughout: the Spirit is preeminently the Spirit of the Son, who has taken flesh and, as one of us, vicariously offered the response we could never offer, the debt we could never pay, through a death that heals the breach our sin has opened up between us and the one he names as "Father." If one reason that much Christian writing on the arts takes leave of a christological and trinitarian environment of this sort is the fear of smothering the integrity of the arts, we can learn much from the ways in which Herbert's orthodoxy shows no signs of narrowing or deadening his poetic virtuosity.

Similar things could be said of Herbert's absorption in Scripture. The view that the Spirit's effectiveness is proportional to the degree one can abstract oneself from the Bible is rarely expressed openly today. But the relative lack of close attention to scriptural texts in the current theology and arts scene is striking (whether as providing subject matter for the arts or as providing wisdom for artistic thought and practice). That Herbert can be at once so rigorously grounded in the texts he loves, with its "masse / Of strange delights"[43] and at the same time fashion words of such artistry should give us lengthy pause for thought.

43. "The H. Scriptures. I," lines 6 and 7, in Wilcox, *English Poems of George Herbert*, 208.

But perhaps the most remarkable benefit that emerges from this brief conversation with Herbert concerns the arts themselves. Although keenly aware of the corrupting "motions" of the human heart, he refuses to regard the poet or poetry as inherently antagonistic to the motions of the Spirit: they can be redeemed and enabled to flourish in their integrity. Further, the ways in which the Spirit may employ the arts seem to be wide ranging in Herbert's outlook. For example, poetic meter can play a part in reordering our lives (surely a ministry of the Spirit); musical metaphors can lend disclosive spiritual power to poetic verse; poetry itself can assume a musical character in keeping with the theological import of its words and thereby, precisely *as* musical, serve as a vehicle of Spirit-led discovery, unlocking otherwise hidden dimensions of reality. Not least, Herbert is provocative for those who dare to theologize about the Spirit but whose pneumatology relies exclusively on the tried and tested discourses beloved by the contemporary academy. This poetry stirs us to recognize that the arts have capacities far beyond illustrating prearticulated truths and to ask whether theology—including a theology of the Spirit—in some sense *requires* the arts. What Herbert wrote about preaching might just as easily be said of theology:

"A verse may finde him, who a sermon flies."[44]

44. "The Church-porch," line 5, in Wilcox, *English Poems of George Herbert*, 50.

7

Natural Theology and Music

There has been a renaissance of interest in natural theology in recent years. This essay grew out of a paper delivered at a conference in Oxford devoted to the theme, a gathering that included a variety of contributions from a wide range of disciplines. The arts were singled out for special attention because this area of culture was considered one where many have spoken of stirrings of an infinite or quasi-divine presence yet without alluding to any particular God. Some claim that these intuitions, however inchoate, provide unique openings for conversations between Christians and those of little or no faith, and thus for a kind of natural theology. By probing what might or might not be "natural" about natural theology, this essay asks what we are to make of claims of this sort when they appear in connection with music. (Some of the issues dealt with here are engaged with in other chapters in this book, but the new context should enable these themes to be read in a fresh light.)

Whatever the disagreements about the precise meaning of "natural theology" (very broadly, theology that is not focused on God's particular self-revelation in Israel and Jesus Christ), among those who advocate it today, certain key concerns are readily identifiable. Three of the commonest are worth

An earlier version of this chapter appears in Jeremy Begbie, "Natural Theology and Music," *Oxford Handbook of Natural Theology*, ed. Russell Re Manning, 566–80 (Oxford: Oxford University Press, 2013). Used by permission of Oxford University Press.

highlighting straightaway. First, and undoubtedly most prevalent, there is the concern to bear witness "to the nongodforsakenness of the world even under the conditions of sin,"[1] to testify to the active presence of God where God is not overtly acknowledged *as* active and present, perhaps even where any god is openly denied. Second, there is often a pointed concern to do justice to the particularities and integrities of the world—whether of politics, economics, physical and biological processes, or whatever; we must "let things be themselves," resist the temptation to force theological interpretations prematurely. Third, we also often find an apologetic drive to render theological truth winsome and compelling to those who for whatever reason find the particular claims of Christian revelation unsupportable and unconvincing.

Amidst the recent resurgence of interest in natural theology, there are signs that the arts are beginning to play an increasingly prominent role, especially when they are linked to beauty and not least with respect to the three concerns we have just outlined. It is argued that the arts can offer ample testimony to the activity of God in the world at large; that their integrity is far better preserved by this form of theologizing than by some more traditional approaches; and that, in the face of the apologetic demands of late modernity, where the limits of narrowly intellectual approaches are quickly becoming apparent and the need to engage the affective and imaginative dimensions of "sense-making" is acutely felt, the arts can and should play a crucial role.[2]

Music has been drawn into these discussions (though with nothing like the energy and concentration given to the visual and literary arts). As is well known, music is notoriously difficult to write about (as George Steiner puts it, "in the face of music, the wonders of language are also its frustrations"),[3] and the contemporary conversation between music and theology is still in its early stages. Nevertheless, attempts have been made at incorporating music into projects that might be termed "natural theology." In what follows, we will briefly examine two recent examples. We will then go on to ask some theological questions arising from these attempts about the project of natural theology, and go on to offer suggestions for how music might be part of such a project, albeit somewhat reconceived.

1. Stanley Hauerwas, *With the Grain of the Universe: The Church's Witness and Natural Theology* (London: SCM, 2002), 20.

2. See, e.g., Anthony Monti, *A Natural Theology of the Arts: Imprint of the Spirit* (Aldershot, UK: Ashgate, 2003); Alister McGrath, *The Open Secret: A New Vision for Natural Theology* (Oxford: Blackwell, 2008), chap. 11.

3. George Steiner, *Errata: An Examined Life* (London: Phoenix, 1997), 65.

Two Case Studies

A wide-ranging and immensely ambitious theological project has recently
been pioneered by David Brown at the University of St. Andrews. The project includes (indeed, is to a large extent constituted by) what he calls an
expanded and transformed "natural religion."[4] Brown distinguishes his own
approach from "natural theology as currently conceived,"[5] by which he appears
to mean a kind associated with modern analytic philosophy of religion, in
which the range of what is to count as theologically significant is (as Brown
sees it) relatively restricted. But Brown's is still a "natural theology" insofar
as it attempts to offer theological engagement with phenomena far beyond
those spheres in which God is overtly acknowledged and beyond the walls of
any church or official religious institution. Brown urges that theologians and
philosophers come to terms with large tracts of "ordinary" human experience
that are redolent of God but have been largely ignored by much traditional
theology; he includes such things as sport, humor, dance, gardens, homes,
and, not least, the arts. Indeed, he is quite willing to loosen his terminological
strictures and speak of "natural theology" very broadly; after a section on
the artists Mondrian, Kandinsky, and Klee, he writes: "What in effect they
sought was a new form of natural theology, where claims about the spiritual
nature of the world could be made." He continues, "New and powerful forms
of natural theology have been developing throughout the twentieth century
without either philosophers or theologians having given them the attention
they deserve."[6]

   In fact, the arts play a crucial role in Brown's enterprise. In his early book
Tradition and Imagination, he urges that tradition and Scripture should not
be set over against each other but that Christians should learn to "see the hand
of God in a continuing process that accompanies both."[7] That tradition is
better seen as an ongoing process rather than as a fixed deposit is, of course,
a point many others have made. Especially distinctive of Brown, however, is
the stress he places on the arts. It is not only theologians and ecclesiastical
councils who lead the way in doctrinal development (through the media of
verbal propositions and statements) but also painters, storytellers, and other
artists—the works of creative imagination are integral and indispensable to

   4. David Brown, *God and Enchantment of Place: Reclaiming Human Experience* (Oxford:
Oxford University Press, 2004), 9.
   5. Brown, *God and Enchantment of Place*, 9.
   6. Brown, *God and Enchantment of Place*, 151.
   7. David Brown, *Tradition and Imagination: Revelation and Change* (Oxford: Oxford University Press, 1999), 1.

the process. So, for example, many paintings of the nativity have highlighted elements in the biblical story that are perhaps implicit in the text but which nonetheless need the unique powers of visual art to bring into the open. Brown thus accords the arts a substantial role in the unveiling of God's purposes, a move not unrelated to his questioning of the stress traditionally placed on the normativity of Scripture. He maintains that revelation is to be understood as a historical process entailing works of the human imagination that themselves embody continuing revelation, that traditions of storytelling and art making are not self-contained or static but emerge through interaction with their surrounding cultures and other religious traditions, and that Scripture therefore cannot be understood as a locus of revelation to be privileged over church tradition; the arts can in some cases serve to improve and even correct the biblical texts.

With this notion goes a strong suspicion of "instrumental rationality" as applied to the arts, the tendency to take an interest in the arts only insofar as a "message" or "program" can be distilled from them—and for the Christian, that means a *theological* message or program. Brown writes: "So deep does instrumental rationality run in our culture that the practice of theology also often reflects that same approach, valuing the arts not in their own right but only in so far as they 'preach the gospel.'"[8] He contends that we must take care to attend to them respectfully on their own terms with a view to "the discovery of God," the ways in which they uniquely mediate the divine, without insisting that they serve some identifiable purely practical end in order to be of any worth.

Music is approached from this perspective. Especially important to him is the combination in music of the "material" and the "ethereal"—a combination crucial to his "sacramental" theology as a whole. In his book *God and Grace of Body*, Brown includes a substantial section on music, with chapters on classical and pop music, as well as on blues, musicals, and opera. The scope is deliberately wide, ranging far beyond music that is explicitly "religious"; music does not have to provide overt and specific religious content in order to be religiously significant.[9]

Speaking of classical music, Brown claims that God can be discerned in a wide range of musical styles, "in intelligible order and in the sublime, in suffering that expects resurrection and suffering that does not, in hesitant exploration and in the confident assertion of faith, in humour and in solemnity,

---

8. Brown, *God and Enchantment of Place*, 22.

9. In *God and Mystery in Words*, Brown offers extensive chapters on texted music in worship. See David Brown, *God and Mystery in Words: Experience through Metaphor and Drama* (Oxford: Oxford University Press, 2008), chaps. 3 and 6.

and in the timeless and the temporal."[10] Of J. S. Bach, he says that since for the composer all music was a reflection of the divine, more a matter of discovery than invention, Bach was "in a sense" engaging in "a natural theology of music."[11]

If we are to speak of this and other music in such terms, Brown believes, we should be clear that it is not that "God is being forced upon anyone," but rather that "favourable conditions [are] being set under which experience of the divine does at least become a realistic possibility." This is analogous to the way arguments for the existence of God in traditional philosophy of religion "open up the individual to certain possibilities"—with the added advantage that here the whole person is being engaged ("body, imagination and emotion no less than the intellect").[12] Brown's keenness to find God amid the unchurched leads him to be critical of much Christian treatment of popular music, where a preoccupation with the artist's lifestyle or convictions obscures the implicit religious dimensions of the music (especially when the musician has no explicit faith or theological interest).[13]

Some will take issue with Brown's treatment of particular forms and pieces of music. But the most pointed questions that Brown's enterprise provokes are methodological and criteriological.[14] While undoubtedly intending a perspective that is at least consonant with Christian orthodoxy and to honor the incarnation ("the primordial sacrament") as pivotal—for the incarnation is paradigmatic of God's willingness to be revealed in a way that is subject to the culturally conditioned historical process of creativity—Brown is highly suspicious of any approach that would privilege Scripture as exercising a normative or corrective role in relation to subsequent tradition. What is insufficiently recognized is the way in which the mainstream church has never replaced Scripture with (or subsumed Scripture seamlessly into) postbiblical tradition; rather, in the church's continual return to the texts, Scripture has de facto functioned normatively over later tradition, even if later tradition is accorded the status of a mediator of revelation. As Kathryn Tanner has observed in a vigorous critique of one of Brown's books, for him "the incarnation as an endorsement of human creativity is . . . played off against the Bible,"[15] but this leaves us far from clear why we should accept the incarnation as critical

10. David Brown, *God and Grace of Body: Sacrament in Ordinary* (Oxford: Oxford University Press, 2007), 294.

11. Brown, *God and Grace of Body*, 254.

12. Brown, *God and Grace of Body*, 293–94.

13. Brown, *God and Grace of Body*, 346.

14. See chap. 4 above.

15. Kathryn Tanner, "Review of David Brown, *Tradition and Imagination: Revelation and Change* (1999)," *International Journal of Systematic Theology* 3, no. 1 (2001): 118–21, here 119.

for the revelation of God and his purposes (or for a theology of creativity), for in principle, this could be set aside in light of a later tradition that found its presence in Scripture offensive, uncongenial, or contrary to widely held religious experiences. To be sure, Brown discusses nine types of criteria for discerning the truth of imaginative theology (historical, empirical, conceptual, moral, criteria of continuity, christological, the degree of imaginative engagement, the effectiveness of the analogical construct, and ecclesial),[16] but as he himself admits, much more needs to be said, especially with regard to their relative strength, source, and grounding.[17] It may well be that Brown's eagerness to relate the Christian faith to such a wide variety of cultural perspectives and to respect the integrity of manifold "experiences," together with the dominance of general categories such as "religious experience"/"experience of the divine"/"sacrament" has led him to be less than convincing when it comes to delineating how such key categories are anchored in the distinctive specifics and particularities of Christian faith.

The very title of Anthony Monti's book, *A Natural Theology of the Arts*, will be instantly appealing to those sympathetic to the term "natural theology" and especially so to those eager to approach the arts, including music, from such a standpoint. Setting his discussion against the background of the postmodern "crisis in the humanities," Monti rejects the possibility of the arts being used as part of knockdown demonstrations of theological truth or refutations of nihilism. He advocates a subtler and more indirect enterprise. He believes that the arts by their very nature are theologically loaded, irrespective of their explicit content, and aims to "set out the epistemological, metaphysical and theological grounds for maintaining that artistic creativity can most adequately be understood as an expression of the 'real presence' of God, that this is the ultimate meaning and truth of such activity."[18] Further, he wants to show that "the God who is present in works of art can best be understood in a Trinitarian way."[19] (All three of the typical concerns of "natural theology" we set out above are thus present.)

Monti believes that such a case can be made with the aid of the epistemology of critical realism, a "metaphysics of flexible openness," and an understanding of art as centering on the process of metaphor (which serves to link epistemology and metaphysics). His discussion ranges widely across many disciplines,

---

16. David Brown, *Discipleship and Imagination: Christian Tradition and Truth* (Oxford: Oxford University Press, 2000), 390–406.

17. Brown, *God and Enchantment of Place*, 3.

18. Monti, *Natural Theology of the Arts*, 6.

19. Monti, *Natural Theology of the Arts*, 6.

but his two major conversation partners are John Polkinghorne, with respect to epistemology and cosmology, and me, with respect to metaphor in the arts.

He wishes to speak of the arts as potentially both a "natural theology" and "revelation," in that they provide experiences that fall between, on the one hand, the kind of diffuse awareness (e.g., a sense of contingency or finitude) that forms the subject matter of "natural theology" as traditionally understood and, on the other hand, the kind of "pointed" and specific experience typical of specific revelations (e.g., a sense of God speaking directly to us).

In the process, Monti offers extensive discussions of music and its potential theological import. Indeed, in music, he holds, "spiritual truth" is enfleshed "most fully." Making use of the work of musicologist Victor Zuckerkandl, he argues that music subverts the assumption that order is only possible in the fixed and static and presents us with "the unprecedented spectacle of an order that is wholly flux," a pointer to the ontology of "flexible openness" characteristic of the created world as viewed through Christian eyes.[20] In addition to these general comments, he offers detailed discussions of, among other pieces, Mozart's *Jupiter* Symphony and the late quartets of Beethoven. He remarks on the ease with which metaphysical/religious language is often used of the latter. Especially notable in Monti is the place given to the future, to the eschatological potential of art to prefigure, albeit provisionally, the life of the world to come. Here he draws at length on my own work on the relation between music and time, the way in which music's temporal features can serve to embody and disclose something of the eschatological character of the Christian faith.[21] Monti's theology is marked by a temporal, forward-driving character and is thus able to take rather more seriously than Brown the engagement of God with the temporal and transient, not only with the material and fleshly.

Where Monti is weakest is in clarifying and maintaining certain key distinctions, a symptom, one suspects, of the diverse array of theological witnesses he draws into his argument. In particular, the term "natural theology" often seems to be used as a synonym for something like "natural" or "general revelation" (revelation beyond the history of Israel culminating in Jesus Christ). However, theology, whatever else it includes, entails intellectual deliberation on phenomena, whereas general revelation denotes a disclosure (a quite different category). This makes it somewhat confusing to speak, as he does, of the arts *as* natural theology[22] (Brown can do the same), even if the arts may

20. Monti, *Natural Theology of the Arts*, 82–84.
21. Monti, *Natural Theology of the Arts*, 139–70.
22. Monti, *Natural Theology of the Arts*, 92, 123.

well offer experiences of a more diffuse sort that many would claim ought to be the subject matter of natural theology.

Clearly, with Monti we are in more resolutely orthodox territory than with Brown. Monti is far more concerned than Brown that his project should serve and strengthen a robust trinitarian faith; in one place, he writes that his natural theology "finds its fulfilment in, rather than substitutes itself for, the revelation of the Triune God."[23] While Brown would probably admit to something similar for his own project, his purpose is less to bolster this or that version of the faith and far more to make effective theological contact with the sheer breadth of human experience. In any case, in Monti there is no hint that postbiblical tradition could correct Scripture, though there is ample evidence of such tradition amplifying, applying, particularizing, and embodying Scripture's witness and in this way functioning as revelation.

On the Naturalness of "Natural Theology"

Arising out of this brief consideration of Brown and Monti, perhaps the most important question to address is, what distinguishes natural theology from any other theology? Presuming the answer lies in the word "natural," our question then becomes, what is "natural" about "natural theology"? More pointedly, to what extent is this naturalness theologically shaped and conditioned, rather than determined and presumed *a priori*, in advance of theological considerations?

What needs stressing here is what many would regard as a truism, that the term "natural" is highly fluid in common usage and historically polyvalent. It is also never ideologically neutral; indeed, it would be theologically naive to pretend that such a concept of nature or "the natural" was available, let alone to attempt to employ such a concept as foundational for theology.[24] We are justified therefore in expecting a measure of clarity about the term if we are to gain any sense of what might be entailed in a natural theology that engages the arts.

Rather than attempt to delineate all the historical construals of "natural" in "natural theology,"[25] I propose to explore its meaning in relation to some basic trajectories in New Testament theology, present in the earliest strands

23. Monti, *Natural Theology of the Arts*, 6, 9.

24. See Alan J. Torrance, "Introduction," in *Christ and Context: The Confrontation between Gospel and Culture*, ed. Hilary Regan and Alan J. Torrance (Edinburgh: T&T Clark, 1993).

25. For a succinct and useful survey of different types of natural theology, see David Fergusson, "Types of Natural Theology," in *The Evolution of Rationality: Interdisciplinary Essays in Honor of J. Wentzel van Huyssteen*, ed. F. LeRon Shults (Grand Rapids: Eerdmans, 2006), 380–93.

of the texts, which here I am going to have to presume, rather than defend, as being basic to classical Christian orthodoxy. We will relate these trajectories to four very broad senses of "natural" as commonly found when the expression "natural theology" is employed in theological discourse today, senses that can and do often overlap. All four are present in both Brown and Monti.

First, theology can be described as "natural" in that it seeks to attend to *the reality of the physical world as a whole, the world explored and examined by the natural sciences.* Clearly, there is no neutral perspective on this reality. The perspective enjoined by the New Testament is one shaped at its profoundest level by what has been disclosed and enacted in Jesus Christ; the Son through whom all things were made has become a creature, submitted to creation's brokenness, and has been raised as an anticipation of an ultimate refashioning of all things. Among other things, this elicits a perception of the cosmos not as brute fact but as the outcome of unconstrained love, fashioned out of nothing, ontologically distinct from yet wholly contingent upon the Creator and oriented to a final re-creation.

Second, theology can be "natural" in that it seeks to attend to *what is primordially human.* In this respect, the New Testament texts direct our attention not to a generic humanity but preeminently to a specific human person, Jesus Christ, the last Adam, who, it is claimed, embodies the primordial divine intention for humans and, in and through this person, to the future, corporate, eschatological fulfillment of the human race.

Third, theology can be "natural" in that it seeks to attend to *those constructive activities we designate as human "culture," irrespective of whether or not they are undertaken by Christians.* Scripturally, we are pressed here to conceive these initially in light of the vocation given to humans to be image bearers of God, realized in the person and agency of Christ, the one true *imago Dei.* This vocation is to discover, respect, develop, and heal what we are given in creation, with and for the sake of others.[26]

To these three we may add a fourth sense of "natural," one we have not mentioned yet: theology can be "natural" in that it seeks to enlist a *properly functioning human reason.* Natural theology then becomes that form of theology that aspires—to be no more precise for the moment—to be rational. In New Testament terms, this would appear to mean one shaped first of all by the re-forming of human rationality, embodied in Christ, and in which humans are invited to participate by the Spirit. From this point of view, the much-cherished belief in a universal rational faculty, purportedly independent

---

26. Jeremy S. Begbie, *Resounding Truth: Christian Wisdom in the World of Music* (Grand Rapids: Baker Academic, 2007), 207–9.

of the contingencies of time, space, and culture, immune to corruption, and free of tradition and thus capable of laying down in advance unalterable criteria for what is to count as "rational" knowledge of and speech about God begins to look distinctly dubious.[27] To recognize this need not lead to an approach that advocates a theological rejection of reason (*contra rationem*), or an addition to reason (*supra rationem*), but rather one that takes its cue from the redemption of the whole person in Jesus Christ, of which our reasoning powers are but one dimension.[28] The thrust of, say, the apostle Paul's anthropology suggests that this redemption of our rational capacities is intrinsic to the salvation of which the Christian faith speaks. Indeed, the momentum of God reconciling and re-creating his creatures in Christ *includes*, through the Spirit, the gift of being able to apprehend it and, indeed, *requires* such a gift, for on what theologically legitimate grounds are we to claim that some zone or mode of human reasoning is entirely immune to the distortions and deformations of human sin? (This is not, of course, to claim that all human reasoning outside the church is distorted and false—this would be yet another theologically unwarranted *a priori* assumption—but only to note that all human reasoning is *prone* to the effects of sinful bias, that no quarter of our minds can be cordoned off and claim in advance some kind of diplomatic immunity from prosecution.)

What should be clear by now is that whichever of these senses of "natural" we presume when speaking of "natural theology," if it is to remain recognizably and distinctively Christian it can only be defined out of a center in what has happened in Jesus Christ. If we are to follow the pressure and core thrust of the New Testament's witness, we will be compelled to put a question mark beside any "natural theology" that is constructed *prior to* or *wholly apart from* attention to what has been embodied in Jesus Christ, crucified, risen, and ascended.

Before returning to music, another formal matter needs to be addressed. Earlier we said that one of the most common motivations of natural theology's

27. Alister McGrath, *A Scientific Theology*, vol. 2, *Reality* (Edinburgh: T&T Clark, 2001), 55–118. See also Alasdair MacIntyre, *Whose Justice? Which Rationality?* (Notre Dame, IN: University of Notre Dame Press, 1988); Ernest Gellner, *Reason and Culture: The Historic Role of Rationality and Rationalism* (Oxford: Blackwell, 1992); Raymond Murphy, *Rationality and Nature: A Sociological Inquiry into a Changing Relationship* (Boulder, CO: Westview Press, 1994); Roy A. Clouser, *The Myth of Religious Neutrality: An Essay on the Hidden Role of Religious Belief in Theories* (Notre Dame, IN: University of Notre Dame Press, 2005).

28. Murray Rae, *Kierkegaard's Vision of the Incarnation: By Faith Transformed* (Oxford: Clarendon Press, 1997), 113; Alan J. Torrance, "Auditus Fidei: Where and How Does God Speak? Faith, Reason, and the Question of Criteria," in *Reason and the Reasons of Faith*, ed. Paul J. Griffiths and Reinhard Hütter (London: T&T Clark, 2005), 27–52.

supporters is the concern to do justice to the particularities and integrities of the world. This is especially conspicuous among those at work in theology and the arts, and some may think that the kind of theological lines we are opening up here move in the opposite direction. It is imperative, surely, that we first listen to the artist, give due space to the witness of music and painting, dance and drama, and only then introduce normative theological considerations of the kind we have just been discussing. (This, as we saw, is very much how David Brown sees the matter.)

Certainly, the ease with which the church has stifled the arts in the name of a supposed orthodoxy is one of the most shameful aspects of its history. But it is questionable to suggest—as it often is—that a respect for "reality" (artistic or otherwise) is best gained by aspiring to a vantage point supposedly free of interpretation (an impossibility in any case), or that if an interpretative stance *is* declared it must be *other* than that provided by the Creator's disclosure of his purposes for created reality in Jesus Christ. If we do choose to adopt an alternative (and by implication, superior) ultimate viewpoint for interpreting and discerning artistic practices, it is incumbent upon us to identify the criteria by which we have made such a decision and to recognize that in so doing we will have relativized the norms presented to us as ultimate in the witness of the New Testament.

Having said all this, if we do take our bearings strictly from the orientation of the New Testament—the transformative reconciliation of all things in the person of Christ—it would be disingenuous to dismiss as a matter of principle all proposed candidates for "natural theology." Precisely *because* of a commitment to God as the redeeming Creator (who self-identifies in Jesus Christ), we are bound to take seriously the concern of many proponents of natural theology that we noted at the outset—and evident in numerous texts in the Old and the New Testaments—to bear witness "to the nongodforsakenness of the world even under the conditions of sin." If the God of Jesus Christ and the Holy Spirit is indeed the God who is active to reconcile the totality of the space-time continuum to himself, how could we do otherwise?

Whether we call this "natural theology" or, as I would prefer, one responsibility of a theology of creation is a matter of debate. A continued attachment to the term "natural theology" is arguably confusing, in that it will too easily trawl with it (or smuggle in) some of the more questionable characteristics of Enlightenment defenses of the faith[29] or questionable Christian tradition,[30]

29. McGrath, *Open Secret*, chap. 7.
30. Colin Gunton, *A Brief Theology of Revelation* (Edinburgh: T&T Clark, 1995), chap. 3.

in particular, assumptions about what counts as "nature" or "natural" that are insufficiently controlled theologically.[31]

In any case, there is much to be said for concurring with Eberhard Jüngel when he calls for a "*more* natural theology": one that moves outward from Christ as Creator and Redeemer of all things and is thus more fully oriented toward "nature" than are many traditional forms of "natural theology." Such an enterprise will lead us

> deeper into [creation's] needs and difficulties (*aporiai*), but also deeper into its hidden glories! Deeper . . . into compassionate solidarity with those who cry *de profundis* . . . but even deeper into the joy of the unanswered mystery of the fact that we are here and are not rather nothing. Deeper into the joy of being able to see the one and only light of life reflecting in the manifold lights of creation and thus, in its light, being able to see with astonishment creation's own [particular] light.[32]

Music's "Natural" Witness

For the remainder of this chapter, then, bearing in mind the theological orientations we have outlined, we may usefully ask: How might music play a part in the endeavor of theology to bear witness to the nongodforsakenness of creation even under the conditions of sin? We have space to offer only four examples, congruent with the four senses of "natural" we highlighted earlier.

First is music's potential to bear witness to the cosmos *as the creation of the Triune God of Jesus Christ*. We can recall here some features of the instrumental music of J. S. Bach (1685–1750) that I have already cited in an earlier essay.[33] We saw how Bach's practice of *elaboratio* opens up an imagination of the physical world at large that resonates strongly with a trinitarian theology of creation: (1) that the elaboration is governed not chiefly by an external, pre-given logic but first and foremost by the musical material itself—through a searching for material with rich potential and accordingly finding an appropriate form; (2) that we hear in this elaboration difference as intrinsic to unity; and (3) that we hear the simultaneous presence of radical

31. In this light, Colin Gunton contrasts natural theology with a theology of nature, by which he designates "an account of what things naturally are, by virtue of their createdness" (Gunton, *Brief Theology of Revelation*, 56) or, put differently, an interpretation of creation in light of the self-revelation of God in Jesus Christ.

32. Eberhard Jüngel, *Christ, Justice and Peace: Toward a Theology of the State in Dialogue with the Barmen Declaration* (Edinburgh: T&T Clark, 1992), 28–29.

33. See chap. 1.

contingency and radical consistency. I developed each of these features in relation to a vision of the created world created, upheld, and drawn to its end by the Triune God of Jesus Christ.

Second is music's potential to bear witness to *what is primordially human*—which in this context will be the goal of our human existence, the communally shaped humanity enabled by the Spirit and already actualized *pro nobis* in Jesus Christ by the same Spirit. Here we point to just one feature of the experience of music that is especially telling in this regard.

The power of music to effect social cohesion is legendary. It has long been known that rhythmic music possesses striking capacities in this respect. In recent years biomusicologists and others have focused much attention on the phenomena of "entrainment."[34] We tap our feet, sway, bob our heads to music, even more so when we are with others who do the same. Evidence suggests that this skill is unique to humans and that it is universal: "In every culture, there is some form of music with a periodic pulse that affords temporal coordination between performers and elicits synchronised motor responses from listeners."[35] Visual, auditory, and motor cues combine to create a potent and mutually reinforcing mix. And given rhythm's connections with emotion, this is one of the quickest ways in which emotion is spread and shared. We only need think of the chanting of a protest march or mass synchronized movement at a rock concert.

Some argue that entrainment was critical in the evolution of our capacity for communal culture, for rhythmic synchronization makes it possible to experience the world in another's time. This capacity of music goes with another that complements it, what Ian Cross calls its "floating intentionality,"[36] its semantic indeterminacy. Unlike language, music is susceptible to a large (though not unlimited) range of interpretations; it struggles to be specific, to denote with reliability and specificity. This flexibility allows the hearer considerable space to develop her own "reading" and application of the music.

34. Martin Clayton, Rebecca Sager, and Udo Will, "In Time with the Music: The Concept of Entrainment and Its Significance for Ethnomusicology," *European Meetings in Ethnomusicology* 11 (ESEM Counterpoint 1, 2004): 1–82; Ian Cross and Iain Morley, "The Evolution of Music: Theories, Definitions and the Nature of the Evidence," in *Communicative Musicality: Exploring the Basis of Human Companionship*, ed. Stephen Malloch and Colwyn Trevarthen (Oxford: Oxford University Press, 2009), 67–70.

35. Aniruddh D. Patel, *Music, Language, and the Brain* (Oxford: Oxford University Press, 2008), 402. See also Carolyn Drake and Daisy Bertrand, "The Quest for Universals in Temporal Processing in Music," *Annals of the New York Academy of the Sciences* 930 (2001): 17–27; William H. McNeill, *Keeping Together in Time: Dance and Drill in Human History* (Cambridge, MA: Harvard University Press, 1995).

36. Ian Cross and Ghofur Eliot Woodruff, "Music as a Communicative Medium," in *The Prehistory of Language*, ed. R. Botha and C. Knight (Oxford: Oxford University Press, 2009), 87.

Putting these together, we can say that music can grant an extraordinary sense of embodied togetherness (among other things, through entrainment processes), *while at the same time* allowing for—even encouraging—a sense of particularity and uniqueness (through its floating intentionality). Many other factors are involved here, of course, but recognizing that these two are operating together in most corporate musical experience can be highly instructive. For example, in some so-called alternative worship,[37] wordless rhythmic music is extensively used and can engender an intense sense of solidarity yet at the same time allow for widely diverse responses and stances among those participating—which can be highly attractive to those anxious about being enlisted to adhere to specific beliefs, doctrines, or goals. No doubt at some stage one will be looking for a higher degree of specificity that Christian worship requires; nonetheless, music of this sort in this context may be witnessing to, and making possible, something of that liberating, differentiated human unity promised in Christ and granted through the Spirit in his body, the church.

Third is music's potential to bear witness to *felicitous culture*. "Culture" here is understood as the human vocation to take the materials given to hand and mind and develop (elaborate), reconfigure, and, indeed, heal them in ways that praise the Creator. Again, this finds its realization in the person of Christ, the one in whom creation finds its true human priest, and with whom, by the Spirit, we are now invited into strenuous engagement with creation, to extend and elaborate creation's praise, in anticipation of the re-creation of all things that has already been embodied in him.

The dynamics of this can be usefully opened up by briefly returning to Bach. We have already spoken about the possibility of music to witness to the character of the world as created by the Triune God, to its own inherent order, thus offering "insight into the depths of the wisdom of the world" (words used on Bach's behalf).[38] But if there is truth in this, we should not forget it happens through *an active process of making*, principally through *inventio* and *elaboratio*, both of which (as we have seen) are themselves constructive exercises. Bach's *Well-Tempered Clavier* is indeed an exploration of the twelve-note chromatic scale, which is indeed derived from the harmonic series, but the scale Bach used (and the slightly differently tuned one we commonly use today) are in fact adjustments, "temperings" of what the physical

37. "Alternative worship" is a generic term for a range of experiments in worship that emerged first in the late 1980s, mainly among adults in their twenties and thirties, with an emphasis on, among other things, multisensory experience and the power of ritual and narrative.

38. J. A. Birnbaum, quoted in Christoph Wolff, *Johann Sebastian Bach: The Learned Musician* (New York: Norton, 2000).

world gives us. If these pieces *are* derived from the harmonic series, they are constructively derived. In fact, Bach substantially reshaped almost everything he touched, from simple motifs to whole styles and genres. He is one of the least "passive" composers in history.

What this provokes us to imagine is a subtle relationship between given, physical order and artistic order, the former being the inhabited environment, trusted and respected, in which the latter can be born, even if through sweat and struggle. It is a vision of "faithful improvisation," of the artist, as physical and embodied, set in the midst of a God-given world vibrant with a dynamic order of its own, not simply "there" like a brute fact to be escaped or violently abused but there as a gift from a God of overflowing generosity, a gift for us to interact with vigorously, to form and (in the face of distortion) transform, and in this way fashion something as felicitous as the *Goldberg Variations*,[39] art that can anticipate by the Spirit the *shalom* previewed and promised in Jesus Christ.

I would suggest that an improvisatory model along these lines is considerably more adequate to a trinitarian account of creativity than the more antagonistic (and unitarian) schemes often used, in which humans are seen, if not as pitted against each other, then as engaged in some kind of zero-sum game.[40]

Fourth is music's potential to witness to *the thought forms appropriate to a renewed rationality*—to the "re-schematizing" of the mind (Rom. 12:2) made possible through sharing in the mind of Christ through the Spirit. Here we focus on just one way in which this can happen: the perception of musical space.[41]

Whatever the commonalities between visual perception and aural perception, in one respect at least they are quite distinct: in our visual field, objects occupy bounded locations and cannot overlap without their integrity being threatened. We are unable to perceive red and yellow in the same place at the same time *as* red and *as* yellow. By the same token, objects in our visual field cannot occupy more than one place at the same time. However, if we hear a tone, it does not occupy a bounded location in our aural field; it fills the whole of the space we hear. A second tone, added to that tone—say, a major third above—will occupy the same (aural) space, yet (provided it is not too loud

39. See, e.g., Peter Williams, *Bach: The Goldberg Variations* (Cambridge: Cambridge University Press, 2001).

40. George Steiner's allusive *Real Presences*, a book frequently alluded to in discussions of natural theology and the arts, can be challenged from this perspective. George Steiner, *Real Presences: Is There Anything in What We Say?* (London: Faber & Faber, 1989). See Jeremy S. Begbie, *Theology, Music, and Time* (Cambridge: Cambridge University Press, 2000), 235–41.

41. This discussion is greatly expanded in chapter 8 of this volume.

or soft) we can hear it as a distinct, irreducibly different tone. The sounds neither merge nor exclude each other but interpenetrate.

The fruitfulness of this kind of perceptual simultaneity ought to be clear. Arguably, the Christian theological tradition has been hampered by relying exclusively or excessively on visual conceptuality in its struggles to "think together" discrete and supposedly incommensurable realities—God's freedom and the world's, divine and human agency, interpersonal integrity, the two natures of Christ, and, supremely (lying behind them all), the oneness and threeness of God. Discussion of these issues typically leads to an oscillation between the extremes of exclusion and merger, an inability to preserve the ontological integrity of disparate particulars. But if the perception of musical tones is allowed to jolt the imagination out of some of its visually dominated defaults, many of these classic *aporiai* are massively alleviated, for we are given a way of thinking of unity and particularity together without compromising either.

The fruitfulness is extended further if we consider the phenomenon of "sympathetic resonance," the way in which one vibrating string enables the vibration of another at a distance from it. Ways of conceiving God's free agency as the means by which the world is freed to be itself begin to open up, avoiding the implication that God's freedom in action entails the negation of the world's. Likewise, the intratrinitarian life of Father, Son, and Spirit, whose very nature is that of other-directed *ecstasis*, is rendered more intellectually accessible when conceived in the light of "enabling resonance" and would seem far more appropriate than the distinctly limited notions favored in some trinitarian theology, especially when such notions inadvertently suggest individual agents who "decide" or "determine" to love or give themselves away. Something analogous applies to human persons in relation and is strengthened if combined with what we discovered about entrainment, the rhythmic enabling of one person to move "in sync" with another.

There are undoubtedly numerous other possibilities for music to be associated with a "natural theology" (appropriately conceived); we have merely touched on a few. Whether theologians today avail themselves of the opportunities music affords, in a climate not always conducive to theology "out of the box," remains to be seen.

8

Room of One's Own?

Music, Space, and Freedom

Immersion in the world of music can bear surprising intellectual fruit. In this essay, I attempt to show how attention to something as apparently unremarkable as hearing two musical notes together can help to liberate theology from some of its worst and most damaging habits. The focus here is on one of the cardinal themes of modernity: the quest for freedom. The perception of musical sound offers untold resources for opening up a scriptural imagination of freedom, in a way that dramatically reconfigures classic debates.

Too often . . . we have simply assumed that two elements operate in a zero-sum relationship to one another, without asking ourselves whether they might be better understood as bearing a "musical" character.

David Cunningham, *These Three Are One*

An earlier version of this chapter appears in Jeremy S. Begbie, "Openness and Specificity: A Conversation with David Brown on Theology and Classical Music," in *Theology, Aesthetics, and Culture: Responses to the Work of David Brown*, ed. Robert MacSwain and Taylor Worley, 145–56 (Oxford: Oxford University Press, 2012). Used by permission of Oxford University Press.

I am particularly grateful for conversations on this theme with Imogen Adkins, whose important doctoral work on the spatiality of music will, I hope, soon be published, and for the perceptive comments of Elizabeth Eichling. The first part of my title echoes that of a famous 1929 essay by Virginia Woolf, widely regarded as pivotal for feminist literary criticism: Virginia Woolf, *A Room of One's Own* (Norwalk, CT: Easton Press, 2003).

Three tones sound. In each of them space encounters us and we encounter space. None of them is in a place; or better, they are all in the same
place, namely, everywhere. . . . Simultaneously sounding tones do not run
together into a mixed tone. No difference of places keeps them apart; yet
they remain audible as different tones. . . . The tones connected in the
triad sound *through one another* . . . or let us say that they interpenetrate
one another.

> Victor Zuckerkandl, *Sound and Symbol:*
> *Music and the External World*

Few passions characterize modernity more clearly and potently than the quest
for freedom. It has become so central to the identity and lifeblood of European
and American culture over the last few hundred years that the story of modernity simply cannot be told without it. And as myriad studies have amply
shown, the manner in which freedom is conceived today is inextricably intertwined with modernity's ambivalent posture with regard to the Christian God.

In what follows, I approach the theme of freedom by addressing what is
widely regarded as a pervasive tendency in the way it has been treated in modern and late modern thinking. What will strike the reader as unusual is that
my response to it is largely musical: I draw on an aural phenomenon that is
basic to most of our experiences of musical sound. My proposal is that many
theologies that have grappled with the manifold issues surrounding freedom
have been hampered by particular ways of imagining the "space" in which
freedom is believed to be realized, and that what would seem to be a relatively
insignificant feature of musical perception can yield remarkable resources
for exposing, engaging, and alleviating the obstacles and complications that
these habits of mind have generated. This is, in other words, an exercise in
music therapy for theologians.

One of Ludwig Wittgenstein's most celebrated aphorisms runs thus: "A
picture held us captive. And we could not get outside it, for it lay in our
language and language seemed to repeat it to us inexorably."[1] Wittgenstein
has in view his own early representative approach to language, according to
which meaningful language consists of propositions composed of names and
logical connectives, and the use of such language is essentially a matter of
naming or picturing facts. He came to realize that such an account was severely
inadequate. But the quotation is eminently applicable to the way theology

---

1. Ludwig Wittgenstein, *Philosophical Investigations* (Oxford: Blackwell, 1953), para. 48e,
here 115.

has too often been pursued—inadvertently captive to habits of thought that are embedded and reiterated in our verbal language but which distort rather than deepen our perception of the realities we engage. And Wittgenstein's term "picture" here is especially apt. For although in this essay we are not concerned with visual images in particular, we are concerned with modes of thought that take their shape chiefly from the ways in which visual perception operates.[2] Some of these, I want to show, have confined theology in ways that are unnecessary as well as damaging, not least when it comes to theologizing about freedom. Insofar as the captivity is dependent on the visual character of our conceptualizing, attempts to free ourselves by substituting one form of visualization for another will hardly help; what is needed (to "get outside") are fresh modes and models of thought that permit the realities in question to declare themselves more fully and clearly. The perception of musical sounds holds considerable potential in this regard.[3] Indeed, the sheer effectiveness of music in this regard makes its relative absence in most contemporary theology puzzling as well as regrettable.[4]

2. I shall leave aside the question—important as it is—of whether there can be any such thing as a *purely* visual argument. On this, see Steven W. Patterson, "'A Picture Held Us Captive': The Later Wittgenstein on Visual Argumentation," *Cogency* 2, no. 2 (Spring 2010): 105–34. Alistair McFadyen writes impressively about the dependence of modern accounts of sin and freedom on the conceptuality of physical spatiality. Alistair I. McFadyen, "Sins of Praise: The Assault on God's Freedom," in *God and Freedom: Essays in Historical and Systematic Theology*, ed. Colin E. Gunton (Edinburgh: T&T Clark, 1995), 32–56. In this essay, I am indebted to Mc-Fadyen's article. However, my argument is that the spatial models that need questioning are not merely "physical" but *visually* oriented. McFadyen does not here consider that there may be *other* ways of conceiving space.

3. With regard to Wittgenstein's saying, Gordon Baker writes: "The cure is to encourage surrender of the dogmatic claims 'Things *must/cannot* be thus and so' by exhibiting other intelligible ways of seeing things (other *possibilities*), that is, by showing that we can take off the spectacles through which we now see whatever we look at. . . . To the extent that philosophical problems take the form of the conflict between 'But this isn't how it is!' and 'yet this is how it *must* be!' . . . they will obviously be dissolved away once the inclination to say 'must' has been neutralized by seeing another possibility." Gordon Baker, "*Philosophical Investigations* Section 122: Neglected Aspects," in *Wittgenstein's Philosophical Investigations: Text and Context*, ed. Robert L. Arrington and Hans-Johann Glock (London: Routledge, 1991), 35–68, 48–49 (italics original). Even here, we should note, there is a marked dependence on the discourse of sight.

4. Jürgen Moltmann makes some revealing remarks in an autobiographical sketch: "Every comprehensive theology takes us beyond the category of time into the categories of space, place, expanse, and limit. We then arrive at spaces of time and space-times in our existence in the world. Developing in this direction, I found numerous theological studies on the concept of God and time, but almost none that addressed the theological concept of God and space. As we know from modern physics, time and space are complementary, but they are not symmetrical for us humans. You can experience different times at the same place, but you cannot exist at the same time in different places. In space we exist beside each other simultaneously. In time, however, we exist after one another successively." Jürgen Moltmann, "God in the World—the World in God: Perichoresis in Trinity and Eschatology," in *The Gospel of John and Christian*

Zero-Sum Theology

We begin with the obvious. Distinct objects in our visual field occupy bounded locations, discrete zones, such that they cannot overlap without their integrity being threatened. We cannot see a patch of red and a patch of yellow in the same space *as* red and *as* yellow. We see either red *or* yellow; or (if the colors are allowed to merge) we see a mixture of the two: orange. This, we should stress, is not an observation with the interests of physical science uppermost, that is, about objects inhabiting a three-dimensional, physical world; the point is about the phenomena of visual perception, about the way things appear to us.

The spatiality here is one of juxtaposition and mutual exclusion: different entities can be next to each other but cannot be in the same place at the same time. This is the space according to which we can distinguish "somewhere" from "elsewhere"; things take up bounded places within it—space becomes, in effect, the aggregate of places. It is the space by virtue of which we can measure intervals between things; it is divisible. It also carries with it the possibility of differing magnitude; objects can be larger than and smaller than others, and if one object enters the bounded area occupied by another, its increased area necessitates the other's decrease. The order or structure of this space will be conceived in terms of the relation of parts to one another against the background of a spatial whole. Further, we might add, this is the spatial experience not only of the eye but also of touch, which gives rise to geometrical measurement.[5]

Needless to say, the space of visual perception is often taken to be indicative of bona fide space, space as it "really is." It is certainly congruent with some of the leading philosophical and scientific conceptions of space in intellectual and scientific history. One of the most influential, with a long (and varied) history, conceives space as a type of receptacle or container, with objects or events located "inside" it, in their appropriate places. But whatever its specific formulation, conceiving space according to the patterns of visual experience is habitual for most of us, so much so that we probably never stop to wonder if other options are even available.

If left unchecked, however, this conceptual habit spawns considerable problems, not least in the popular imagination, as even a glance at the history

---

Theology, ed. Richard Bauckham and Carl Mosser (Grand Rapids: Eerdmans, 2008), 369–81, here 371. What is perplexing is that, to my knowledge at least, when he does write about space theologically, trinitarian space included, Moltmann does not draw on music even though so many of his inclinations move in this direction. See, for example, his reflections in *God in Creation: An Ecological Doctrine of Creation* (London: SCM, 1985), sec. 6; see also 13–17.

5. Here I am drawing on Zuckerkandl, *Sound and Symbol*, vol. 1, *Music and the External World* (London: Routledge & Kegan Paul, 1956), esp. 275–76, 282–85, 293–94.

of theology quickly shows. And this is perhaps nowhere clearer than in the modern theological imagination of freedom.[6]

As long as we remain wedded to "pictures" of distinct quasi-material objects in bounded domains, difficulties are almost bound to arise when we come to ask how an infinitely free God can be both external and internal to the world's space—"transcendent" and "immanent," to use the traditional terminology—difficulties that arguably obfuscate the testimony of Scripture. God's "thereness" and "hereness" will tend to be understood against the background of a "hyper-space," discrete portions of which both God and the world inhabit. It is not hard to see how this can encourage and support a philosophy of univocity—ontological and linguistic—in which God and the created world are regarded as belonging to the same genus. Repeated protests in recent theology against the notion that "being" can be predicated univocally of both God and the world, such that God is conceived as "a being" of the same order as other "beings" (albeit an infinitely greater one), begin to make more sense.

Accordingly, because in this kind of scheme the spaces that God and the world occupy cannot overlap or interpenetrate without threatening the other's integrity, there will be a propensity to regard transcendence and immanence as competing options. Kathryn Tanner speaks critically of "contrastive transcendence," a transcendence defined negatively in terms of what God is not, such that God is envisaged as essentially disengaged from the world; God's freedom is thus fundamentally freedom *from* all that is not God.[7] By the same token, divine immanence will be understood as the polar opposite of transcendence, denoting an involvement with the world that borders on imprisonment. Evidently, conceiving or speaking of a God who is *both* ontologically other than the world and yet actively engaged with it becomes deeply problematic.[8]

6. In a contribution to a recent series of essays on transcendence, David Wood writes: "The spatiality of our understanding of transcendence is rarely as crude as imagining 'another place' (or another time) where transcendence happens. *But we should never underestimate the power of the most vulgar models.*" Wood, "Topologies of Transcendence," in *Transcendence and Beyond: A Postmodern Inquiry*, ed. John D. Caputo and Michael J. Scanlon (Bloomington: Indiana University Press, 2007), 169–203, here 171 (italics mine).

7. Kathryn Tanner, *God and Creation in Christian Theology: Tyranny or Empowerment?* (Oxford: Blackwell, 1988), chap. 2. Over thirty years ago, Colin E. Gunton argued cogently that many of our difficulties with the concept of transcendence arise through the domination of visual patterns of perception. Gunton, "Transcendence, Metaphor and the Knowability of God," *Journal of Theological Studies* 31, no. 2 (1980): 501–16.

8. Some have pointed to a tension in the work of René Descartes (1596–1650) between a notion of God as cause and sustainer of the world and the idea that "true extension" can only be understood in terms of the measurable space of the physical world. Since God does not have extension in this sense, Descartes finds it hard to elucidate the nature of God's causal agency

Even if we find a way of negotiating or living with these obstacles such
that the transcendent God is held to be involved "in" the world in some sense,
it is no less challenging to conceive how this God can be active within the
world's space without undermining its integrity. The more of God, the less
the world is able to realize its true being—or so it would seem—for the two
cannot occupy the same "place." The notion of intermittent salvific divine
intervention might be appealing here: God does *some* things but not *all* things;
God is active in some places but not in all places. This notion, however, only
intensifies the danger of imagining that God's action necessarily violates the
world's freedom, like a burglar breaking into a house. The ease with which we
slip into "God-of-the-gaps" patterns of thinking illustrates well the power of
visual-spatial models—that which we cannot explain through the cause and
effect "internal" to the world we attribute to the "external" agency of God,
the deus ex machina. Tanner captures well the effect on construals of divine
agency when a contrastive transcendence holds sway:

> Divinity characterized in terms of a direct contrast with certain sorts of being
> or with the world of non-divine being as a whole is brought down to the level
> of the world and beings within it in virtue of that opposition: God becomes
> one being among others within a single order. Such talk suggests that God
> exists alongside the non-divine, that God is limited by what is opposed to it
> [*sic*], that God is as finite as the non-divine beings with which it [*sic*] is directly
> contrasted. A cosmology influenced by such suggestions will characterize a
> divine agency in terms appropriate for a finite one. Like that of a finite agent,
> God's influence will be of a limited sort: it may not extend to everything,

---

"in" the world. See William C. Placher, *The Domestication of Transcendence: How Modern
Thinking about God Went Wrong* (Louisville: Westminster John Knox Press, 1996), 131–32;
F. LeRon Shults, *Reforming the Doctrine of God* (Grand Rapids: Eerdmans, 2005), 18–22. It is
well known that Isaac Newton struggled hard to find an appropriate "place" for God's causality within the created world. He posited an absolute space and time, extending infinitely and
immutably in all directions, and could speak of absolute space as the "sensorium" of God, by
virtue of which God is truly present to everything. Isaac Newton, *The Principia: Mathematical
Principles of Natural Philosophy*, trans. I. Bernard Cohen and Anne Miller Whitman (Berkeley:
University of California Press, 1999), 6. Newton denied that he was a pantheist, but Placher
comments that "given a geometrical understanding of space and univocal meanings for terms
like 'present' and 'existence,' he was hard put to explain why his thought would not lead in
that direction." Placher, *Domestication of Transcendence*, 141. On this, see the illuminating
essay by Geoffrey Gorham, "Early Scientific Images of God: Descartes, Hobbes, and Newton,"
in *Turning Images in Philosophy, Science, and Religion: A New Book of Nature*, ed. Charles
Taliaferro and Jil Evans (Oxford: Oxford University Press, 2011), 25–45. Thomas F. Torrance
interprets Newton in the context of theories of space as receptacle, with God conceived as the
infinite container of all things. This effectively rules out any particular acts of God within the
container: God "can no more become incarnate than a box can become one of the several objects
it contains." Torrance, *Space, Time and Incarnation* (London: Oxford University Press, 1969), 39.

it may presuppose what it does not produce, it may require the intervening agencies of others.[9]

The other option easily suggested by the visual-spatial conceptuality is the opposite extreme: a merger of God and world such that Creator and creature are to some degree ontologically identified or synthesized, a metaphysical move that has taken numerous forms in modernity. Although there can be no denying their immense attractiveness and the sophistication with which they are often presented, such schemes are obviously vulnerable to the charge that both God and creature will lose their distinctive integrity and thereby their freedom.[10]

Intertwined with these developments are particular conceptions of infinity. Relevant here is the distinction between "mathematical" and "metaphysical" infinity; in the former case, infinity is understood according to the indefinite extension of a series, in the latter, as intensive and qualitative. According to LeRon Shults, in the seventeenth and eighteenth centuries the latter was eclipsed through an overemployment of the categories of extension and quantity, deployed in creaturely senses. God's infinity was typically construed in terms of infinite extension (in accordance with the pattern of the extension of finite things) and thus negatively: God is infinite in that God is without limit.[11] Thus God becomes "a being that is simply extensively greater than creatures." Such a being becomes "caught in the dialectic of 'more' or 'less,'" in the tension between transcendence and immanence—either far from or close to other beings."[12] Here, in other words, divine and human space and their

9. Tanner, *God and Creation*, 45–46.

10. The kind of questions we are putting to models of "contrastive transcendence" are obviously pertinent, though in different ways, to theological schemes such as "panentheism" with its particular dependence on the preposition "in" (all things are "in" God). Critical issues concerning what is to be invested ontologically in the language of containment here can hardly be avoided. For discussion, see Chan Ho Park, "Transcendence and Spatiality of the Triune Creator" (PhD diss., Fuller Theological Seminary, 2005), esp. 52–61. Similar questions have understandably been asked of Jürgen Moltmann's highly spatial notion of divine creation as withdrawal (*zimzum*); see Park, "Transcendence and Spatiality," 108–25.

11. Shults, *Reforming the Doctrine of God*, esp. 22–26, 98. Some will point to precursors of this in medieval thought. So, for example, Conor Cunningham argues that Duns Scotus bequeathed a notion of infinity as essentially quantitative. Cunningham, *A Genealogy of Nihilism: Philosophies of Nothing and the Difference of Theology* (London: Routledge, 2002), 28–32. He quotes Anne Davenport's assessment; although the infinite "cannot be reached by finite steps, it belongs conceptually to the same univocal 'measure' of excellence to which the finite belongs." Cunningham, *Genealogy of Nihilism*, 30; the quote is from Anne Ashley Davenport, *Measure of a Different Greatness: The Intensive Infinite, 1250–1650* (Leiden: Brill, 1999), 280.

12. Shults, *Reforming the Doctrine of God*, 98. Karl Barth writes: "We assign [God] the highest place in the world; and in so doing we place him fundamentally on one line with ourselves and with things." Barth, *The Epistle to the Romans* (Oxford: Oxford University Press,

relation are being conceived in creaturely, visual-spatial terms, as entailing the mutual exclusion of places and the articulation of difference and distinction through juxtaposition.

How Can God and Humankind Be Free Together?

Very much the same considerations apply to the way we correlate divine and human freedom.[13] Divine and human agency become ontologically comparable (agency is predicated of God and humans univocally) and compete for the same space, operating in inverse proportion. For God to be in my space means that I will be either displaced or diminished in some manner. The more God's power is affirmed, the more human agency is rendered inconsequential—the more of God, the less of us (and vice versa). The linking of human agency with the modern doctrine of autonomy[14] spawns the view that anything that is not in its entirety the agent's undetermined act is, just to that extent, a denial of the agent's freedom. It is little wonder that some of the most virulent currents of modern atheism trade heavily on the belief that worshiping God entails a self-abnegation that insults, indeed robs, us of our dignity. "To enrich God," declared Ludwig Feuerbach, "man must become poor; that God may be all, man must be nothing."[15] We must move into the space once occupied by this fictional deity and recover our diminished or "displaced" dignity. In drawing out the lines of thought here, David Bentley Hart is characteristically forthright:

> What we habitually understand democratic liberty to be—what we take, that is, as our most exalted model of freedom—is merely the unobstructed power of choice. The consequence of this, manifestly, is that we moderns tend to elevate what should at best be regarded as the moral life's minimal condition to the

---

1968). Walter Lowe comments: "So entrenched is the tendency Barth postulates that even the term 'infinite' leads us to imagine a (limitless) extension of the finite. . . . To draw a term from the postmodern thinker Emmanuel Levinas, the qualifier 'infinite' does not assure exemption from the hegemony of 'the Same.'" Lowe, "Postmodern Theology," in *The Oxford Handbook of Systematic Theology*, ed. J. B. Webster, Kathryn Tanner, and Iain R. Torrance (Oxford: Oxford University Press, 2007), 617–33, here 618.

13. In this essay I do not consider at any length the relation of human freedom to creation at large, where, regrettably, freedom is too often pitted against its polar opposite, determinism. For especially penetrating discussions, see Robert W. Jenson, *Systematic Theology: The Works of God*, 2 vols. (New York: Oxford University Press, 1999), 2:22–23; Peter Van Inwagen, *An Essay on Free Will* (Oxford: Clarendon Press, 1983).

14. J. B. Schneewind, *The Invention of Autonomy: A History of Modern Moral Philosophy* (Cambridge: Cambridge University Press, 1988).

15. Ludwig Feuerbach, *The Essence of Christianity*, trans. George Eliot (New York: Harper & Row, 1957), 26.

status of its highest expression, and in the process reduce the very concept of freedom to one of purely libertarian or voluntarist spontaneity. We have come to believe . . . that the will necessarily becomes more free the more it is emancipated from whatever constraints it suffers.[16]

Armed with such assumptions—that freedom is at its base level being freed *from* the other, that all restrictions are arbitrary and extrinsic and as such a threat to our freedom, that freedom is, in effect, no more than "the ability to do otherwise"—it is almost impossible not to regard belief in an infinite deity as inherently inimical to human flourishing. Indeed, some would contend that it belongs to the very core of modernity that freedom not only can be but must be defined without any reference to God.

Understandably, theologians have been quick to distinguish an authentic Christian vision of freedom from such scenarios. But they have been rather less swift in exposing the "zero-sum" schemes[17] that have so often fueled the debates about freedom *within* the Christian tradition. The issue is not only *whether* God is or is not invoked in speaking of freedom but also *what kind* of God is invoked and what kind of relations this God is assumed to establish with humans and the world at large.[18] Even if we hold to some sort of convergence of divine and human agency, it is repeatedly suggested by implication that each must be allowed its own exclusive portion of the available space. We

16. David Bentley Hart, *In the Aftermath: Provocations and Laments* (Grand Rapids: Eerdmans, 2009), 77.

17. See David B. Burrell, *Freedom and Creation in Three Traditions* (Notre Dame, IN: University of Notre Dame Press, 1993), 2.

18. A sizable body of opinion would link modern "libertarian" theories of freedom to early modern "voluntarism" of one sort or another, in which the dominating scenario is that of the sovereignty and total autonomy of the will (divine and/or human). The connections may not be simple or directly causal, but they are almost certainly there. The consequences for a voluntarist doctrine of God include a pointed stress on divine inscrutability together with acute problems in conceiving divine purposes as anything other than arbitrary. As far as human freedom is concerned, the issues are well summarized by David Burrell, in his "Can We Be Free without a Creator?," in *God, Truth, and Witness: Engaging Stanley Hauerwas*, ed. L. Gregory Jones, Reinhard Hütter, and C. Rosalee Velloso da Silva (Grand Rapids: Brazos Press, 2005), 35–52. Classical schemes in which the purpose or end of human life is always in view remind us that even "freedom to choose" makes sense only in light of a teleology, "the goal-directedness of human development" (42). Modernity typically defines freedom without reference to God and thus (commonly) without reference to an ultimate *telos*. God quite naturally becomes conceived as the infinite being who curbs, inhibits, or even suppresses human "freedom." With "the unique relation that both distinguishes creator from creatures and unites them" forgotten, "many contemporary accounts of freedom inevitably regard the creator as another operator in the scene, and so a rival to created agency." Burrell continues: "The resultant 'creator' can no longer be the God whom Jews, Christians, and Muslims worship, but can only be 'the biggest thing around'" (45).

only need think of some of the historic struggles over doctrines of salvation: if freedom is understood as being essentially about absolute self-determination, a polarity typically arises between, on the one hand, a conception of God's unmerited saving grace as an untrammeled, unrestricted divine causality at work in the world (at its worst, turning God into a tyrant) and, on the other hand, a notion of human "decision" envisaged as an entirely unprompted, self-generated response to God (an expression of "my personal space") such that divine agency becomes effectively dispensable.

Between these two extremes lie numerous attempts to divide things up so that both agencies have at least something of their own to contribute to the soteriological package. We are thus pressed rather too easily toward a "contractual" rather than a "covenantal" soteriology. A covenant, theologically speaking, is an unconditional pledge not dependent on the worth of the other party or parties; a contract is an agreement dependent on the fulfillment of certain conditions. A contract tacitly implies a finite, creaturely space shared by two agents, in which both agree—in effect—to occupy different zones ("if you do this much, I'll do that"). As Alan Torrance, Douglas Campbell, and others have shown, contractual soteriology can drastically misrepresent Scripture's witness to the character of divine grace: God's love becomes conditioned on the fulfillment of certain prior actions, the imperatives of obedience become logically prior to the indicatives of grace, and human agents are presumed to have it within themselves to effect at least the first stage of their own repentant faith in God (as if standing outside their own space, seeing clearly the problem between them and God, and then taking the first step toward reconciliation).[19] William Placher makes pertinent comments about those who have attempted to give due place to human integrity over against a divine "grace" that has in effect become conceived as an overpowering, even deterministic force. Having surveyed a number of theologians of the seventeenth century, he comments:

> Lutheran synergists, Catholic Molinists, Arminians, and covenant theologians—
> the differences are important, but the similarities are quite striking. All thought
> of God and human beings as operating in some sense on the same level, so that,

19. See Alan J. Torrance, "The Theological Grounds for Advocating Forgiveness and Reconciliation in the Sociopolitical Realm," in *The Politics of Past Evil: Religion, Reconciliation, and the Dilemmas of Transitional Justice*, ed. Daniel Philpott (Paris: University of Notre Dame Press, 2006), 45–85; Douglas A. Campbell, *The Quest for Paul's Gospel: A Suggested Strategy* (London: T&T Clark, 2005), chap. 8; Campbell, *The Deliverance of God: A Rereading of Justification in Paul* (Grand Rapids: Eerdmans, 2009), esp. 15–35; James B. Torrance, "Covenant and Contract: A Study of the Theological Background of Worship in Seventeenth-Century Scotland," *Scottish Journal of Theology* 23 (1970): 51–76.

if human beings were to do something toward their salvation, then one had to reduce the divine contribution.[20]

In this light it is no surprise that much modern theology has warmed readily to "kenotic" (self-emptying) models of the God-human relation, where God in some manner "limits" himself so as not to suppress or diminish human agency.[21] Sarah Coakley sums up the conception of freedom that she believes lies behind some of these schemes. There is, she says, a

> "space" granted to humans by God to exercise freedom—for good or ill. . . . The "freedom" thus exercised by humans must be of the "incompatibilist" sort, that is, the type supposedly free from conditioning control by another. The visual picture here . . . is of a (very big) divine figure backing out of the scene, or restraining his influence, in order that other (little) figures may exercise completely independent thinking and acting.[22]

Coakley notes the gendered connotations of the doctrine of God at work here: that of "a normative 'masculine' self who gains independence by setting himself apart from that which gave him life and indeed continues to sustain him."[23]

The only other viable option—on these kinds of presuppositions—is some form of synthesis: a dissolution of the divine into the human or vice versa, where, needless to say, the integrity of each is endangered.

Similar remarks could be made about the pervasiveness of visual-spatial construals of interpersonal freedom. The huge damage done to theology by the dominance of libertarian philosophies—where freedom becomes a matter of obtaining and moving into a vacant place of one's own, unconstrained and

20. Placher, *Domestication of Transcendence*, 162–63. Placher also observes how those on the other side, keen to champion the "sovereignty" of divine grace (Jansenists, Lutheran Pietists, Puritans), were paradoxically prone to domesticating it in practice, preoccupied as they were with the question of assurance. Placher, *Domestication of Transcendence*, chap. 6. We are, of course, touching on massively complex and contested territory with a fraught history in relations between Protestants and Roman Catholics. For a subtle account of many of the issues at stake, concerned with showing that "grace and free will do not need to come into a conflictual competition in the mystery of the *initium fidei*," see Reinhard Hütter, "St. Thomas on Grace and Free Will in the *Initium Fidei*: The Surpassing Augustinian Synthesis," *Nova et Vetera* 5, no. 3 (2007): 521–54.

21. For a recent account and defense, see David W. Brown, *Divine Humanity: Kenosis Explored and Defended* (London: SCM, 2011).

22. Sarah Coakley, "Kenosis: Theological Meanings and Gender Connotations," in *The Work of Love: Creation as Kenosis*, ed. John C. Polkinghorne (Grand Rapids: Eerdmans, 2001), 205.

23. Coakley, "Kenosis," 205. See also Sarah Coakley, "Feminism," in *A Companion to Philosophy of Religion*, ed. Philip L. Quinn and Charles Taliaferro (Oxford: Blackwell, 1997), 601–6.

unconditioned as far as possible by other persons, and maximizing the extent of that space as much as is practically possible—is a theme amply rehearsed in a wide range of current literature.[24]

Two in One Space

These tangled problematics find concentrated expression in Christology, and understandably so. Classical Christianity has held that in Jesus Christ we are given the utterly free movement of God toward us and a wholly free movement of a human being toward God. How can this be? In the visually conceived world, the ancient orthodoxy of the church according to the Council of Chalcedon of 451 CE that Christ is both human and divine (without confusion or change, separation or division) is notoriously hard to articulate or conceive in a way that does justice to the New Testament's irreducibly awkward witness to the co-presence of both in this one historical person. The critical danger, again, is in assuming that deity and humanity are ontologically comparable categories, instances of the same genus jostling for the same space—in this case the three-dimensional, physical space of Jesus of Nazareth. Typically we find the two "natures" are either thought to exist in some kind of precarious equilibrium—like a tightrope walker with a double-weighted bar, poised far above heresy, or else some sort of compromise must be negotiated through attenuation of one of the natures—it is claimed, for example, that in the incarnation the eternal Son underwent some type of pulling back, nonexercise, or even abandonment of his divine powers or attributes (as in some nineteenth- and twentieth-century "kenotic" Christologies) or that the humanity of Jesus had to be a curtailed version of the authentic article in order to cope with a potentially overpowering divine presence.[25] These options, of course, threaten to weaken or even undermine salvation, for how can *God* redeem *humanity* if neither retains their fullness?

24. Among the finest treatments are those found in Richard Bauckham, *God and the Crisis of Freedom: Biblical and Contemporary Perspectives* (Louisville: Westminster John Knox Press, 2002); and Colin E. Gunton, ed., *God and Freedom: Essays in Historical and Systematic Theology* (Edinburgh: T&T Clark, 1995). Roger Lundin's comments on Heidegger's concept of the modern "age of the world picture" are telling: "In the realm of the *world picture*, we can do little more than cultivate a mutual toleration of our incommensurable perspectives." Roger Lundin, *Believing Again: Doubt and Faith in a Secular Age* (Grand Rapids: Eerdmans, 2009), 179 (italics original).

25. The irony is that the New Testament passage from which such Christologies ultimately derive—Phil. 2:5–11—most probably does not carry any of these connotations, even if we do maintain (as I believe we should) that Paul is here affirming a conception of the "preexistence" of Christ. For a clear discussion, see Gordon D. Fee, "Exploring Kenotic Christology: The

Essays on Chalcedon by Richard Norris and Sarah Coakley have suggested that the debates on either side of the council (and in some modern Christologies) can give the impression that "deity" and "humanity" are two entities on the same ontological level, "differing items of the *same* order," "competing for the same space."[26] If so, this shows that spatial problems of this type are by no means unique to our era. But they have undoubtedly been exacerbated in modernity by a strong tendency to think in the visual-spatial terms we have been describing. Whatever one's final assessment of modern kenotic Christologies, for example, it is hard to deny that unguarded use of the terminology of "retraction," "setting aside," "self-limitation," and so forth will tend to encourage the projection of inappropriate aspects of visualizable, creaturely space into theological ontology, generating unnecessary and damaging antinomies. Significantly, Coakley comments that such Christologies tend to be vitiated by the assumption that divinity and humanity are categories that "can be collapsed into one flat package" and then (not surprisingly) considered incompatible. Writing in connection with Kathryn Tanner's work, she observes, "Christology that intends to be 'orthodox' radically loses its way if it starts from the assumption that the humanity and divinity of Christ are like two vying (but potentially well-matched?) contestants striving to inhabit the same space."[27]

Self-Emptying of God," in *Exploring Kenotic Christology*, ed. C. Stephen Evans (Oxford: Oxford University Press, 2006), 25–44.

26. Sarah Coakley, "What Does Chalcedon Solve and What Does It Not? Some Reflections on the Status and Meaning of the Chalcedonian 'Definition,'" in *The Incarnation: An Interdisciplinary Symposium on the Incarnation of the Son of God*, ed. Stephen T. Davis, Gerald O'Collins, and Daniel Kendall (Oxford: Oxford University Press, 2002), 143–63, here 147. See Richard Norris, "Chalcedon Revisited: A Historical and Theological Reflection," in *New Perspectives on Historical Theology: Essays in Memory of John Meyendorff*, ed. Bradley Nassif (Grand Rapids: Eerdmans, 1996), 140–58. Norris believes that in the debates surrounding Chalcedon the two natures came to be conceived in "reified" or concretized terms as differing items of the same ontological order, what he calls "interchangeable contraries," forgetting that *"there is no overarching category in which both [Creator and creature] can be classified"* (156, italics original). He thinks that Chalcedon itself is more reticent: there the question posed is not "how to fit two logical contraries together into one, as its ancient and modern interpreters have all but uniformly supposed, but how to dispense with a binary logic in figuring the relation between God and creatures" (158). Coakley takes Norris to task for what she sees as his Lindbeckian thesis about Chalcedon as merely "regulatory," his Neo-Kantian epistemological assumptions, and his inconsistency in assuming that an ontological statement is present in Chalcedon even as he is denying it. Coakley, "What Does Chalcedon Solve?," 149–52. But she believes Norris is right in (among other things) holding that "to gloss the human and divine 'natures' as inherently two of the same kind, and/or in 'contradiction' with one another, is not implied by the text of the [Chalcedonian] 'Definition' *per se*" (148). She goes on to say, however, that neither can this interpretation be entirely ruled out (148).

27. Sarah Coakley, "Does Kenosis Rest on a Mistake? Three Kenotic Models in Patristic Exegesis," in *Exploring Kenotic Christology: The Self-Emptying of God*, ed. C. Stephen Evans (Oxford: Oxford University Press, 2006), 246–64, here 261, 262. She continues: "We are not trying

Few have explored the consequences of receptacle or container notions of space and time more fully than the Scottish Reformed theologian T. F. Torrance.[28] With considerable acuity, he notes the way we are encouraged to imagine the relation between God and created space—and thus between the incarnate Christ and the Father—in creaturely-spatial terms. He attacks both finite and infinite versions of receptacle philosophies.[29] In the case of the finite version, the incarnation is imagined as the Son of God's complete entry into a finite container, with an implied abandonment of heaven. Crudely, the Son must be either "up there" with the Father or "down here" with us; he cannot be in both "places" at the same time. For Torrance, the Lutheran objection to the Calvinists' insistence that the eternal Son is *both* in heaven upholding the universe *and* living on earth as Jesus of Nazareth—namely, that this implies that part of the Son was still "outside" Jesus of Nazareth (the so-called Calvinist extra [*extra Calvinisticum*])—illustrates the point well. Torrance is thus wary of Lutheran theologies that speak of the total self-emptying of the infinite Son into a finite body-receptacle and of Christologies that posit a communication of the property of ubiquity (omnipresence) to Christ's humanity in order to render it capable of receiving the divine fullness. Such systems are bound to compromise one or other of the natures.[30] He is equally suspicious of the notion of space as infinite receptacle and especially of portraying God himself in such terms, for this would make the incarnation impossible to affirm (how could God be both container and contents?) and opens the door to Arianism and/or deism.[31]

Three in One Space

A common criticism of Chalcedon is that its affirmations are insufficiently trinitarian. Certainly, it is no surprise to find the various aporias we

---

to squeeze together, or coalesce, two sets of features which (annoyingly?) present us with logical opposites; rather, we are attempting to conceive of a unique intersection precisely *of* opposites, in which the divine—that which is *in se* unimaginably greater and indeed creator and sustainer of the human—is 'united,' *hypostatically*, with that 'human,' forming one concrete subject." Coakley, "Does Kenosis Rest on a Mistake?," 262 (italics original). The term "opposites" is perhaps unfortunate here, given Coakley's commitments to noncompetitive understandings of the God-world relation.

28. Torrance, *Space, Time and Incarnation*; Thomas F. Torrance, *Space, Time, and Resurrection* (Grand Rapids: Eerdmans, 1976). For exceptionally clear discussions of Torrance on these matters, see Paul D. Molnar, *Incarnation and Resurrection: Toward a Contemporary Understanding* (Grand Rapids: Eerdmans, 2007), 90–96; Molnar, *Thomas F. Torrance: Theologian of the Trinity* (Farnham, UK: Ashgate, 2009), 124–35.

29. Torrance, *Space, Time and Incarnation*, 62–63.

30. Torrance, *Space, Time and Incarnation*, 30–36.

31. Torrance, *Space, Time and Incarnation*, 39, 63.

have noted reaching acute expression in conceptual struggles concerning the trinitarian "space" of God, the very fount of all freedom. There have, of course, been a multitude of renderings of the Trinity in visual art, many of which bear commanding and effective witness to God's triunity. That is not at issue here. However, if we are to think oneness and threeness together in a manner appropriate to the New Testament but at the same time in a way that is not attentive to the dangers of being overdetermined by visual thought patterning, we are likely to be led into complications parallel to those we have just observed in Christology. For, to ask the obvious, how can three occupy the same (visualizable) space and be perceptible *as three*? Modern theology's struggles in this respect are hardly unprecedented, but they are certainly conspicuous to any student of trinitarian doctrine of the last two or three hundred years, and a good case could be mounted for claiming that they have been exacerbated by the inclinations of thought and language we have highlighted. Strenuous attempts to maintain threeness typically result in some form of precarious equilibrium: the divine persons are strongly affirmed in both their particularity and their undivided unity but left there in lifeless tension. Repeated appeals to "mystery" in this context sound decidedly thin and unsatisfying, especially when compared to the fulsome and dynamic interpenetrative interplay of Son and Father attested in, say, John's Gospel. And not surprisingly, various forms of compromise have been on offer—theologies that veer toward heavily "socialized" (near-tritheistic) trinitarianism, on the one hand, or varieties of modalism, on the other hand (distinction *ad extra*, undifferentiated oneness *ad intra*).

In none of what I have said above am I assuming straightforward, direct causal links between particular doctrines and visual patterns of thought and language. Things are far more complex and intricate. Visual conceptualization may well be one factor at work in the way freedom has been imagined in modernity, but there are undoubtedly many more.[32] My proposal is fairly modest, but I hope not thereby insignificant: that in modernity, an unwarranted reliance on conceptual frameworks that favor spatial visualization and its associated language have likely aggravated and in some places perhaps generated a range of problems that have repeatedly frustrated and distorted

---

32. Even the perceived role and capacity of "the visual" in modernity has undergone substantial changes. For an intriguing treatment of early modernity in this regard, see Stuart Clark, *Vanities of the Eye: Vision in Early Modern European Culture* (Oxford: Oxford University Press, 2007). Clark argues that the relation between what we see and what we know "was particularly unsettled in late Renaissance Europe. In one context after another, vision came to be characterized by uncertainty and unreliability, such that access to visual reality could no longer be normally guaranteed. It is as though European intellectuals lost their optical nerve." Clark, *Vanities of the Eye*, 2.

Christian theology in its attempt to explicate the New Testament's rendering of the character of freedom, divine and human.

If we move from the visible to the audible, however, a different world unfolds.

Sound Space

I play a note on a piano. The tone I hear fills the whole of my aural field, my heard space. It does not occupy a bounded location. It "saturates our hearing."[33] It is "everywhere" in that space; there is nothing "outside" it, no spatial zone where the sound is not. I then play a second higher tone along with the first. This second sound fills the entirety of the *same* (heard) space, yet I hear it as distinct, irreducibly different. In this aural environment, two different entities, it would seem, can be in the same space at the same time. And they are not each in a place that we can describe as "here" rather than "there." Each seems to be "everywhere."

Appeals to physics here—that sound waves, considered as physically locatable phenomena, do occupy measurable places in space—are understandable but beside the point. The focus of our interest is in sound as a perceptual experience and, arising from that, as a determinant in shaping thought and language. We are concerned not with the three-dimensional space in which musical instruments, singers, and sound waves are situated but rather with sonic space *as heard*, the kind of space we are given to hear as we perceive musical tones.[34]

Sounds as "Secondary Objects" and "Pure Events"

What kind of existence do these sounds (as heard) have? Clearly, sounds are not ordinary three-dimensional objects, like dogs and trees, nor ordinary events, like dogs barking or trees swaying. Yet are they not objects and events of *some* sort? Roger Scruton has recently argued that sounds are best regarded as "secondary objects" and "pure events."[35] Concentrating on the

33. Roger Scruton, *The Aesthetics of Music* (Oxford: Clarendon Press, 1997), 13.

34. It is also worth emphasizing that in this essay we are not considering the spatial representation of music or musical form (as in a score or diagram); on this understanding of musical "space," see Mark Evan Bonds, "The Spatial Representation of Musical Form," *Journal of Musicology* 27, no. 3 (2010): 265–303.

35. Scruton, *Aesthetics of Music*, 6–13; Roger Scruton, *Understanding Music: Philosophy and Interpretation* (London: Continuum, 2009); Scruton, "Sounds as Secondary Objects and Pure Events," in *Sounds and Perception: New Philosophical Essays*, ed. Matthew Nudds and Casey O'Callaghan (Oxford: Oxford University Press, 2009), 50–68.

"intentional objects"[36] of audition—what we hear when we identify something *as* "a sound"—he contends that "sounds are *'audibilia,'* which is to say that their essence resides in 'the way they sound.'"[37] They are secondary in that their existence, nature, and qualities depend on the way they are perceived; at the same time, they are not properties or qualities but objects with qualities, analogous to smells.[38] When we call a sound rough or pleasant, we are attributing a quality to the sound, not to the object that produced it nor to the physical changes the object undergoes; we can identify and describe the sound without referring to its physical source. If I describe the intentional object of my sight, the description will be (in part at least) a description of the physical object. The remark "I see a red car" both describes my perception and (to some extent) describes the car across the street. But to describe a sound as soft says nothing about the object that produced the sound: "The auditory field, unlike the visual field, does not depict its cause."[39]

According to Scruton, having acknowledged sounds as secondary objects, we can go on to speak of sounds as "pure events"—they are happenings but do not happen *to* particular, identifiable entities.[40] When a building collapses, the event happens to the building, but the sound the building makes as it disintegrates is not an event in the building's life or a change in which the building shares; it is an event in itself, a "pure event."[41] On this account, then, sounds can be detached from the source that produces them and the physical disturbances they entail. It is unnecessary to refer to the source or cause of a sound in order to identify and describe it, and organizing sounds so that we can make sense of them does not necessarily entail any knowledge of what produced them. Sounds can be "intrinsically ordered in our hearing, without reference to an order of physical objects and events."[42]

36. Intentionality concerns the directedness of the mind in perception, its "aboutness"; "intentional objects" are objects of one's "mental acts" (thinking, judging, etc.). See T. Crane, "Intentionalism," in *The Oxford Handbook of Philosophy of Mind*, ed. Brian P. McLaughlin, Ansgar Beckermann, and Sven Walter (Oxford: Clarendon Press, 2009), 474–93.
37. Scruton, "Sounds as Secondary Objects," 57.
38. A distinction is commonly made between "primary qualities," properties of objects that are possessed by an object independent of any observer (such as size, solidity, and shape), and "secondary qualities," properties that provoke sensations in the observer (such as taste and smell). Secondary qualities concern the way things *appear* to us.
39. Scruton, *Understanding Music*, 26.
40. Scruton, *Understanding Music*, 61–62.
41. Hence Scruton's rejection of "physicalist" accounts of sound, viz., those that understand sounds as identical with the events that generate them. See, e.g., Casey O'Callaghan, *Sounds: A Philosophical Theory* (Oxford: Oxford University Press, 2007); Robert Casati and Jerome Dokic, *La Philosophe du Son* (Nimes: Jacqueline Chambon, 1994). See Scruton, *Understanding Music*, 20–23, and chap. 2.
42. Scruton, "Sounds as Secondary Objects," 28.

Here an important distinction should be kept in mind between noises and (musical) tones. The conductor Sir Thomas Beecham is supposed to have quipped that "the English people may not understand music, but they absolutely love the noise that it makes."[43] Hearing sounds as music, Scruton argues, is qualitatively different from hearing noises. In the latter case, our inclination is usually to follow them through to their source. When I hear crashing from my daughter's bedroom upstairs, I want to know the object or event that has caused it. I could detach the noise from any thought about what created it (as with any sound) and consider it on its own, but it would be odd to do so. I am interested in the noise primarily because of what it can tell me about an object or event. I use the sound to orient me in visual space, to help me locate myself with respect to the tangible and measurable three-dimensional world. But this is not normally the case with musical tones: I am interested in these not because they tell me about their source (though they may do that) but because of what they can do by virtue of their intrinsic relations to one another, their own musical order (pitch, melody, harmony, and rhythm). Indeed, recognizing music as such *depends* on our ability, at least to some extent, to detach sounds from their physical causes: the power of music relies on this ability. Musical sounds—as heard—are not subject to the three-dimensional order of visible, tangible, and measurable objects.[44]

43. Derek Watson, ed., *The Wordsworth Dictionary of Musical Quotations* (Ware, UK: Wordsworth Editions, 1994), 331.

44. Scruton, *Understanding Music*, 30. Scruton alludes to the "octave illusion" presented by Diana Deutsch: two different successions of tones are played simultaneously, one into each ear through headphones. What is "heard" by the listener in each ear is not what is actually played into each ear. "The auditory *Gestalt* is not merely incongruent with the physical events that produce it. It is organized according to principles that are intrinsic to the world of sounds." Scruton, *Understanding Music*, 27; Diana Deutsch, "An Auditory Illusion," *Nature* 251 (1974): 307–9; Deutsch, "The Octave Illusion Revisited Again," *Journal of Experimental Psychology: Human Perception and Performance* 30, no. 2 (2004): 355–64.

Andy Hamilton has challenged Scruton's "acousmatic" thesis—namely, that "to hear sounds as music involves divorcing them from the worldly source or cause of their production." Hamilton, "The Sound of Music," in *Sounds and Perception: New Philosophical Essays*, ed. Matthew Nudds and Casey O'Callaghan (Oxford: Oxford University Press, 2009), 146–82. Hamilton says Scruton "wrongly denies that the non-acousmatic aspect is genuinely musical." Hamilton, "Sound of Music," 160. He contends that listening to music always involves, at least to some extent, a combination of acousmatic and non-acousmatic experience, and *both* are genuinely musical. Our awareness of a particular instrument at a concert, or a player's movements, or the physical impact of a sound through our body may in fact be critical to the total musical enjoyment: "'Real-life' causality is a genuinely musical part of musical experience." He adds: "For 'genuinely musical' here, one could substitute 'genuinely aesthetic.'" Hamilton, "Sound of Music," 172. At issue here, of course, is what is to count as intrinsic to bona fide "musical experience" or to authentic "musical listening"—Scruton's understanding of these are arguably

The Space of Sounds

What kind of "space" is this, then? "The essential feature of a spatial dimension," according to Scruton, "is that it contains places, which can be *occupied* by things, and between which things can move."[45] A tone cannot "move" from one pitch to another without changing its character. The pitch spectrum is not a dimension analogous to the dimensions of physical space:

> There is no clear orientation of sounds in auditory space: no way of assigning faces, ends, boundaries, and so on to them, so as to introduce those topological features which help us to make sense of the idea of "occupying" a place. . . . The acousmatic experience offers a world of objects which are ordered only *apparently*, and not in fact.[46]

Scruton concedes that musicians regularly use spatial language—notes "move up and down" and so forth. Musical perception is *necessarily* metaphorical: we hear tones *as* rising, falling, and so on; we hear *in* the tones a spatial order.[47] And all language that results from such hearing is no less metaphorical. But, he insists, we should avoid investing these metaphors with inappropriate content.

Are matters quite so clear-cut? One question worth considering, for example, is whether musical space enables the perception of aspects of the physical world's space that are opaque to visual-spatial models. Is the only kind of existent spatial order that which we can visualize? Moreover, acknowledging that the spatiality of musical perception does not correspond to the spatial order of three-dimensional objects and that the language we use of musical-auditory space will indeed entail metaphor does not in any sense rule out the truth-disclosing potential of the spatial language and concepts generated by the distinctive spatiality of musical experience. There is after all no *a priori* reason to believe that all our spatial language and concepts must

---

too restrictive and somewhat idealized. For our purposes, we simply note that hearing/listening to music necessarily *involves* the capacity to abstract sounds (tones) from their sources and causes and to hear them as related to one another in meaningful, internally related configurations, even if we allow that other acousmatic experience may be (and usually is) relevant to hearing the sounds *as music*. Without this capacity, there could be no musical experience. Whether our ability to abstract from "real-life causality" can ever be complete and whether such a total perceptual disengagement would even be desirable are quite another matter. In any case, here we are concerned not with musical perception in its wider, physical contexts but only with one, albeit crucial, dimension of it.

45. Scruton, *Aesthetics of Music*, 14 (italics original). Scruton asserts bluntly: "The distinction between place and occupant is . . . fundamental to the concept of space" (47).

46. Scruton, *Aesthetics of Music*, 14 (italics original).

47. Scruton, *Aesthetics of Music*, chap. 3.

have their truth-bearing capacity assessed entirely according to the extent that they measure up to what we have already decided from our visual experience is to be deemed "essential" space (space "in fact"). In any case, the type of spatial language and conceptuality especially critical for our purposes is not that of "up" and "down" and so on but the type we employ to make distinctions between objects that exist simultaneously or concurrently but which we nevertheless recognize as distinct.

Interpenetration

Bolder and rather more penetrating in this regard is the remarkable work of the Austrian musicologist Victor Zuckerkandl (1896–1965).[48] He describes the space manifest in musical tones as a space of "interpenetration." When one tone is heard along with a different tone, it does not drive the first away, nor is it in a different place, nor does it merge with the first to create a new tone. Both are heard as full and distinct. They do not occupy discrete places. The space we hear is not an aggregate of places; "somewhere" cannot be distinguished from "elsewhere." We cannot measure heard tones geometrically or point to boundaries to distinguish them. There is no spatial magnitude of elements; one tone cannot take up "more space" than the other. There is no possibility of "the more of the first tone, the less of the other" (presuming one does not drown out the other through greater loudness). Spatial order here is not the relation of spatial parts to one another against the backdrop of a spatial whole, since we are not encountering the space of juxtaposition and mutual exclusion; the distinction between parts and whole is irrelevant in this context. The tones can "sound through" one another, interpenetrate. They can be *in* one another, while being heard *as* two distinct tones.[49]

48. Zuckerkandl, *Sound and Symbol*, vol. 1, *Music and the External World* (Princeton: Princeton University Press, 1973); Zuckerkandl, *Sound and Symbol*, vol. 2, *Man the Musician* (Princeton: Princeton University Press, 1976). John Shepherd and Peter Wicke are the only music scholars I have found to appreciate the importance of Zuckerkandl's work for our understanding of the experience of sound, time, and space. Shepherd and Wicke, *Music and Cultural Theory* (Cambridge: Polity Press, 1997), 122–23, 129–36, 141, 150–52, 154, 159, 160.

49. Zuckerkandl, *Sound and Symbol: Music and the External World*, chaps. 14, 15, and 16. It might be objected that visual art can suggest this very powerfully. Indeed, it can *suggest* it or evoke it—as in the impressive "polyphonic" art of Paul Klee (1879–1940), which does seem to radiate a sense of the overlaying of diverse colors. See Hajo Düchting, *Paul Klee: Painting Music* (Munich: Prestel, 1997), 65–79; Andrew Kagan, *Paul Klee: Art and Music* (Ithaca, NY: Cornell University Press, 1983). But the fact remains that in this case we do not perceive distinct colors in the same place; we perceive difference only by comparing "edged" units of color. This is not in any way to downplay Klee's artistry but only to highlight the divergence between two types of perception.

"Coming From" and "Coming Toward"

Zuckerkandl also writes of sonic space as "coming from," "coming toward." A color I see is the property of a physical object; it is "with" the object, "out there." But as we have noted (via Scruton), a perceived tone is not "with" the thing that produced it. It has detached itself from the physical object, and as such it is impinging upon me, always coming toward me. Its happening (as "pure event," in Scruton's sense) *is* its coming toward me. Here, says Zuckerkandl, I am experiencing space not simply in the form of an inert vessel or container through which a sound travels but space in the form of "coming toward"—a living space, in other words: "Space that has become alive as a result of sound! Hence not sound that has come alive in space . . . but space that becomes an occurrence through tone,"[50] or, we might say: space as an intrinsic dimension of tone. This is why a single tone is not dull in the same way that, say, staring at a blank sheet of white paper is. In the latter case we get bored because there is "nothing there." But "it would never occur to [a person] to say that he hears *nothing* when he hears only one tone";[51] rather he hears a sound coming toward him. It is this quality that gives sound a depth—not the visual depth generated by physical distance but the dynamic depth of "coming toward me," "coming from": "depth in auditory space is only another expression for this 'coming from . . .' that we sense in every tone."[52]

Resonant Order

If the language of "coming from" and "coming toward" may be somewhat obscure, more readily accessible is Zuckerkandl's account of musical-spatial order. In the interpenetration of sounds in our heard space, as we have seen, the integrity of each heard sound is not effaced but, in principle at least, is preserved. In the case of musical tones in particular, another momentum is often at work, such that the integrity of each sound is not only preserved but enriched.

If I hear a truck outside, the wind blowing through the trees, and a baby crying all at the same time, the sounds may well interpenetrate, creating a differentiated aural space, but we would hardly claim that an auditory *order* was present.[53] The noises bear no internal relation to one another; they just

50. Zuckerkandl, *Sound and Symbol: Music and the External World*, 277.
51. Zuckerkandl, *Sound and Symbol: Music and the External World*, 283.
52. Zuckerkandl, *Sound and Symbol: Music and the External World*, 289.
53. This kind of everyday experience is nonetheless a testimony to the interpenetrative capacities of simultaneously heard sounds in contrast to visual perception. This is brought out

happen to be together in the one aural space. But in the case of a three-note major triad, the three tones are perceptibly related, not just to me as the hearer but internally to one another. They are mutually *resonant*; they "set each other off," enhancing, "enlarging" one another as particular and distinct. Thus we perceive an ordered chord, not three noises.

This order arises because of the way regularly constituted vibrating bodies, such as strings, participate in a phenomenon known as the harmonic series, a collection of distinct frequencies present in the vibrating body. Certain strings will resonate strongly with some (but by no means all) other strings. If I play middle C on a piano and open up the string an octave above by silently depressing the appropriate key, the upper C string will vibrate (very quietly) even though it has not been struck. This is because the upper C is the second harmonic (or first overtone) of the "fundamental" lower C.[54] The upper C has been provoked to sound through "sympathetic resonance."

This is clearly not a case of mutual diminution; rather, the *more* the lower string sounds, the *more* the upper string sounds. The tones we hear are not in competition, nor do they simply allow each other room. The lower sound establishes the upper, frees it to be itself, enhances it, without compromising its own integrity. Moreover, when certain other strings are opened up alongside both these strings—for instance, to make an extended major chord—we will hear those other strings coming to life.

A chord of this sort therefore opens up a distinctive kind of spatial order we may call "resonant order," in which tones are heard to relate intrinsically

---

well by John Hull in his book *Touching the Rock*, when he reflects on the experience of losing his sight. Deprived of sight, he asks:

> What is the world of sound? I have been spending some time out of doors trying to respond to the special nature of the acoustic world. . . . The tangible world sets up only as many points of reality as can be touched by my body, and this seems to be restricted to one problem at a time. I can explore the splinters on the park bench with the tip of my finger but I cannot, at the same time, concentrate upon exploring the pebbles with my big toe. . . . The world revealed by sound is so different. . . . On Holy Saturday I sat in Cannon Hill Park while the children were playing. . . . The footsteps came from both sides. They met, mingled, separated again. From the next bench, there was the rustle of a newspaper and the murmur of conversation. . . . I heard the steady, deep roar of the through traffic, the buses and the trucks. . . . [The acoustic world] stays the same whichever way I turn my head. This is not true of the [visually] perceptible world. It changes as I turn my head. New things come into view. The view looking that way is quite different from the view looking this way. It is not like that with sound. . . . This is a world which I cannot shut out, which goes on all around me, and which gets on with its own life. . . . Acoustic space is a world of revelation. (John Hull, *Touching the Rock: An Experience of Blindness* [London: SPCK, 1990], 61–64)

54. This will not work if the upper note is, say, a D flat, for D flat is only very distantly related to C harmonically.

to one another in such a way as to generate and reinforce each other. This ordered space is responsible for the dynamism we are used to intuiting in most of the music of Western culture; because of the internal relatedness of tones to one another through the harmonic series, even single chords will have certain "attractions" toward and "gravitational pulls" from other tones and chords. The playing out of music in time is a playing out of this tonal order.[55]

This musical space we have been describing—an interpenetrating, coming from–coming toward, resonantly ordered space—makes possible something we will only meet in music: that of radically different words being audible simultaneously while at the same time being pleasurable and intelligible. In act 2 of Giuseppe Verdi's *Otello*, for example, there is a famous quartet when what happens in the Shakespeare play on separate occasions is brought together.[56] Four voices sing simultaneously, yet of different things, in one texture. If merely spoken this would be nearly impossible to understand, let alone enjoy. But when the simultaneous words are taken into the spatial order of musical tones, the effect is comprehensible and captivating. Zuckerkandl speaks of this as generating a "supermeaning, the meaning of a whole."[57] Another example: in U2's song "The Fly," the lower voice sings of trying to hang on to love like a fly climbing up a wall, while at the same time the upper voice (called "gospel" voice) sings in falsetto of love coming down from above. Two very different sets of words are concurrently sung and both given new meaning—and thus a "supermeaning"—in and through their sonic simultaneity.[58]

Music, then, is capable of evoking a space for the hearer that is, so to speak, "edgeless," an inherently expansive space that has no close parallel in the world of the eye.[59] The experience is well described by Maurice Merleau-Ponty:

> When, in the concert hall, I open my eyes, visible space seems to me cramped compared to that other space through which, a moment ago, the music was being unfolded, and even if I keep my eyes open while the piece is being played, I have

55. For an illuminating exposition of the tonal order of Western music, see, e.g., Brian Hyer, "Tonality," *Oxford Music Online*, http://www.oxfordmusiconline.com (subscription required).

56. James A. Hepokoski, "Verdi's Composition of *Otello*: The Act II Quartet," in *Analyzing Opera: Verdi and Wagner*, ed. Carolyn Abbate and Roger Parker (Berkeley: University of California Press, 1989), 125–49.

57. Zuckerkandl, *Sound and Symbol: Music and the External World*, 332.

58. U2, "The Fly," on *Achtung Baby*, Island, 1991, compact disc.

59. It may well be argued that in the case of visual perception and the visually perceivable world there is a parallel, that of resonances between colors. However, as far as *interpenetration* and *coming from–coming toward* are concerned, it is hard to see a visual parallel to these aspects of sound as perceived.

the impression that the music is not really contained within this circumscribed and unimpressive space.[60]

Sound Doctrine

We are proposing, then, that the space of musical tones is a space of interpenetration, of coming from–coming toward, and of resonant order. Clearly, this resists being construed in terms of receptacle spatiality; this space is not a container but rather the space *of*, space as an intrinsic dimension or condition of objects and events, space understood in accordance with that which "has" space. With this in mind, let us revisit the theological loci we highlighted earlier.

Transcendence and Immanence Transposed

To return to the Creator-creature relation: once we are freed from the supposition of an area of super-space in which God and the world are both situated, the ontological and conceptual machinery of contrastive transcendence will seem far less apposite, with its tendency to posit transcendence and immanence as polar opposites and then to elaborate various compromises and mediations between them. The way is opened up for far more biblically grounded accounts, congruent with God's covenantal commitment disclosed in his triune self-revelation. God's transcendence transcends a merely creaturely understanding of transcendence—it transcends the contrasts by which finite beings are distinguished and differentiated and cannot be conceived as a spatial relation in the visual, tangible, measurable sense. Rather God stands in a *creative* (covenantally propelled) relation to created space. Because God is radically *for* the world, we can speak of a "dynamic transcendence": the transcendence of a God who creates all things out of nothing, sustains and redeems all things toward their eschatological fulfillment. This is a transcendence of the Giver, fundamentally oriented *to* and *for* the world's flourishing. God's triune being is a being toward, known by the creature as a "coming from" or "coming toward." Tanner observes that

> a non-competitive relation between creatures and God is possible, it seems, only if God is the fecund provider of *all* that the creature is in itself; the creature in its giftedness, in its goodness, does not compete with God's gift-fullness and goodness because God is the giver of all that the creature is for the good.

60. Maurice Merleau-Ponty, *Phenomenology of Perception* (New York: Humanities Press, 1962), 257–58.

This relationship of total giver to total gift is possible, in turn, only if God and creatures are, so to speak, on different levels of being, and different planes of causality. . . . God does not give on the same plane of being and activity as creatures, as one among other givers and therefore God is not in potential competition (or co-operation) with them. . . . God, from beyond this plane of created reality, brings about the *whole* plane of creaturely being and activity in its goodness.[61]

Divine immanence accordingly can be (re)conceived as a creative involvement with the world that is not confined to interventions in this or that particular zone or place. If God is not characterized fundamentally by contrast with this or that being, God may be directly and immediately involved with the entirety of the space-time continuum, albeit in diverse ways. Such an immanence does not merely *permit* transcendence but *requires* it. Only a God who is nonidentical with the creation—both in the sense that God creates all things out of nothing (not as an extension of his being), and in the sense that the God-world distinction transcends even the contrastive distinctions by which finite beings are distinguished—can be truly and savingly present *to* and *for* the world in its entirety, directly and immediately. Similarly, transcendence entails immanence; if divine transcendence is positively understood as the transcendence of the triune plenitude, the transcendence of divine covenantal commitment to fellowship, no portion of created reality can lack divine engagement. Musical conceptuality lends itself very naturally to perceiving and articulating these dynamics, for it sidesteps the pernicious notion of a prior, conditioning super-space and operates with an "otherness" driven not by negation and opposition but by gracious fullness and by the promotion and enhancement of the particularity of the other. All three features of musical tone perception are seen to be relevant here. *Interpenetration*: we are freed from thinking in terms of the divine and created as mutually exclusive zones. *Coming from–coming toward*: *creatio ex nihilo* is the outcome of God's own triune "space" in action (not a movement into [or out of!] a preexisting space);

---

61. Kathryn Tanner, *Jesus, Humanity and the Trinity: A Brief Systematic Theology* (Edinburgh: T&T Clark, 2000), 3, 4. Compare Henk J. M. Schoot: "God is not transcendent in the sense that he needs a difference to be the unique one he is. God is not different within a certain genus, on the basis of a common similarity. . . . God is 'outside' of any genus, and thus God is not different from creatures the way in which creatures mutually differ. God differs differently. . . . Such an account undermines the opposition between transcendence and immanence, because God is not transcendent in such a way that he is simply 'outside of' or 'above' the world, and thus not transcendent in such a way that it would exclude his 'descent' into the world." Schoot, *Christ the 'Name' of God: Thomas Aquinas on Naming Christ* (Leuven: Peeters, 1993), 144–45. See also Karl Barth, *Church Dogmatics*, trans. Geoffrey W. Bromiley and Thomas F. Torrance, IV/1 (Edinburgh: T&T Clark, 1958), 186–87.

God's sustenance and gracious approach toward us in Jesus Christ do not happen through some intervening "gap" between God and creation (as some cosmologies suggest) but rather as a result of God's own "space" toward the world, the space that *is* God-toward-us, God-for-us, God's own dynamic, triune depth, his eternally coming-forthness. *Resonant order*: God not only allows the created world "room" but establishes it in its very otherness, augmenting it in its distinctive particularity through engaging intensely with it.

Accordingly, working from a center in the Triune God's self-disclosure entails refusing to imagine God's infinity simply in terms of the absence of limits, according to a prior model of infinitely extended (immaterial) substance (which is to posit God in relation to other things in places, namely, "beyond" them). God encompasses and permeates all things, carrying them to their goal. Some consider the work of Gregory of Nyssa (ca. 335–ca. 394) especially significant here,[62] insofar as he demonstrates the dangers of applying creaturely extensive terms to God and of supposing a univocity of being with regard to God and the world, and inasmuch as he offers a positive vision of infinity (which includes a kind of "extension") arising from the trinitarian liveliness of the God who is unconditionally and actively committed to the created world. For Gregory,

> the God who is infinite and no being among beings is also the personal God of election and incarnation, the dynamic, living, and creative God he is, precisely because being is not a genus whereunder God as "a being" might be subsumed, but is the act through which beings are given form by the God who is never without form and beauty.[63]

The transcendence of one tone or chord over another (say, of a fundamental over its first overtone) is the transcendence of irreducible difference, certainly, but a difference that brings life, abundance, fullness to the other tones. There is much to suggest that only within some such musical-conceptual context will the extensive language of quantity, measure, "greater than," and so forth find its proper place in discussions of divine infinity.[64]

None of this is to suggest that every dilemma and difficulty regarding the Creator-creation relation can be instantly or wholly resolved through engaging

---

62. Shults, *Reforming the Doctrine of God*, 101–2; David Bentley Hart, *The Beauty of the Infinite: The Aesthetics of Christian Truth* (Grand Rapids: Eerdmans, 2003), 235–36.

63. Hart, *Beauty of the Infinite*, 235.

64. It is important not to favor a qualitative *as opposed to* a quantitative understanding of infinity. Because God's being is a differentiated triune life, we may properly employ the extensive language of quantity to God, which itself relies on the notion of "place." See Hart, *Beauty of the Infinite*, 235.

musical phenomena, but it is to say that some of the perceived problems will be shown to be pseudo-problems, some of them will prove to be far less intractable than initially thought, and many can be recast in forms that lead to far greater understanding.

Agency in Concord

Similar things can be said with regard to divine and human agency and to interhuman agency. As with transcendence and immanence, little is to be gained from attempting to secure some perilous equipoise between divine and human agency (as if both belonged to the same causal system), just as there would be little point in speaking of the sympathetic resonance of a tone with another as a phenomenon of "balance." Nor need we assume univocity of predication, as if God's agency and human agency had to be understood as basically of the same ontological category, occupying different zones in the same space, with the resulting tendency to set them in competitive opposition. Creaturely dependence on God cannot be understood in the terms appropriate to visually perceptible objects. Karl Rahner writes:

> The relation between God and creature is characterized, precisely in contrast to any causal independence otherwise met within the world, by the fact that self-possession and independence increase in direct, not in inverse proportion.[65]

Kathryn Tanner thus speaks of God's "creative agency":[66] God liberating human particularity through direct engagement such that we are enabled to live according to the liveliness intended for us, the specific form of our intended resonance of life with God. Saving faith is not thereby rendered void, nor need it be regarded as the act of some supposedly wholly unconstrained will, but rather as being enabled by God to participate, through the resonating agency of the Spirit, in God's own resonance. Such *is* human freedom.

We hardly need spell out the consequences of this for thinking through the church's corporate freedom, where we are freed *by* the other *for* the other and, in this manner, find (against our expectations and self-willed desires) our God-intended resonant space. Freedom is never possession but always gift, not the result of individual choices but graciously bestowed. And we might add

65. Karl Rahner, *Encyclopedia of Theology: The Concise Sacramentum Mundi* (New York: Seabury Press, 1975), 598. In another place, Rahner speaks of the tendency in some quarters to presume that God can only "become greater and more real by the devaluation and cancellation of the creature." Karl Rahner, *Theological Investigations*, vol. 1 (Baltimore: Helicon Press, 1961), 188.

66. Tanner, *God and Creation*, chap. 2.

that understanding freedom in this way is by no means to exclude or belittle the agency of God in and through others in the body of Christ who shape human agency and enhance our freedom: "Other agents may *affect* human agency, but it is God who *effects* it, who constitutes its effectiveness."[67]

To expand the point: constraints, far from being the enemy of freedom, are in fact its condition, notwithstanding the obvious but crucial fact that some constraints are radically dehumanizing. Theologically, this means that no adequate account of freedom can be given *except* by speaking of the loving constraints of the Creator for the creature, the constraints of our physical embeddedness and finitude, and the ecclesial constraints of the body of Christ. Denial of constraint is a denial of our humanness.[68]

Is this not the kind of environment in which we should set the classic debates about "free response" in relation to divine grace? In his introduction to a collection of essays on divine and human agency in the writings of the apostle Paul, John Barclay notes the need to "unthink" some of our presuppositions.[69] With Paul's writings in mind, he asks:

Is it helpful to frame [divine and human agency] in terms of chronological anteriority, or is the placement of one agency "within" the other a better metaphor? It appears that human agency is the *necessary expression* of the life of the Spirit, and certainly not its antithesis; the two are not mutually exclusive as if in some zero-sum calculation.

He continues:

Everything depends on how one conceives the "human agent" reconstituted in Christ. Although in one sense we may speak properly of a "dual agency," in

67. John M. G. Barclay, "Introduction," in *Divine and Human Agency in Paul and His Cultural Environment*, ed. John M. G. Barclay and Simon J. Gathercole (London: T&T Clark, 2006), 1–8, here 7.

68. For further discussion, see Jeremy S. Begbie, *Theology, Music and Time* (Cambridge: Cambridge University Press, 2000), 198–245. "Nothing could be more misleading than the popular philosophy that freedom is constituted by the absence of limits. There is, to be sure, a truth which it intends to recognize, which is that the 'potency' of freedom requires 'possibility' as its object. . . . Where the popular philosophy becomes so misleading is in its suggestion that we can maximize freedom by multiplying the number of possibilities open to us. For if possibilities are to be meaningful for free choice, they must be well-defined by structures of limit." Oliver O'Donovan, *Resurrection and Moral Order: An Outline for Evangelical Ethics* (Leicester: Inter-Varsity Press, 1994), 107. Understanding authentic freedom "requires not only belief that we possess an actual nature, which must flourish to be free, but a belief in the transcendent Good towards which that nature is oriented. . . . We are free not because we can choose, but only when we have chosen well." Hart, *In the Aftermath*, 79.

69. Barclay, "Introduction," 4.

non-exclusive relation, this would be inadequately expressed as the co-operation or conjunction of two agents, or as the relationship of gift and response, if it is thereby forgotten that the "response" continues to be activated by grace, and the believers' agency *embedded within* that of the Spirit.[70]

We recall the distinction between covenant and contract. Whereas a contract is an arrangement whereby conditions are fulfilled by two parties in order to secure certain ends such that each party occupies his or her own active "space," a covenant (whether bilateral or unilateral) is driven by an unconditional commitment that goes not just halfway, so to speak, but "all the way" to engage and "embrace" the space of the other. Reconciliation, the New Testament's *katallage*, finds its concentrated depth in the incarnate Son's journey into that far country of our entrapment, wholly identifying, *as* the eternal Son, with our predicament. This is the enfleshment of God in the midst of our dissonance, a reaching-forth of the Triune God, that is not satisfied with some midpoint but spans and encompasses the *total* divine-human "space" such that, through Christ's dying and rising, a radically new divine-human resonance can be established, so that we, "embedded" in the Spirit's agency, might be retuned to the one he knows and calls "Abba."

This notion of the resonant interpenetration of agencies can of course be extended to interpersonal agency. Paul's vision of the church in 1 Corinthians 12 as both one and many—to cite just one pertinent text—is not that of a mosaic of bounded places in which the whole is simply the sum of the parts, still less an aggregation of interest groups self-protected against the encroachment of others, nor—the chronic tendency of many Western churches—a homogenous mass in which all diversity has been effectively wiped out in the name of "oneness," but rather a diverse body of mutually resonating members, in which, through an ex-centric dynamic set in motion by the Spirit, particularity is established, sustained, and enabled to flourish just *as* persons are united in fellowship.[71]

70. John M. G. Barclay, "'By the Grace of God I Am What I Am': Grace and Agency in Philo and Paul," in *Divine and Human Agency in Paul and His Cultural Environment*, ed. John M. G. Barclay and Simon J. Gathercole (London: T&T Clark, 2006), 140–58, here 156 (italics original).

71. In his prison writings, Dietrich Bonhoeffer employs the model of polyphony with regard to the relation between our love for God and our other, earthly affections; he also uses it to speak of the divine and the human in Christ, alluding to Chalcedon. These thoughts are not developed systematically, but there can be little doubt that he is intuitively sensing the theologically possibilities of drawing on the "interpenetrating" and mutually animating character of multivoiced music. Dietrich Bonhoeffer, *Letters and Papers from Prison* (London: SCM, 1972), 302–3. For discussion, see Jeremy S. Begbie, *Resounding Truth: Christian Wisdom in the World of Music* (Grand Rapids: Baker Academic, 2007), 160–62. A case could be made to the effect that Bonhoeffer had realized some of the potentially distorting consequences of visual-spatial

Christological Counterpoint

All of this bears very obviously on Christology. Indeed, it is precisely a failure to think out of a center in the christological redemption of the space-time order that accounts for so many endemic hindrances in this field.[72] With musical conceptuality, our tendency to regard divine and human agency in Christ as inherently opposed, and the somewhat questionable Christologies proposed to deal with the supposed opposition, will be less likely to take hold. We will be more capable of conceiving the person of Christ not as the Son entering a finite receptacle but as the co-presence of God's space and the space of the creation: the Son sharing created space while yet remaining the Father's eternal Son and thus primordially inhabiting God's eternal trinitarian space. We will begin to be more alert to the dangers of regarding the relation between the incarnate Son and the Father according to the determinants of visual, tangible, measurable space (the earthly Christ "here" in our space and the Father "there" in God's space), more inclined to preserve the kind of "in-one-anotherness" of Son and Father evoked in John's Gospel.[73] We will also perhaps be less inclined to think in terms of maintaining an uneasy equilibrium or negotiating some kind of give-and-take compromise between the divine Son and the humanity he assumes, and more disposed to think in terms of the interpenetrating resonance of God's agency and human agency, the latter achieving its freedom by being embedded in the freedom of the former.[74]

To press this a little further, the "divine nature" could well be explicated in terms of the incarnate Son in full reciprocal resonance with his Father, enabled through the agency of the Spirit and now interpenetrating our space so as to be made accessible and available to us. Likewise with respect to Christ's "human nature": in the incarnate Son our assumed humanity has been liberated by the Spirit to resonate with the Father, our privilege being to participate by the Spirit in this perfectly resonant response to the Father already made on

---

thought patterns (such as those entailed in the notion of the deus ex machina). See Lundin's comments in *Believing Again*, 206–10.

72. See the illuminating account of "double agency" in the work of Karl Barth in George Hunsinger, *How to Read Karl Barth: The Shape of His Theology* (New York: Oxford University Press, 1991), chap. 7. Against the charge that Barth's conception of divine sovereignty and human responsibility is incoherent (with its concern to hold asymmetry, intimacy, and integrity together), Hunsinger highlights the christological configuration of Barth's mind on the matter: "Barth's account of fellowship in particular and of divine and human agency in general cannot possibly be understood unless it is seen that this conception falls within the terms of the Chalcedonian pattern." Hunsinger, *How to Read Karl Barth*, 185.

73. I owe the phrase "in-one-anotherness" to my former colleague Richard Bauckham.

74. For an illuminating discussion along these lines (that draws on Zuckerkandl), see Colin E. Gunton, *Yesterday and Today: A Study of Continuities in Christology* (London: Darton, Longman & Todd, 1983), chap. 6, esp. 111–19.

our behalf. In these ways—answering the common complaint that Chalcedon lacks trinitarian vigor—an enriched Chalcedonian imagination is released, one that can arguably follow through the New Testament's christological and trinitarian momentum more fully and faithfully.

Trinitarian Soundings

We have journeyed into trinitarian territory. And this is hardly surprising, since the doctrines of transcendence and immanence, divine and human agency, and Christology all presuppose God's trinitarian "space" as their implicit grammar.

It is almost routine in current theology to argue that the theological dilemmas and quandaries concerning freedom we have identified have arisen through a lack of attention to God's triunity; less common are analyses of patterns of thinking that have generated or exacerbated the problems in the first place or proposals for more effective alternatives. What could be more appropriate than to conceptualize and articulate God's triunity in terms suggested by hearing a three-note chord—that is, as a resonance of life-in-three, with the three reciprocally interpenetrating, without exclusion yet without merger, irreducibly distinct yet together constituting the one divine space; the life of each "coming forth" and "going toward" the others; each animating, establishing, and enhancing the others in their particularity?[75] It is hard to read Zuckerkandl's account of listening to a three-note chord without also hearing harmonies of trinitarian doctrine:

> Three tones sound. In each of them space encounters us and we encounter space. None of them is in a place; or better, they are all in the same place,

---

75. Clearly, applying spatial language to God's immanent life requires considerable caution. For very good reasons, much of the Christian tradition has insisted on affirming the nonspatiality (and nontemporality) of God. However, I am inclined to side with Murray Rae's recent and highly nuanced treatment of the issue. Rae is fully aware of the dangers of conceptual moves that result in a projection of the creaturely spatiality into the divine (for example, arguing that if "Jesus exists in creaturely space . . . there must be some kind of analogy of creaturely spaciousness that belongs to the being of God himself"). But he nevertheless proposes (with Barth, but against John Webster and Ian Mackenzie) that we may legitimately speak of God possessing his own space, on the basis of "the differentiation of the persons of the Trinity, revealed in the economy as belonging to the being of God himself." Rae, "The Spatiality of God," in *Trinitarian Theology after Barth*, ed. Myk Habets and Phillip Tolliday (Eugene, OR: Wipf & Stock, 2011), 70–86, 78. God's antecedent, trinitarian differentiation is the ontological condition of God's differentiation from creation and a condition of all differentiation between creaturely entities. "Space" is being conceived here preeminently out of a center in God's own space, not according to a notion of "space" imported from elsewhere. In this essay, my methodological intention is similar: I have no wish to let music provide an *a priori* conception of space to which a theology of freedom is then expected to conform. Rather, music can offer a mode of clarification and correction to a theology that seeks to be primarily oriented and conformed to the self-disclosure of God's own trinitarian "space."

namely, everywhere. . . . Simultaneously sounding tones do not run together into a mixed tone. No difference of places keeps them apart; yet they remain audible as different tones. . . . The tones connected in the triad sound *through one another* . . . or let us say that they interpenetrate one another.[76]

Conclusion

I have pursued one main line of argument in an effort to demonstrate the fruitfulness of drawing on the conceptuality and language of musical perception for reconfiguring the way we commonly theologize human freedom. Clearly, many caveats are in order. For example, in the case of the mutual resonance of two strings, we are speaking of two objects belonging to the same ontological class, something obviously not applicable to the Creator-creature relation. Further, we need to be wary of an indiscriminate reduction of all relations to the same type or level—an undoubted danger amid the current vogue for "relationality" evident in some theological quarters.[77] The intratrinitarian relations, the relation of human and divine in the hypostatic union, the relation between Christ and the church, between persons in the church—all of these need to be carefully differentiated. The trinitarian *perichoresis* cannot be mapped onto concrete human relations without substantial caution.[78] Nor

76. Zuckerkandl, *Sound and Symbol: Music and the External World*, 297, 298, 299. If this essay were expanded further, of course, we could explore much more fully the ways in which dynamic multivoiced music (such as a fugue) might help us develop aspects of trinitarian theology. See Jenson, *Systematic Theology*, 2:236; Jonathan P. Case, "The Music of the Spheres: Music and the Divine Life in George Steiner and Robert W. Jenson (Part II: Intersections)," *Crucible* 3, no. 2 (2011), http://www.ea.org.au/Crucible/Issues/Past-Issues/Vol-3-No-2-September-2011.aspx.

77. For discussion of these matters, see John C. Polkinghorne, ed., *The Trinity and an Entangled World: Relationality in Physical Science and Theology* (Grand Rapids: Eerdmans, 2010).

78. For strong exhortations to caution regarding *perichoresis*, see Oliver Crisp, "Problems with Perichoresis," *Tyndale Bulletin* 56 (2005): 118–40; Randall E. Otto and E. Randall, "The Use and Abuse of Perichoresis in Recent Theology," *Scottish Journal of Theology* 54, no. 3 (2001): 366–84. On the hazards of applying trinitarian relations to the church, see Mark Husbands, "The Trinity Is Not Our Social Program: Volf, Gregory and Barth," in *Trinitarian Theology for the Church: Scripture, Community, Worship*, ed. Daniel J. Treier and David Lauber (Downers Grove, IL: InterVarsity Press, 2009), 120–41.

In recent years, some have voiced strong concerns about the language of "participation" or "sharing" (*koinonia*) used of our redeemed relation to the Triune God, fearing (among other things) that it will lead to a compromising of the Creator/creature distinction, the priority of God's covenantal action, and the necessity of the cross. See, e.g., John Webster, "The Church and the Perfection of God," in *The Community of the Word: Toward an Evangelical Ecclesiology*, ed. Mark Husbands and Daniel J. Treier (Downers Grove, IL: InterVarsity Press, 2005), 75–95, 80–87. Bruce L. McCormack, "What's at Stake in Current Debates over Justification?," in *Justification: What's at Stake in the Current Debates*, ed. Mark Husbands and Daniel J. Treier (Downers Grove, IL: InterVarsity Press, 2004), 81–117. Properly qualified, however, I see no compelling

can the infinite freedom of the Triune God be compared to humans' finite freedom without considerable qualification.[79] Also, due attention needs to be given to the asymmetry of the God-human relation, the precedence and priority of God, not least because of the peril of sliding back into treating divine and human agency as two agents on the same level. And of course we have said little about sin, evil, and the cross—the related theme of dissonance would require extensive discussion if this were to be expanded. Further still, vibrating strings are clearly not persons or agents, even if perceiving them may serve to release us from thinking or speaking of God's agency as a form of impersonal efficient causation, or of grace as subpersonal substance, or of divine personhood as separable from divine action.

It is also worth bearing in mind that for the purposes of our argument we have been abstracting an experience of musical sound from what is always in practice a constellation of experiences, multisensual and multimedia, involving far more than hearing and far more than the musical sounds themselves; music is always experienced along with sights and smells, memories and hopes, passions and politics. And, of course, we have been abstracting "thinking about" music from its concrete enactment. Any sequel to our discussion would need to consider the implications for the way the church, for example, actually uses music in its worship and witness.

Notwithstanding all this, however, the central contention of this essay still, I believe, stands: namely, that musical perception can yield quite distinctive and highly fruitful resources for reshaping the way we commonly think about and articulate human freedom, resources that directly address and sometimes significantly alleviate numerous dilemmas that have profoundly shaped both modernity's and modern theology's construction of freedom, both within and outside the church. Attending to the phenomenology of musical perception

---

reason to abandon the language of participation as an appropriate way of conveying at least one dimension of the meaning of *koinonia*. And musical interpenetration, along with generative or sympathetic resonance (where one sounding body is definitely primary), may have much to offer in offsetting the anxieties expressed about the concept. We saw earlier the importance of understanding human agency not in terms of a self-generated and self-sustained response to an extrinsic divine action but as being drawn into the trinitarian initiative of grace, enacted in the Son and now available to us through the agency of the Spirit. Our response, accordingly, is a sharing in Christ's response on our behalf, in the power of the Spirit, and in such a way that its distinctiveness, its particularity, is not effaced but brought to fulfillment. For a recent and highly nuanced treatment of these and related themes, see J. Canlis, *Calvin's Ladder: A Spiritual Theology of Ascent and Ascension* (Grand Rapids: Eerdmans, 2010).

79. See, e.g., Bauckham, *God and the Crisis of Freedom*, 198–209; and the illuminating essay by Brian Hebblethwaite, "Finite and Infinite Freedom in Farrer and von Balthasar," in *Human and Divine Agency: Anglican, Catholic, and Lutheran Perspectives*, ed. F. Michael McLain and W. Mark Richardson (Lanham, MD: University Press of America, 1999), 83–96.

can not only assist us in circumventing many of these difficulties; it can also substantially deepen and extend our apprehension of freedom in the process. This is not, of course, to suggest or imply that engagement with music resolves every theological predicament relating to freedom. Still less is it to imply that inasmuch as music could contribute to theology it would reduce or defuse what ought to remain a mystery. Our intention is quite the opposite: at its best, by eliciting more fully the dynamics of, say, the realization of our freedom as we participate in the infinite freedom of God, engagement with music can render that mystery all the more resistant to reductionist strategies that rob those dynamics of their true depth, power, and wonder.

Before we close, two additional points are worth making. First, at the risk of underlining the obvious, spatial thought and language are unavoidable in theology.[80] Despite a distinct move away from spatiality in some theological quarters in recent times—a strong attraction to narrative and drama is especially noticeable, for example—spatial concepts and discourse are inescapable, not least because they pervade Scripture. The question is not *whether* we employ spatial modes of thinking and speaking but rather *what we are investing in them*, what we imagine is being delivered by them and through them. Engaging with music may mean that we come to hear far *less* in our spatial language and thought—and it may also mean that we hear far *more*.

Second, some will suspect that my argument is designed to provide further fuel for the habitual denigration of all things visual that is often thought to belong to the lifeblood of Protestantism. Or, on a wider front, some might imagine a wholesale support for a line of argument found in much writing in recent years that points to a widespread and damaging dominance of visuality in Western culture at large, indeed a hegemony that has led, some claim, to various forms of alienation, control, and normalization ("ocularcentrism," or what Marie-José Mondzain has called "optocracy").[81]

80. "It is simply impossible for me to form a spatial conception of Heaven and Hell. . . . But the imagination can function only spatially; without space the imagination is like a child who wants to build a palace and has no blocks." Czesław Miłosz, Bogdana Carpenter, and Madeline G. Levine, eds., *To Begin Where I Am: Selected Essays* (New York: Farrar, Straus & Giroux, 2001), 320.

81. Marie-José Mondzain, *Image, Icon, Economy: The Byzantine Origins of the Contemporary Imaginary* (Stanford, CA: Stanford University Press, 2005), 162. See, e.g., Martin Jay, *Downcast Eyes: The Denigration of Vision in Twentieth-Century French Thought* (Berkeley: University of California Press, 1994); David Michael Kleinberg-Levin, *Modernity and the Hegemony of Vision* (Berkeley: University of California Press, 1993); Kleinberg-Levin, *The Philosopher's Gaze: Modernity in the Shadows of Enlightenment* (Berkeley: University of California Press, 1999); Alain Corbin, *Time, Desire, and Horror: Towards a History of the Senses* (Cambridge: Polity Press, 1995); Walter J. Ong, *Ramus, Method, and the Decay of Dialogue: From the Art of Discourse to the Art of Reason* (Cambridge, MA: Harvard University Press, 1983); Chris

It would certainly be fascinating to explore this literature on visuality (vis-à-vis Protestantism and beyond) alongside the kind of contrast between visual and musical-sonic perception I have elaborated above. But for the moment, three comments will need to suffice. First, to assume that a comprehensive opposition to all things visual lies at the core of Protestantism is unsupportable; the intense visual sensibility of the Protestant tradition has by now been well established, and the issues surrounding its suspicion of images are far more varied, multileveled, and nuanced than is often supposed.[82] Second, my purpose has been not to exalt one sense at the expense of another (that would be yet another misguided zero-sum game) but rather to show that an overreliance on, or overdetermination by, one sensory mode may well encourage, perhaps even engender, certain habits of thought and language that theology could well do without. Third, I am inclined to think that in the years to come theology will have to develop a richer and subtler approach to the relation between different sensory modes, media, and art forms than has been noticeable to date. In a perceptive essay, Ben Quash comments on Hans Urs von Balthasar's stress on the "polyphonic" texture of Scripture:

> All [its] genres are valuable. Each has its own surplus of meaning to contribute to the others. Each genre will have particular strengths at opening up and exploring particular aspects of reality. Each will have a particular range and depth of penetration. Thus the theologian who has the ability to command a wide set of genres will find his or her capacity to conceptualize, to interpret, and to participate in the life of the Christian community and the wider world, enriched in consequence.[83]

Much the same could be said of different modes of sense perception and associated art forms. Of course, to suggest *a priori* that all art forms or

---

Jenks, "The Centrality of the Eye in Western Culture: An Introduction," in *Visual Culture* (London: Routledge, 1995), 1–25; Robert Paul Doede and Paul Edward Hughes, "Wounded Vision and the Optics of Hope," in *The Future of Hope: Christian Tradition amid Modernity and Postmodernity*, ed. Miroslav Volf and William H. Katerberg (Grand Rapids: Eerdmans, 2004), 170–99. From a somewhat extreme theological perspective, see Jacques Ellul, *The Humiliation of the Word* (Grand Rapids: Eerdmans, 1985); far more measured are the perceptive comments of Roger Lundin in *Believing Again*, 193–210.

82. See, e.g., William A. Dyrness, *Reformed Theology and Visual Culture: The Protestant Imagination from Calvin to Edwards* (Cambridge: Cambridge University Press, 2004); David Morgan, *Protestants and Pictures: Religion, Visual Culture and the Age of American Mass Production* (New York: Oxford University Press, 1999); Christopher R. Joby, *Calvinism and the Arts: A Re-assessment* (Leuven: Peeters, 2007).

83. Ben Quash, "Real Enactment: The Role of Drama in the Theology of Hans Urs von Balthasar," in *Faithful Performances: Enacting Christian Tradition*, ed. Trevor A. Hart and Steven R. Guthrie (Aldershot, UK: Ashgate, 2007), 13–32, here 28.

sensory modes must be accorded equal weight and value in theology would be disingenuous. We cannot decide this sort of thing in advance. In response to the frequent calls today for a "recovery" of the visual (or perhaps the aural) in churches, it is worth asking: "Why? On what theological grounds?" In any case, the senses invariably operate by implicating one another in highly complex ways, and many art forms are experienced along with other art forms and perceived with different senses simultaneously. (Most of the images that bombard a teenager today come with sound, for example, despite all that is said about ours being a "visual" culture.) The challenge, then, is not to set this or that sense (or art form) on a pedestal but to cultivate an alertness to the distinctive theological capacities and limitations of each, with a view to each making its own particular contribution to the enrichment of Christian life and thought, alert to the ways they can and do interact with one another.

Having said all this, I think it appropriate that we end by returning to the main thread of the essay and quote a delicious evocation of the powers of musical sound. In Peter Shaffer's play *Amadeus*, Mozart bubbles over with enthusiasm to Emperor Joseph II about his new opera, *The Marriage of Figaro*:

> MOZART: I have a scene in the second act—it starts as a duet, just a man and wife quarrelling. Suddenly the wife's scheming little maid comes in unexpectedly—a very funny situation. Duet turns into trio. Then the husband's equally screaming valet comes in. Trio turns into quartet. Then a stupid old gardener—quartet becomes quintet, and so on. On and on, sextet, septet, octet! How long do you think I can sustain that?
>
> JOSEPH: I have no idea.
>
> MOZART: Guess! Guess, Majesty. Imagine the longest time such a thing could last, then double it.
>
> JOSEPH: Well, six or seven minutes! maybe eight!
>
> MOZART: Twenty, sire! How about twenty? Twenty minutes of continuous music. No recitatives.
>
> VON SWIETEN: Mozart—
>
> MOZART: [ignoring him] Sire, only opera can do this. In a play, if more than one person speaks at the same time, it's just noise. No one can understand a word. But with music, with music you can have twenty individuals all talking at once, and it's not noise—it's a perfect harmony.[84]

---

84. Peter Shaffer, *Amadeus* (play), http://www.dailyscript.com/scripts/amadeus.html.

9

The Future of Theology amid the Arts

Some Reformed Reflections

I have always been wary of championing one particular theological tradition too loudly, for fear of suggesting that there could be a time when we would cease to learn from others. The ecumenical exchange that marks the current theology and the arts scene is surely to be encouraged. At the same time, it does little good to be overly modest about streams of wisdom familiar to us that may in fact be badly needed—to refresh long-standing debates, perhaps, or redirect debates to resources easily overlooked. When I was invited to deliver a lecture as part of a Wheaton College series devoted to exploring the current interplay between faith and learning, I decided to highlight what I think are the strengths of a broadly Reformed or Calvinist outlook for engaging the arts theologically today, bearing in mind how frequently this tradition has been caricatured and scorned. Pulling material together for the lecture and the ensuing book chapter brought many surprises.

The ferment of "theology and the arts" shows no signs of waning. It burgeons in colleges, universities, and churches. Theological internet watchers observe

This chapter was originally published as Jeremy Begbie, "The Future of Theology Amid the Arts: Some Reformed Reflections," in *Christ Across the Disciplines: Past, Present, and Future*, ed. Roger Lundin, 152–82 (Grand Rapids: Eerdmans, 2013).

I am very grateful to Tanner Capps, David Taylor, Bo Helmich, Suzanne McDonald, Adrienne Dengerink Chaplin, Nicholas Wolterstorff, Kevin Vanhoozer, and James K. A. Smith for their valuable comments on earlier drafts of this essay.

its fast-expanding presence, and publishers are beginning to see it as a serious niche market. Here I want to home in on just one feature of this encouraging groundswell of interest, especially noticeable in recent years—what appears to be a distinct unease or awkwardness about Protestantism, especially of the Reformed variety. Undoubtedly it would be easy to exaggerate this, but I doubt if I am the only one to have had the sense at many gatherings that although Christians of this ilk are usually welcome at the table, the best they can do is catch up with the profounder and unquestionably more fruitful wisdom of others—which by and large means those of a Roman Catholic, Anglo-Catholic, or Eastern Orthodox persuasion.

The reasons are not hard to see. The weaknesses of the Reformed tradition have been regularly rehearsed: an exaggerated fear of idolatry, an excessive suspicion of the arts (a "frigid Philistinism"),[1] a tendency to distrust all images, a paucity of reflection on beauty, a frequent inability to take physicality seriously, and so on—the territory is familiar to any who explore the field. To be sure, much scholarship has questioned the caricatures and sought to provide more balanced perspectives.[2] But this has not prevented many in the Reformed stream, not least evangelicals, from assuming that the theological grass will be greener elsewhere—especially in modern Roman Catholic writing or in the pre-Reformation wisdom of Aquinas, Dionysius, or Augustine.

This eagerness to move outside one's camp is in many ways surely healthy. When I first put my toe in the Christianity and arts river in the early 1980s, I recall three main currents of writing were available: the Roman Catholic (drawing on Maritain, Rahner, and others), the liberal Protestant (looking especially to Tillich), and the Dutch Neo-Calvinist (Rookmaaker, Seerveld, with Wolterstorff sitting a little to one side). Serious dialogue among them seemed relatively rare. Today, the currents converse and mingle freely, often pulling others into the mix: nowadays artistic evangelicals are as likely to get their inspiration from Hans Urs von Balthasar and Henri de Lubac as they

---

1. I borrow the phrase from Trevor A. Hart, in his "Protestantism and Art," in *The Blackwell Companion to Protestantism*, ed. Alister E. Mcgrath and Darren C. Marks (Oxford: Blackwell, 2006), 268–86, here 268.

2. See, e.g., Paul Corby Finney, ed., *Seeing beyond the Word: Visual Arts and the Calvinist Tradition* (Grand Rapids: Eerdmans, 1999); William A. Dyrness, *Visual Faith: Art, Theology, and Worship in Dialogue* (Grand Rapids: Baker Books, 2001); Randall C. Zachman, *Image and Word in the Theology of John Calvin* (Notre Dame, IN: University of Notre Dame Press, 2007); Christopher R. Joby, *Calvinism and the Arts: A Re-Assessment* (Leuven: Peeters, 2007); David Vandrunen, "Iconoclasm, Incarnation and Eschatology: Toward a Catholic Understanding of the Reformed Doctrine of the 'Second' Commandment," *International Journal of Systematic Theology* 6, no. 2 (2004): 130–47; Belden C. Lane, *Ravished by Beauty: The Surprising Legacy of Reformed Spirituality* (Oxford: Oxford University Press, 2011).

are from Rookmaaker or Seerveld.[3] This crisscrossing of perspectives has undoubtedly borne immense fruit. However, amid the ecumenical conviviality I am inclined to think that shame about parts of the Reformed inheritance has been overplayed, and that the riches this tradition can hold before the wider church with regard to the arts are too easily overlooked. Indeed, I believe that in some respects this tradition is sorely needed in the present conversations.

This is not, of course, to imply that the critical wisdom in this area belongs solely to the Reformed churches or that its traits and concerns are wholly absent elsewhere. In any case, the tradition itself is hugely complex and varied. I harbor no assumptions about being able to identify a single monolithic Reformed theology and have no interest in defending all that has emerged within the tradition. (It may be worth noting that I have never been a member of a Presbyterian or centrally Reformed church or denomination.) Still less am I interested in shoring up what some would say is a waning Protestantism in our culture. I am concerned rather with certain casts of mind—conceptual concerns and strategies, especially insofar as they arise from close attention to the theological dimensions of biblical texts—that are more typical of the Reformed tradition than any other and that I believe deserve to be heard in the current debates. If, as some think, we have witnessed a modest resurgence of interest in "Calvinism" (in the United States at least),[4] perhaps that can provoke us to ask whether some of these casts of mind might have more to offer the current conversations about faith and art than has often been supposed. In this connection, a remark of Trevor Hart's about the relevance of strands of Reformation thinking is worth quoting:

> In an age where, for many, aesthetic experience has effectively substituted itself for religious faith as a perceived window onto "spiritual" realities . . . we may find that Reformation perspectives possess a curious freshness, reminding us of things which some theological approaches to art (not least some in the Protestant tradition) appear to have forgotten or broken faith with.[5]

3. For one account of the "state of play" in theology and the arts (as in 2007), see William A. Dyrness, "The Arts," in *The Oxford Handbook of Systematic Theology*, ed. John B. Webster, Kathryn Tanner, and Iain R. Torrance (Oxford: Oxford University Press, 2007), 561–79.

4. *Time* magazine has described New Calvinism as one of "10 Ideas Changing the World Right Now." David Van Biema, "The New Calvinism," *Time Magazine Online* (March 12, 2009), http://www.time.com/time/specials/packages/article/0,28804,1884779_1884782_1884760,00 .html. See also Collin Hansen, *Young, Restless, Reformed: A Journalist's Journey with the New Calvinists* (Wheaton: Crossway Books, 2008). Whether this represents a major shift or movement is a moot point. James K. A. Smith, "Barna Report on the 'New Calvinism,'" *Fors Clavigera* (blog), November 16, 2010, http://forsclavigera.blogspot.com/2010/11/barna-report -on-new-calvinism.html.

5. Hart, "Protestantism and Art," 270.

I want to explore this "curious freshness" with respect to some key elements of the Reformed heritage. To structure the discussion, I will focus on just three areas of interest I find prominent in much contemporary writing about theology and the arts, at popular, semipopular, and academic levels: beauty, sacrament, and language.

The Allure of Beauty

After seasons of exile, the theme of beauty seems to be enjoying something of a comeback. In artistic circles, there are signs of an energetic interest, and the philosophical world has seen a steady stream of studies.[6] Among theologians it is proving ever more popular. Impatient with what Edward Farley calls "the new problematic of beauty" engendered in particular by the eighteenth century's "relocation of beauty from an external property to a human sensibility,"[7] many want to reinstate beauty by speaking of it as integral to the created world and indeed to the identity of God.[8] Hence the appeal of Balthasar's theological aesthetics, of Augustine and Aquinas on beauty,[9] and

6. See, e.g., Elaine Scarry, *On Beauty and Being Just* (Princeton: Princeton University Press, 1999); Bill Beckley and David Shapiro, *Uncontrollable Beauty: Toward a New Aesthetics* (New York: Allworth Press, 1998); Arthur C. Danto, *The Abuse of Beauty: Aesthetics and the Concept of Art* (Chicago: Open Court, 2003); Glenn Parsons and Allen Carlson, eds., *Functional Beauty* (Oxford: Oxford University Press, 2008); Roger Scruton, *Beauty* (Oxford: Oxford University Press, 2009); Brett Ashley Kaplan, *Unwanted Beauty: Aesthetic Pleasure in Holocaust Representation* (Urbana: University of Illinois Press, 2007); Alexander Nehamas, "The Return of the Beautiful: Morality, Pleasure, and the Value of Uncertainty," *Journal of Aesthetics and Art Criticism* 58, no. 4 (2000): 393–403; Nehamas, *Only a Promise of Happiness: The Place of Beauty in a World of Art* (Princeton: Princeton University Press, 2007).

7. Edward Farley, *Faith and Beauty: A Theological Aesthetic* (Aldershot, UK: Ashgate, 2001), 33.

8. See, e.g., Bruno Forte, *The Portal of Beauty: Towards a Theology of Aesthetics* (Grand Rapids: Eerdmans, 2008); Richard Harries, *Art and the Beauty of God: A Christian Understanding* (London: Mowbray, 2000); David Bentley Hart, *The Beauty of the Infinite: The Aesthetics of Christian Truth* (Grand Rapids: Eerdmans, 2003); John Milbank, Graham Ward, and Edith Wyschogrod, *Theological Perspectives on God and Beauty* (Harrisburg, PA: Trinity Press International, 2003); Aidan Nichols, *Redeeming Beauty: Soundings in Sacral Aesthetics* (Aldershot, UK: Ashgate, 2007); Patrick Sherry, *Spirit and Beauty: An Introduction to Theological Aesthetics* (London: SCM, 2002); Daniel J. Treier, Mark Husbands, and Roger Lundin, eds., *The Beauty of God: Theology and the Arts* (Downers Grove, IL: InterVarsity Press Academic, 2007); Richard Viladesau, *The Beauty of the Cross: The Passion of Christ in Theology and the Arts from the Catacombs to the Eve of the Renaissance* (Oxford: Oxford University Press, 2005); Viladesau, *Theological Aesthetics: God in Imagination, Beauty, and Art* (New York: Oxford University Press, 1999), chap. 4.

9. See, e.g., John Milbank, "Beauty and the Soul," in *Theological Perspectives on God and Beauty*, ed. John Milbank, Graham Ward, and Edith Wyschogrod (Harrisburg, PA: Trinity Press International, 2003), 1–34; Carol Harrison, "Taking Creation for the Creator: Use and

the increasing fascination with Jacques Maritain.[10] Along with this often goes an almost immediate association of the arts with beauty—to care about the arts, it is assumed, is to care about beauty, and vice versa.

To call any of this into question might seem odd, even bizarre—especially in a culture so obviously in need of beauty, and at a time when Protestant Christians habitually neglect beauty in favor of the other two "transcendentals," truth and goodness. Nevertheless, I believe it is worth sending some friendly warning shots across the bow of this fashionable theological steamer. The first is a formal point about the assumed mutual entailment of beauty and the arts. It may well be that beauty (variously defined) can and should be considered a desirable quality in the arts. But to suppose that the presence of or aspiration toward beauty is a necessary condition for something to be considered *as* art is much more debatable, as is the stronger view that the arts are to be distinguished from other cultural activities and products by their investment in beauty. It is not hard to think of exemplary art that most would not call beautiful (e.g., paintings by Max Beckman, Igor Stravinsky's *Le Sacre du Printemps*) and not hard to find a significant concern for beauty in other fields, say, in mathematical physics. Prior to the eighteenth century the links between what we now call the arts and beauty were not nearly as strong as is often presumed; certainly, this goes for most of the classic theologies of beauty. Thus I have a certain sympathy with Reformed philosopher Nicholas Wolterstorff when he questions an automatic correlation of art and beauty (and the cluster of ideas that tend to be associated with this correlation)[11] and with Calvin Seerveld, who is also strongly opposed to any necessary coupling of the two, from a Dutch Neo-Calvinist perspective.[12] Exercising a little caution here means we will be much more likely to notice that when

Enjoyment in Augustine's Theological Aesthetics," in *Idolatry: False Worship in the Bible, Early Judaism and Christianity*, ed. Stephen C. Barton (London: T&T Clark, 2007), 179–97.

10. Rowan Williams, *Grace and Necessity: Reflections on Art and Love* (London: Continuum, 2005); Matthew J. Milliner, "The New Maritainians," *Public Discourse* (website), May 14, 2010, http://www.thepublicdiscourse.com/2010/05/1307; John G. Trapani, *Poetry, Beauty, and Contemplation: The Complete Aesthetics of Jacques Maritain* (Washington, DC: Catholic University of America Press, 2011).

11. For Wolterstorff, "aesthetic excellence" is characterized by unity, internal richness, and "fittingness-intensity." He believes that beauty (which he understands in terms of proportion, consonance, brightness, and affording pleasure upon contemplation) is not the necessary and sufficient condition of aesthetic excellence. We judge many works of art as aesthetically excellent that we would not normally judge as beautiful—and still regard them as works of art. Nicholas Wolterstorff, *Art in Action: Toward a Christian Aesthetic* (Grand Rapids: Eerdmans, 1980), 156–74, esp. 161–63. Wolterstorff has amplified this considerably in *Art Rethought: The Social Practices of Art* (New York: Oxford University Press, 2015), esp. chap. 19.

12. Calvin Seerveld, *Rainbows for the Fallen World: Aesthetic Life and Artistic Task* (Toronto: Tuppence Press, 1980), 116–25.

Balthasar expounds a "theological aesthetics,"[13] he is principally concerned not with the arts (though he certainly engages the arts at length) but with beauty as a dimension of theology, or that when David Bentley Hart writes so eloquently about "aesthetics," he has in mind largely the beauty of God and God's creation (he makes only fleeting references to the arts).[14]

The second point concerns the controls shaping our concepts of beauty. The Reformed tradition is well known for its stress on the noetic effects of the fall, its insistence that sin does not rise to the neck and suddenly halt just below the cerebellum—it is urged that our conceptual categories require a continual re-formation by the Spirit to be conformed to the pattern of Christ, a reconfiguration that is internal to the dynamic of redemption. In this light, I suggest that if we *are* to speak of beauty as belonging to God and/or the created world and conceive it (provisionally at least) according to some version of the so-called great theory[15]—according to which beauty is characterized, for example, by proportion and consonance of parts, brightness or radiance, perfection or integrity, and as granting pleasure upon contemplation—the concept will need to be subject to a constant reshaping through the church's repeated return to God's reconciling self-disclosure.[16]

It is just this alertness to theological criteria grounded in the self-identification of God that should be borne in mind when reading the Reformed theologian Karl Barth on beauty.[17] Barth could not bring himself to speak of beauty as a "perfection" of God; beauty is rather the form of God's glory in his self-revelation, that about God's self-presentation which attracts rather

13. Hans Urs von Balthasar, *The Glory of the Lord: A Theological Aesthetics*, vol. 1, *Seeing the Form*, trans. Erasmo Leivà-Merikakis (Edinburgh: T&T Clark, 1982), 118.

14. Hart, *Beauty of the Infinite*.

15. See Wladyslaw Tatarkiewicz, "The Great Theory of Beauty and Its Decline," *Journal of Aesthetics and Art Criticism* 31 (1972): 165–80.

16. Balthasar properly insists that it is to the economy of salvation that we must go to discover God's beauty (and thus the ultimate measure of all beauty), since the incarnation, death, and raising of Jesus display God's love in its clearest and most decisive form; here, above all, we witness the mutual self-surrendering love of the Father and the Son in the Spirit for the healing of the world. He cautions that we "ought never to speak of God's beauty without reference to the form and manner of appearing which he exhibits in salvation-history." And later: "God's attribute of beauty can certainly . . . be examined in the context of a doctrine of the divine attributes. Besides examining God's beauty as manifested by God's actions in his creation, his beauty would also be deduced from the harmony of his essential attributes, and particularly from the Trinity. But such a doctrine of God and the Trinity really speaks to us only when and as long as the θεολογια does not become detached from the οικονομια, but rather lets its every formulation and stage of reflection be accompanied and supported by the latter's vivid discernibility." Balthasar, *Glory of the Lord*, 1:124, 125.

17. Karl Barth, *Church Dogmatics*, trans. Thomas F. Torrance and Geoffrey W. Bromiley, II/1 (Edinburgh: T&T Clark, 1970), 650–66.

than repels, which redeems, persuades, and convinces, evokes joy rather than indifference. If we judge him as overcautious, we should not do so without first heeding his anxiety about an "aestheticism" that would turn a preset notion of beauty into an absolute to which the God of Jesus Christ is expected to conform.[18]

In very compressed terms, then, we might propose that divine beauty be conceived as the form of love of the Son for the Father and the Father for the Son,[19] a dynamic self-surrender that implies neither merger nor homogeneity but the "distance" of love. Insofar as the Spirit is the personal unity of the mutual outgoingness of Father and Son, the impulse toward self-sharing in God's life, and the one who establishes particularity, we might cautiously describe the Spirit as the "beautifier" in God.[20] The integrity and proportion of God's beauty is the ceaseless self-giving of the Father to the Son and the Son to the Father in the ecstatic dynamism of the Spirit. Further, if Christ is the measure of God's beauty, then he is so also of creaturely beauty. Here—in the one conceived and empowered by the Spirit, born in a stable, hounded to a shameful death, vindicated by God on the third day, and exalted as a "spiritual body," the stuff of the earth made new—creation's beauty is brought to its culmination. Further still, it makes good sense to see the Spirit as related directly to the axis of attraction and longing, allure and desire, which seems integral to our perception of the radiance of both divine and created beauty.

What, then, of beauty and the arts? Even if we reject a *necessary* mutual entailment of the two, this does not mean rejecting the category of beauty (carefully qualified) as naming a *desideratum* in the arts. On this point, I limit myself to three comments, with the Reformed tradition especially in view.[21] First, a vision of beauty re-formed along the lines suggested above will celebrate the ability of the arts *to voice creation's praise*, and thus its beauty,

18. "We must be careful not to start from any preconceived ideas, especially in this case a preconceived idea of the beautiful. . . . God is not beautiful in the sense that he shares in an idea of beauty superior to him, so that to know it is to know him as God. On the contrary, it is as he is God that he is also beautiful, so that he is the basis and standard of everything that is beautiful and of all ideas of the beautiful." Barth, *Church Dogmatics* II/1, 656.
19. Undoubtedly, the Reformed luminary Jonathan Edwards (1703–1758) has a considerable amount to offer when accounting for beauty in trinitarian terms, whatever hesitations we may have about a Platonic seam in his thought. He writes of "primary beauty," whose chief instance is God's own triune benevolence, the mutual generosity and "infinite consent" that constitutes the life of God. Roland André Delattre, *Beauty and Sensibility in the Thought of Jonathan Edwards: An Essay in Aesthetics and Theological Ethics* (New Haven: Yale University Press, 1968), chaps. 7 and 8; Amy Plantinga Pauw, *The Supreme Harmony of All: The Trinitarian Theology of Jonathan Edwards* (Grand Rapids: Eerdmans, 2002), 80–85; Farley, *Faith and Beauty*, chap. 4.
20. For an exposition of the Spirit in relation to beauty, see Sherry, *Spirit and Beauty*.
21. For fuller treatment of these issues, see chaps. 1 and 2 in this book.

in its very createdness. This was another key concern of Barth, exemplified in his (doubtless inflated) adulation of Mozart. For Barth, Mozart's music embodies the ability of creation to praise its Creator, *as created*. This composer, he writes, "simply offered himself as the agent by which little bits of horn, metal and catgut could serve as the voices of creation."[22] In another place he says of Mozart:

> The sun shines but does not blind, does not burn or consume. Heaven arches over the earth, but it does not weigh it down, it does not crush or devour it. Hence *earth remains earth*, with no need to maintain itself in a titanic revolt against heaven.[23]

This is not a demeaning of creatureliness in the name of divine transcendence, as is so often thought;[24] the point is that creation fulfills its character precisely insofar as it *is* limited, not divine (yet fully real); its distinctive beauty and goodness are inseparable from its createdness.[25]

There is another dimension here worth highlighting. For Barth, Mozart enables creation's praise while still conceding that its beauty has been marred and corrupted. Some writers and artists broadly in the Reformed tradition have thus spoken of a "broken beauty,"[26] where the artistic evocation of beauty bears the marks of the world's tragedy that Christ has penetrated and healed at Golgotha. John Walford has shown how some seventeenth-century Dutch landscape painters portray the natural world in anything but idealized terms; here is a beauty that takes account of the marks of distortion (transience, decay, storm damage).[27] Ultimately such beauty can

22. Karl Barth, *Church Dogmatics*, trans. Geoffrey W. Bromiley and Thomas F. Torrance, III/3 (Edinburgh: T&T Clark, 1960), 298.

23. Karl Barth, *Wolfgang Amadeus Mozart*, trans. Clarence K. Pott (Grand Rapids: Eerdmans, 1986), 53 (italics mine).

24. Novelist John Updike remarks that Barth's insistence on God's Otherness "seemed to free him to be exceptionally (for a theologian) appreciative and indulgent of this world, the world at hand." John Updike, foreword to Barth, *Wolfgang Amadeus Mozart*, 7–12, here 7.

25. In a number of places I have attempted to outline a view of creativity that takes full account both of God's trinitarian agency and humans' full participation in that agency, and in such a way that created order is neither ignored nor abrogated but enabled to articulate fresh praise. See, e.g., Begbie, *Voicing Creation's Praise: Towards a Theology of the Arts* (Edinburgh: T&T Clark, 1991), 167–258; Begbie, *Resounding Truth: Christian Wisdom in the World of Music* (Grand Rapids: Baker Academic, 2007), chap. 8.

26. E. John Walford, "The Case for a Broken Beauty: An Art Historical Viewpoint," in Treier, Husbands, and Lundin, *Beauty of God*, 87–109. See also Theodore L. Prescott, *A Broken Beauty* (Grand Rapids: Eerdmans, 2005).

27. E. John Walford, *Jacob van Ruisdael and the Perception of Landscape* (New Haven: Yale University Press, 1991), chap. 4, esp. 99–100. In the course of a wide-ranging book, written from what he describes as a "Reformed" perspective, William A. Dyrness asks what "Reformed

be discerned and interpreted correctly only through the lens of the crucifixion. And this takes us to our second main comment about a re-formed
vision of beauty for the arts: insofar as it refuses to marginalize the cross
and all that is implicated there, it *spurns sentimentality*, any downplaying
of the moral corruption that threatens creation and creaturely activity.[28]
God's self-presentation in Christ intrudes starkly on all sanitized theologies
of beauty. Divine love speaks its most exalted word just *as* it plunges into
unspeakable degradation. In Christ's humiliation and execution, we witness
God's supreme self-revealing, the ultimate triumph over sin and death. God
enacts beauty *this* way.

Of course, Reformed thinkers are not the only ones to argue in this manner, and they have often failed to do so, despite the fact that many of their
theological distinctives strongly resist a sentimental ethos. From a Roman
Catholic perspective, for instance, Richard Viladesau has written along these
lines;[29] Balthasar has insisted that a theology of beauty can do no other than

---

Protestantism" can bring to a "poetic theology." Dyrness, *Poetic Theology: God and the Poetics of Everyday Life* (Grand Rapids: Eerdmans, 2011), chap. 6; see also p. 9. Following up his
belief that "a critical aesthetic category of a Protestant aesthetic is dramatic action," he writes
that Protestants have "inherited a particular aesthetic framework that is different from . . . that
of the Catholic and Orthodox traditions" (153). He speaks of three categories illuminating
this framework: "brokenness, hidden character, and the prophetic." The element of "brokenness" (166–73) is congruent with what I have been developing here. I am unclear about the
central meaning of "hiddenness" (173–77), since Dyrness includes such diverse things under
this umbrella—e.g., Calvin Seerveld's "allusiveness," Wolterstorff's "fittingness," and the way
in which art's beauty is often concealed. At times Dyrness's main point seems to be about simplicity, the way in which art hides its artifice. In any case, the third category, the "prophetic"
(177–80), alludes to a protest against the world's brokenness and to the way in which art
should "encourage viewers and hearers to reconstrue the pattern of their lives, to re-interpret
or *re-read* that pattern in accordance with the biblical truth, and, more importantly, to discern
their lives in accordance with what is seen and heard" (177, italics original). There is clearly an
eschatological dimension to this third category.

28. See chap. 2 above.

29. Viladesau, *Beauty of the Cross*; Richard Viladesau, *The Triumph of the Cross: The
Passion of Christ in Theology and the Arts from the Renaissance to the Counter-Reformation*
(Oxford: Oxford University Press, 2008); Viladesau, "The Beauty of the Cross," in *Theological Aesthetics after Von Balthasar*, ed. Oleg V. Bychkov and James Fodor (Aldershot,
UK: Ashgate, 2008), 135–51; Viladesau, "Theosis and Beauty," *Theology Today* 65 (2008):
180–90. He writes: "In Christ our understanding of the transcendental quality of beauty is
raised to a deeper and more inclusive level, one that embraces even what appears (from a
merely inner-worldly perspective) to be irrational, disordered, lacking in attractiveness and
goodness." He explains: "Though the other may not be beautiful, generous self-giving love
for the needy other is perceived by the eyes of faith as a (morally, spiritually) beautiful act
in the 'theo-drama' in which we are involved, a drama created by God's artistry." Viladesau,
"Theosis and Beauty," 188. (I am not entirely convinced, however, that the metaphysics Viladesau espouses in this and other writings is adequately focused and grounded to support this
vision.)

proceed by way of the cross;[30] and the celebrated composer James MacMillan has consistently sought to defy the seduction of sentimentality through resolute attention to the crucifixion.[31]

A third comment: a re-formed vision of beauty will *be charged with promise*. If the risen and exalted Christ prefigures the final re-creation of all things, then earthly beauty at its richest will share in that prefigurement. Reformed theologian Eberhard Jüngel writes: "The beautiful . . . carries within itself the *promise* of truth to come, a future *direct* encounter with the truth. . . . The beautiful is a *pre-appearance directed to a goal*."[32] The agent of this pre-appearance is the Holy Spirit, the evidence and guarantee of the glory yet to come. For a contemporary example of this in action, a recent sculpture from Mozambique comes to mind. It bears the title *The Tree of Life* and for a short time stood in the atrium of the British Museum in London. A tree grew in the garden of Eden but access was forbidden. In Revelation 22 the tree reappears, standing on each side of the river of the water of life that flows from God's throne, its leaves for the healing of the nations. This sculpted tree is constructed entirely from weapons reclaimed after Mozambique's civil war. We recall Isaiah's vision of peace: "They shall beat their swords into plowshares, and their spears into pruning hooks" (Isa. 2:4).[33]

The Power of Sacrament

The appeal to "sacrament," the "sacramental," and "sacramentality" abounds in the theology and arts arena of the last decade, especially in connection with the visual arts.[34] To conceive of the arts as in some sense sacramental

30. Balthasar asks: "How could we . . . understand the 'beauty' of the Cross without the abysmal darkness into which the Crucified plunges?" Balthasar, *Glory of the Lord*, 1:117. David Luy highlights the affirmation, "never dimmed" in Balthasar's work from the outset of his theological aesthetics, "that the horrific event of the crucifixion, the agony of Jesus through his passion and death, represents at once the paradigmatic expression of the divine, and the apex of God's glory shining in the world." Luy, "The Aesthetic Collision: Hans Urs von Balthasar on the Trinity and the Cross," *International Journal of Systematic Theology* 13, no. 2 (2011): 154–69, here 154.

31. See Begbie, *Resounding Truth*, 176–82.

32. Eberhard Jüngel, "'Even the Beautiful Must Die'—Beauty in the Light of Truth," in *Theological Essays*, vol. 2, ed. J. B. Webster (Edinburgh: T&T Clark, 1989), 59–81, here 76 (italics original).

33. "Tree of Life," *British Museum*, https://en.wikipedia.org/wiki/Tree_of_Life_(Kester).

34. Among numerous examples, see David Brown and Ann Loades, eds., *The Sense of the Sacramental: Movement and Measure in Art and Music, Place and Time* (London: SPCK, 1995); David Brown and David Fuller, *Signs of Grace: Sacraments in Poetry and Prose* (Ridgefield, CT: Morehouse, 1996); David Brown, *God and Enchantment of Place: Reclaiming Human*

appears to be a relatively recent move in intellectual history—something rarely acknowledged by those who like to make the move today.[35] In any case, today it has become extraordinarily popular, especially among the artistically inclined who have been reared in "low" Protestant churches and who suddenly find themselves awakened to pre-Reformation, Roman Catholic, and Orthodox sensibilities.

What motivates this enthusiasm to speak of the arts as "sacramental"? One factor seems to be an eagerness to recover a sense of the physicality of the arts—in particular, to validate the worth and integrity of the physical and its capacity to mediate the nonphysical, against quasi-gnostic tendencies in some theology to undervalue or even denigrate materiality. Another is that the supposed sacramentality of the arts gives us a way of conceiving God's presence in culture at large—if art by its very nature is sacramental, it can act as a conduit of divine presence far beyond ecclesiastical boundaries.[36]

Metaphysical concerns can also be at work. Behind much talk of art and sacrament, modernity's much-discussed "disenchantment" of the cosmos is presumed, the modern drive to reduce the world to a bare, godless mechanism. Today, as Roger Lundin remarks, "question the wisdom of calling poetry a sacrament, and you will be accused of denying mystery and disenchanting the world."[37] The movement known as Radical Orthodoxy comes to mind in this connection, with its commitment to a rehabilitated Christianized Platonism and to narrating modernity and postmodernity as a tale of poignant decline.

Experience (Oxford: Oxford University Press, 2004), chap. 1; David Brown, *God and Grace of Body: Sacrament in Ordinary* (Oxford: Oxford University Press, 2007), 3–4, 246–47, 371; Albert L. Blackwell, *The Sacred in Music* (Cambridge: Lutterworth Press, 1999), 16, 28; Scott Cairns, "Elemental Metonymy: Poems, Icons, Holy Mysteries" (paper delivered at the Calvin College Interdisciplinary Conference in Christian Scholarship, Grand Rapids, September 27–29, 2001).

35. See the remarks of Roger Lundin, *Believing Again: Doubt and Faith in a Secular Age* (Grand Rapids: Eerdmans, 2009), 24–29. Wolterstorff's "unsupported hunch" is that the link first appears in John Keble (1792–1866), though he underlines the caution with which Keble makes the connection. Nicholas Wolterstorff, "Evangelicalism and the Arts," *Christian Scholar's Review* 17, no. 4 (1988): 449–73, 460–62.

36. This notion is a characteristic stress of the voluminous writing of David Brown, an ardent advocate of the "sacramental" potential of the arts. (See chap. 4 of this volume.) According to Brown, music, for example, through its combination of the "ethereal and material" is a finite reality through which "God's presence in our midst [can] once more be made known." Brown, *God and Grace of Body*, 247.

37. Lundin, *Believing Again*, 25. Whether the arts can in some sense "re-enchant" the world is a theme much discussed in recent literature; see, e.g., David Morgan, "The Enchantment of Art: Abstraction and Empathy from German Romanticism to Expressionism," *Journal of the History of Ideas* 57, no. 2 (1996): 317–41; Gordon Graham, *The Re-Enchantment of the World: Art versus Religion* (Oxford: Oxford University Press, 2007).

In the late medieval period, Europe is said to have abandoned a "participatory" worldview such that created reality came to be treated as an autonomous zone of inert, flat materiality. This desacralization (or "desacramentalizing") of the cosmos inevitably led by virtue of its own destructive logic to various manifestations of nihilism. Radical Orthodoxy proposes a counter-ontology in which the material world is seen as "suspended" in the uncreated immaterial, "engraced" *ab initio*.[38] These proposals owe a hefty debt to the French Jesuit Henri de Lubac (1896–1991),[39] with his call for a renaissance of a conception of the "supernatural" as always already present with and within "ordinary" creation. Lubac has lately received fervent support from Hans Boersma of Regent College, Vancouver, who pleads that evangelicals, among others, embrace a "sacramental ontology" for the sake of an effective Christian witness in a late-modern or postmodern society.[40]

For our purposes, we should note the way the arts are drawn into these sweeping theological vistas, to point to strategies of resistance to our culture's drift into a nihilist void. One of Radical Orthodoxy's original group, Philip Blond, maintains that the painter Kazimir Malevich (1878–1935) offers a highly evocative sense of the form(s) inherent to the visible, physical world. Citing two of Malevich's works of the late 1920s and early 1930s, Blond tells us that

> even where the face of a human figure is left blank, the colors surrounding it edge around and mark out in the absence of a face the shape of what might fulfill such a request. . . . In this sense, all of Malevich's work was indeed *iconic*, a visible testament to *the presence of the ideal in the real*, and the belief that the artist could depict such a fact.[41]

38. John Milbank, Catherine Pickstock, and Graham Ward, *Radical Orthodoxy: A New Theology* (London: Routledge, 1999); James K. A. Smith, *Introducing Radical Orthodoxy: Mapping a Post-Secular Theology* (Grand Rapids: Baker Books, 2004).

39. Substantial writing on Lubac has appeared in recent years; see, e.g., John Milbank, *The Suspended Middle: Henri de Lubac and the Debate concerning the Supernatural* (Grand Rapids: Eerdmans, 2005); Rudolf Voderholzer and Michael J. Miller, *Meet Henri de Lubac* (San Francisco: Ignatius Press, 2008); Bryan C. Hollon, *Everything Is Sacred: Spiritual Exegesis in the Political Theology of Henri de Lubac* (Eugene, OR: Cascade Books, 2009).

40. Hans Boersma, *Nouvelle Théologie and Sacramental Ontology: A Return to Mystery* (Oxford: Oxford University Press, 2009); Boersma, *Heavenly Participation: The Weaving of a Sacramental Tapestry* (Grand Rapids: Eerdmans, 2010).

41. Philip Blond, "Perception: From Modern Painting to the Vision in Christ," in Milbank, Pickstock, and Ward, *Radical Orthodoxy*, 220–42, here 231 (italics mine). For another example of an attempt to read Malevich theologically, especially with reference to the category of "presence," see Charles Pickstone, "Art's Last Icon: Malevich's *Black Square* Revisited," in *Visual Theology: Forming and Transforming the Community through the Arts*, ed. Robin Margaret Jensen and Kimberly J. Vrudny (Collegeville, MN: Liturgical Press, 2009), 3–10.

Blond insists that recognizing such presence calls for nothing less than a theological construal: "It is *worldly form* as God-given (as culminated and expressed in the union of word and flesh in Christ) that is revelatory, and nothing else. . . . The world shows and exhibits its participation in universal theological forms that can and must be seen."[42]

With regard to music, Albert Blackwell has drawn on a broad range of sources to demonstrate its "sacramental potential," arguing that the term "sacramental" is applicable to *"any finite reality through which the divine is perceived to be disclosed and communicated, and through which our human response to the divine assumes some measure of shape, form, and structure."*[43] Blackwell delineates two broad traditions of sacramental encounter that have been applied to music: the "Pythagorean" and the "incarnational," the former focusing on the intellectual apprehension through music of the world's mathematical constitution, the latter on the sensual, bodily experience music affords.[44]

I find myself deeply sympathetic to the concerns that make the notion of sacramentality so appealing to those engaging the arts. At the same time, awkward questions are bound to arise, and they are not eased by the fact that I have not yet found a sufficiently robust and theologically compelling case for extending the language of sacramentality to the practices and products of the arts. That is not to say a case could never be made, only that to my knowledge a good one has not yet appeared, especially with respect to non-visual and nonliterary art.

If the Reformed tradition has a particular contribution here, it is its repeated concern to orient (or reorient) our thinking about sacrament/sacramentality in rather more obviously scriptural directions than we find in much of the "art and sacrament" discourse presently in vogue. Specifically, we are pressed in the direction of what some call a "covenant ontology," where created reality is resolutely interpreted as grounded in the Father's love for the Son in the Spirit, which is to say in a manner made possible by and consistent with what has been disclosed and accomplished in Jesus Christ. Many Reformed theologians have expounded this kind of perspective (with different accents) but with little evident impact so far in the theology and arts world.[45] Much

---

42. Blond, "Perception," 235 (italics mine).

43. Blackwell, *Sacred in Music*, 28, quoting Richard McBrien, *Catholicism*, vol. 2 (London: G. Chapman, 1980), 732 (italics original).

44. Blackwell, *Sacred in Music*, chap. 1.

45. See, e.g., Michael S. Horton, *Covenant and Salvation: Union with Christ* (Louisville: Westminster John Knox Press, 2007); Alan J. Torrance, "Creatio Ex Nihilo and the Spatio-Temporal Dimensions, with Special Reference to Jürgen Moltmann and D. C. Williams," in *The Doctrine of Creation: Essays in Dogmatics, History and Philosophy*, ed. Colin E. Gunton

depends here on holding to what has been uniquely *enacted and achieved* in Christ—himself the culmination of God's covenant with Israel and the foretaste of the new creation to come—and on reading the created world and God's commitment to this world resolutely through this prism.[46]

I confine myself to just three comments that issue from this notion, again with a particular eye to Reformed perspectives. The first concerns that heavily laden word (a close friend of "sacrament") "presence." If we have in view

---

(Edinburgh: T&T Clark, 1997), 83–104; Thomas F. Torrance, *Divine and Contingent Order* (Oxford: Oxford University Press, 1981); Colin E. Gunton, *The Triune Creator: A Historical and Systematic Study* (Edinburgh: Edinburgh University Press, 1998); Kevin J. Vanhoozer, *Remythologizing Theology: Divine Action, Passion, and Authorship* (Cambridge: Cambridge University Press, 2010).

Rowan Williams tellingly writes: "Sacramentality is not a general principle that the world is full of 'sacredness': it is the very specific conviction that the world is full of the life of a God whose nature is made known in Christ and the Spirit." Williams, foreword to *The Gestures of God: Explorations in Sacramentality*, ed. Geoffrey Rowell and Christine Hall (London: Continuum, 2004), xiii–xiv, here xiii. The same conviction appears in a more recent article: "Sacramentality has been too often understood as a rather static manifestation of the sacred (the familiar language about sacramental understanding of the world can mean simply that the world affords glimpses of the holy); but if divine presence is always necessarily divine action, what is sacramental about the Church is its transparency to the divine act of mutual self-gift." Rowan Williams, "Divine Presence and Divine Action: Reflections in the Wake of Nicholas Lash," *The Archbishop of Canterbury* (website), June 30, 2011, http://www.archbishopofcanterbury.org /articles.php/2131/divine-presence-and-divine-action-reflections-in-the-wake-of-nicholas-lash.

It is intriguing to find Pope Benedict XVI speaking of the integration of covenant and creation in his Easter homily of 2011 in ways that draw directly on the language of Karl Barth: "Communion between God and man does not appear as something extra, something added later to a world already fully created. The Covenant, communion between God and man, is inbuilt at the deepest level of creation. Yes, the Covenant is the inner ground of creation, just as creation is the external presupposition of the Covenant. God made the world so that there could be a space where he might communicate his love, and from which the response of love might come back to him." Homily of Pope Benedict XVI, Easter Vigil, Saint Peter's Basilica, April 23, 2011, quoted in Rocco Palmo, "In the Resurrection, 'Creation Has Been Fulfilled,'" *Whispers in the Loggia* (blog), April 23, 2011, http://whispersintheloggia.blogspot.com/2011/04 /in-resurrection-creation-has-been.html. Cf. Karl Barth, *Church Dogmatics*, trans. Geoffrey W. Bromiley and Thomas F. Torrance, III/1 (Edinburgh: T&T Clark, 1958), § 41. I am grateful to Tanner Capps for directing me to these sources.

46. Merely describing Christ as the "primordial sacrament," while doubtless defendable, is hardly enough if we are to prevent Jesus from being seen merely as the supreme instance of a preconceived "sacramentality," ontologically prior to, and epistemically accessible (by a simple act of perception) independently of Christ. Reformed theology will at this point press that Christology and union with Christ determined the central content and dynamic of "sacrament." Much of what I am saying about "sacramental" here could also apply to the term "incarnational." "At times, Protestant advocates of the arts in particular have promoted the incarnation as a general concept of divine blessing of the world rather than as a doctrine of the specific redemptive activity that God has accomplished through the person and work of Jesus Christ." Daniel J. Treier, Mark Husbands, and Roger Lundin, "Introduction," in Treier, Husbands, and Lundin, *Beauty of God*, 10.

the covenanting God of Israel, dedicated unconditionally to the redemption of all things in and through his Son in the Spirit, then the concept of divine "presence" must be rescued from anything that suggests an inert "thereness" or a deity of bland infinitude, a nameless Other. Ironically, there are potent resources within the arts for helping us recover a fuller vision of presence, as I have tried to show elsewhere with respect to music.[47] For the moment, I point to two recent reflections on "presence" by Rowan Williams, who, although not writing from a self-consciously Reformed angle, gives pointed expression to the theological direction I am commending. In a journal on Christianity and the arts, he reflects on the conundrum that "the change associated with Jesus is incapable of representation," yet "for the change to be communicable it must in some way be representable."[48] The key challenge here is "how do you show transcendent difference in the representation of earthly events?"[49] This comes to a head if we consider how we portray Christ visually. We cannot represent divinity as something simply added to humanity ("the human with inspirational extras"),[50] or merely by picturing humanity taken to some extreme. Somehow the artist needs to show how the world is "enlarged" through the coming of Christ, without creatureliness being distorted or overridden in the process. "How does presence *alter* things? That is what the artist tackling this most impossible of tasks is after."[51] And this can be achieved very subtly. Through irony, for example, the sheer oddity of the gospel at work in the world can be shown. Williams alludes to a painting by Roger Wagner, *Menorah* (1993), in which Holocaust victims "are wandering in the neighbourhood of a distantly seen, conventionally depicted crucifixion, the background dominated by . . . immense towers exuding gas, arranged in the pattern of [a] ceremonial [Jewish] candlestick." Our world becomes strange, different, "as a result of having this particular stranger, Jesus, introduced into it."[52] Presence, in other words, is presence for *change*; God makes things different and our perception of things different as part of his judgment and renewal of the world.[53]

47. Jeremy S. Begbie, "Music, Mystery and Sacrament," in *The Gestures of God: Explorations in Sacramentality*, ed. Geoffrey Rowell and Christine Hall (London: Continuum, 2004), 173–91; more widely, Begbie, *Theology, Music and Time* (Cambridge: Cambridge University Press, 2000).

48. Rowan Williams, "Presence," *Art and Christianity* 43 (2005): 1–4, here 2.

49. Williams, "Presence," 3.

50. Williams, "Presence," 3.

51. Williams, "Presence," 4 (italics mine).

52. Williams, "Presence," 3, 4.

53. For something of the background to this, see Williams's article, "Sacraments of a New Society," in *On Christian Theology* (Oxford: Blackwell, 2000), 209–21. In this connection, Wolterstorff is, I believe, fully justified in questioning the drift of David Jones's well-known

In another article Williams warns against imagining that God's presence can be discerned without any transformation on the part of the discerner.[54] He finds himself critical of what he calls "the aestheticizing of the notion of divine presence," where the problem of God's absence is seen

> as being that we cannot discern God and need to be educated in the skills that will allow us to perceive or experience the divine or the sacred. This is not by any means a waste of time . . . but to the extent that it sees the issue as something to do with the latent capacities of the ego and how they are to be fully activated, it carries some difficulties.[55]

The crucial problem is that all too easily an independent, self-directing ego stands at the center of the story, needing to be taught to search for truth. This in turn suggests a passive deity; "the hiddenness of God becomes a sort of accident which could be prevented or surmounted if better conditions prevailed."[56]

Williams insists that "divine presence . . . does not stand still to be 'discovered.'" Divine presence is the redemptive God at work; it is "the action that constitutes the human self as a responding self, as already 'implicated.'"[57] This action is irreducibly threefold, shaped by God's own triunity. Williams outlines a subtle account of this momentum: apprehending God's presence involves being caught up in the eternal responsiveness within God, through the Spirit, sharing in the Son's self-giving response to the Father's self-bestowal.[58] This brings with it *disruption*, a disturbance of the self.

---

essay on art and sacrament. Wolterstorff, "Evangelicalism and the Arts," 455–59. Note also the observations of theologians John Inge and Alistair McFadyen about the tendency of the concept of sacrament to become "static," as they reflect on working with a sculptor on a piece installed at Ely Cathedral. Alistair I. McFadyen and John Inge, "Art in a Cathedral," in *Sounding the Depths: Theology through the Arts*, ed. Jeremy S. Begbie (London: SCM, 2002), 119–58, here 153–57.

54. Williams, "Divine Presence and Divine Action" (no page numbers; subsequent quotations will be referred to by paragraph number).

55. Williams, "Divine Presence and Divine Action," para. 2.

56. Williams, "Divine Presence and Divine Action," para. 2.

57. Williams, "Divine Presence and Divine Action," para. 3.

58. "The Christian narrative and grammar of God is of an inseparably continuous agency, 'bestowing' itself in such a way that it makes itself other to itself; that otherness in turn answers the act of bestowal by returning itself wholly to its source, holding on to nothing but making its identity a gift; and in this reciprocal flow of life, a third level of agency is generated as the act performed by the first two together, not identical with either, nor with the bare fact of their juxtaposition. . . . The central moment, if we can so speak of it, is one in which the unconditioned response to the movement of life into the other becomes generative of a further difference—in which, to use at last the familiar dramatic idioms of doctrine, the Son's self-giving to the will of the Father releases the gift of the Spirit." Williams, "Divine Presence and Divine Action," para. 4.

Divine presence . . . is . . . the recognition of a prior [divine] relatedness, a relatedness that has already established the very conditions for awareness and is acknowledged only in being appropriated in some way, *through the disorientation or displacement of the individual ego.*[59]

Williams is perhaps at his most Reformed when he comments on the intellectual transformation this entails; there is a danger, he says, of not thinking through "what it means to believe—as classical Christian theology has maintained—not only that God is by definition active in every imaginable circumstance but also that God is more particularly active in the life of the mind."[60]

None of this rules out claims to discern divine presence in the world at large. But, Williams cautions,

> where we recognise—as we undoubtedly have to—certain human experiences as moments of openness to the sacred or the holy, to a dimension in reality that is not exhausted by even the fullest accounts of working and function, we have to be wary of turning this into an encounter with something that is essentially just there to be looked at. . . . The holy is what we, knowingly or not, *inhabit*: more exactly, it is what actively inhabits us as a form or shape of life, the unceasing exchange of life from self to other and back again.[61]

59. Williams, "Divine Presence and Divine Action," para. 7 (italics mine).

60. Williams, "Divine Presence and Divine Action," para. 3.

61. Williams, "Divine Presence and Divine Action," para. 9 (italics original). Williams concludes that "the role of the Church, then, is neither to go in eager search of experiences of the divine, hoping to produce some kind of evidence for its convictions about God, nor to deny any true awareness of God outside its own practice and discipline. It is to try and keep alive the connection between the disorienting moment of perceiving the holy and the comprehensive narrative and (we may as well use the word) metaphysic of trinitarian activity" (para. 10).

One way of interpreting Williams here is to see him as wanting to distinguish between two types of *contemplation*: one that presumes a posture of intellectual distance between self and other such that the self's mind remains sovereign and firmly in control (even if the language of "disinterestedness" is employed liberally); and another that presumes a radically dispossessive attitude on the part of the knower, resulting in a relation sustained not by the self but by what is known, an affectively charged relation entailing ongoing transformation. Williams is deeply sympathetic and supportive of the latter (as he has shown in many writings) but eschews the former. In this respect, he parallels those who have questioned the assumption of a certain kind of "disinterested" contemplation as the sine qua non of a proper posture toward art (e.g., Wolterstorff, *Art in Action*, 21–63).

William Dyrness has recently argued (and with good reason) that the Protestant Reformed tradition has been severely marred by *over*reacting to the notion of contemplation. Dyrness, *Poetic Theology*, chap. 7. I am not convinced, however, that a contemporary recovery of affective pre-Reformation contemplative practices of the sort that Dyrness urges (healthy and culture-sensitive as they may be) can be sustained without being intertwined much more closely with the kind of christological and trinitarian perspectives that he keenly endorses earlier in the book, and that—we might note—Williams is also recommending (see Dyrness, *Poetic Theology*, 146–86).

A second comment on art and sacrament: much of the relevant writing is marked by a heavy *reliance on certain binaries*, especially that of visible and invisible (or material and immaterial, real and ideal, finite and infinite) in ways that easily encourage a particular framing of the supposed pathology of the human condition and our conception of created reality as a whole. (This is especially noticeable, for example, in the Philip Blond essay mentioned above.) Sometimes the dichotomy is located within the creaturely realm, sometimes between creature and Creator (and the two senses are often confused). To be oriented more scripturally, however, and more resolutely toward the christological and covenantal, means that the critical ontological distinction is seen to be that between Creator and creation, God and all that is not God, a distinction that is logically prior to any fall or corruption. Concomitantly, the crisis provoked by sin centers not on visibility, materiality, reality versus ideality, or even finitude (though all these things become infected by sin), but on the moral rupture of God and creature, to which the arts are prone as much as any other human endeavor. The climax of the divine response is not merely an epiphany of perceptible (though veiled) divine presence but a materialized drama of reconciliation: the Son assumes human flesh, identifying with us in the depths of our calamity, journeying through crucifixion to resurrection on the third day. In *this* way the breach is healed and the covenant renewed. In 2005, Reformed philosopher Adrienne Dengerink Chaplin offered a pointed critique of Radical Orthodoxy along these lines, centering on the arts. It repays careful reading.[62]

From this perspective, a multitude of possibilities open up for the arts. To cite just one example, we will be far better equipped to address the positive potential of the arts in contexts of injustice—less inclined to seek divine presence in and of itself, and more likely to be open to the irruptive, novel, and transformative possibilities of divine agency, as explored, for example, by the Reformed South African theologian John de Gruchy.[63]

62. Adrienne D. Chaplin, "The Invisible and the Sublime: From Participation to Reconciliation," in *Radical Orthodoxy and the Reformed Tradition: Creation, Covenant and Participation*, ed. James K. A. Smith and James H. Olthuis (Grand Rapids: Baker Academic, 2005), 89–106. Hans Boersma observes that many evangelicals want to construe the God-world relation as having "covenantal shape," but his caricature of this view as "an agreed-on (covenantal) relationship between two completely separate beings" is unfortunate, to put it mildly. Boersma, *Heavenly Participation*, 24. Boersma appears to be confusing covenant and contract, as well as supposing that advocates of a covenant ontology are (generally?) guilty of some sort of deism and of assuming a univocity of being with regard to Creator and creature. Construing the God-world relation in terms of covenant, and centrally in terms of Christ himself, need not in any way weaken a robust vision of creation as being upheld, suffused with, charged with God's active presence.

63. John W. de Gruchy, *Christianity, Art, and Transformation: Theological Aesthetics in the Struggle for Justice* (Cambridge: Cambridge University Press, 2001).

My third comment: if we do wish to employ the conceptuality that surrounds "sacramentality" as a way of speaking of the potential theological efficacy of the arts, we could do much worse than turn for assistance to *Calvin's understanding of the sacrament of the Lord's Supper*, his eucharistic theology.[64] It may have its limitations, but Calvin does at least have the considerable advantage of refusing to presume that the critical theological axis of the Lord's Supper is about the mediation of the invisible in the visible (though of course this is included), or the inherent capacity of material things to convey divine presence, still less the addition of causal powers to material elements. Rather it turns on the ascended and human Christ's transformative action among us, by way of and through our actions with material things.[65] Calvin's doctrine of union with Christ, in which there is no ontological merger, is clearly pivotal here (as in the rest of his theology), along with his account of the Holy Spirit; through the Spirit, the entire eucharistic action becomes a vehicle through which the church encounters and shares in the ascended reality of Jesus Christ, as a foretaste of the fullness of eschatological life to come. This does not entail a denigration of materiality—whether of the elements or of our bodies—but it does open up

64. See John Calvin, *Institutes*, IV:14, 17. For sensitive discussions, see J. Canlis, *Calvin's Ladder: A Spiritual Theology of Ascent and Ascension* (Grand Rapids: Eerdmans, 2010), chap. 4; J. Todd Billings, *Calvin, Participation, and the Gift: The Activity of Believers in Union with Christ* (Oxford: Oxford University Press, 2007), esp. chap. 4; B. A. Gerrish, *Grace and Gratitude: The Eucharistic Theology of John Calvin* (Minneapolis: Fortress Press, 1993); George Hunsinger, *The Eucharist and Ecumenism: Let Us Keep the Feast* (Cambridge: Cambridge University Press, 2008), 34–39; Thomas J. Davis, *This Is My Body: The Presence of Christ in Reformation Thought* (Grand Rapids: Baker Academic, 2008), esp. chaps. 3–8. Laura Smit has written a fascinating essay on Calvin's eucharistic theology, arguing that, along with "[his] understanding of God's overflowing goodness," it can provide "the ground for a Neoplatonic metaphysic and aesthetic that is similar to, but also importantly different from, Radical Orthodoxy's conclusions." Smit, "'The Depth behind Things': Towards a Calvinist Sacramental Theology," in Smith and Olthuis, *Radical Orthodoxy and the Reformed Tradition*, 205–27, here 206. While sympathetic to an application of Calvin's insights on the Eucharist to other fields, I am not convinced it can lend support to the distinctive theology of creation that Smit is keen to approve.

65. See Nicholas Wolterstorff, afterword to Begbie, *Sounding the Depths*, 221–32, here 231. In this context, the notion of agency will require careful handling. I have found that many discussions of art as sacramental center on the question: "Can music, painting (or whatever) mediate divine presence?" This too easily shifts the focus of attention away from personal agency, divine and human, to the inherent causal powers of a physical object, which comes close to being thought of as a kind of agent. With regard to sacramental theology, Wolterstorff helpfully distinguishes "sign-agent" conceptuality, in which new and fresh causal powers are thought to be imparted to the material sign, and "God-agency" conceptuality, in which God is the agent of change—in the case of the Eucharist, sealing or assuring us of his promises. Nicholas Wolterstorff, "Sacrament as Action, Not Presence," in *Christ: The Sacramental Word*, ed. David Brown and Ann Loades (London: SPCK, 1995), 103–22. The latter need not render the causal powers of the material object irrelevant or "empty," but it does shift the center of agency to God and God's transformative purposes.

a way of setting this materiality within the context of an essentially dynamic, christological, and Spirit-driven frame of reference.[66]

Let us pause for a moment to look back over our discussion of beauty and sacrament. It is notable that issues revolving around the doctrine of creation appear more than any others. It is here that the Reformed tradition can make what is perhaps its most telling contributions to the theology and arts conversation today. Needless to say, there is diversity within the tradition here; I am obviously being selective.[67] The key matter, I suggest, is the extent to which we are prepared to pursue a christological and pneumatological reading of the created world at large. The Reformed tradition has been zealous in upholding and guarding the Creator-creature differentiation, the absolute ontological distinction between Creator and created. When sensitively articulated, this has nothing to do with positing a gulf between the two, even less with a diminution of the creature. Nor does it entail denying the possibility of communion between creature and Creator; paradoxically, it is only by upholding the distinction that an accurate understanding of fellowship is possible. The christological orientation of the New Testament should be our guide here; God's covenant purposes for creation have been instantiated in this person, in a historically achieved hypostatic union of Creator and creature, empowered and enabled by the Spirit. God's act in Jesus Christ is the outworking of God's eternal passion to reconcile humanity to himself, and as such is the ground of God's act of creation. Creation out of nothing is therefore not a neutral "let there be" but the outworking of love, rooted in the eternal commitment of the Father to the Son and of the Son to the Father in the Spirit. Divine transcendence is accordingly to be conceived in gracious and positive terms; God's free otherness makes his covenant dedication to the world *as other* possible. Insofar as God is free *from* the world, God is free *for* it. Likewise,

66. John E. Colwell, a Baptist theologian, has recently supported making a distinction between "sacraments" (narrowly understood as specific ecclesial rites) and "sacramental," which he uses to refer to a "dynamic" of grace-ful "mediated immediacy" that characterizes God's own triune being and God's relation to the world. Colwell, *Promise and Presence: An Exploration of Sacramental Theology* (Milton Keynes, UK: Paternoster Press, 2005). It is the great merit of this book that Colwell defines his terms carefully to avoid what would otherwise be considerable confusion.

67. In my view, the most fruitful and compelling vision of a doctrine of creation for late modernity along Reformed lines was offered by the late Colin Gunton in various writings. See, e.g., Colin E. Gunton, *Christ and Creation* (Exeter: Paternoster Press, 1993); Gunton, *The Doctrine of Creation: Essays in Dogmatics, History and Philosophy* (Edinburgh: T&T Clark, 1997); Gunton, *Triune Creator*. Gunton has been criticized on many counts, probably most of all for his highly negative reading of Augustine. But whatever his weaknesses, he had an uncanny and unerring eye for the key theological issues at stake in any field, and never more so than with regard to the doctrine of creation. His work in this area has yet to receive the attention it deserves.

God's engagement with creation is for the sake of the flourishing of the creature as created and finite, not its debasement, still less its absorption into divinity. And from this perspective, the world's tragedy is shown to be at root a moral dislocation that requires a restoration of fellowship or communion.[68] I am suggesting that it is within a theological environment of this sort that the notions of beauty and sacrament are most fruitfully set, especially if we want to relate them effectively to the arts.

It should be conceded that the history of Reformed theology shows it is by no means uniformly strong on these matters. Karl Barth's determination stands out above all, whatever questions may be asked of him. Keith Johnson's acute summary of a key difference between Balthasar (writing in 1951)[69] and Barth is telling:

> Von Balthasar failed to see the full implication of what Eberhard Jüngel calls Barth's "decisive innovation" in his doctrine of creation: Barth's decision to make the human Jesus of Nazareth the condition for the possibility of knowledge of human being as such. What von Balthasar failed to realize is that this innovation enables Barth to posit that God's eternal decision to reconcile humanity in the person of Jesus Christ is the presupposition *of creation*. . . . For von Balthasar, the relationship between humanity and God is an intrinsic feature of humanity as such by virtue of God's act of creation viewed in distinction from God's act in Jesus Christ. . . . Although Barth also believes that creation signifies that the human exists in relationship with God, it does so solely because creation as such cannot be defined in distinction from the covenant of grace.[70]

And for Barth, Johnson continues, "the covenant is not a programme but a *person*: Jesus Christ."[71]

68. There may well be appropriate ways of speaking of "participation" of humans in God, through Christ in the Spirit, and perhaps in a qualified sense of creation as a whole "participating" through the Mediator in the life of God. Radical Orthodoxy is committed to the notion of participation as applying not only to a saving participation of the believer in Christ but to a general metaphysics. It is not clear to me, however, that Radical Orthodoxy's notion of the "suspension" of the material in the divine can do justice to a biblical, dynamic ontology of grace that upholds the irreducible Creator/creature distinction or to an appropriate distinction between creation and redemption. For discussion, see Smith, *Introducing Radical Orthodoxy*, 74–77 and chap. 6; Horton, *Covenant and Salvation*, chaps. 8 and 9; Vanhoozer, *Remythologizing Theology*, 280–83.

69. Hans Urs von Balthasar, *Karl Barth: Darstellung und Deutung seiner Theologie* (Cologne: Verlag Jacob Hegner, 1952); translated as Hans Urs von Balthasar, *The Theology of Karl Barth: Exposition and Interpretation*, trans. Edward T. Oakes (San Francisco: Communio Books, Ignatius Press, 1992).

70. Keith L. Johnson, *Karl Barth and the Analogia Entis* (London: T&T Clark, 2010), 202, 205 (italics original).

71. Johnson, *Karl Barth and the Analogia Entis*, 206 (italics original). After I delivered the lecture from which this essay emerged, sensing in me a certain sympathy with Karl Barth,

The Infirmities of Language

"Where words fail, music speaks."[72] The aphorism attributed to Hans Christian Andersen gives voice to a recurring sentiment in modern and late modern culture, that the nonverbal arts blossom where words fall short—in its stronger forms, that these arts afford access to a realm that lies beyond the reach of any verbal claims to truth or falsity, a realm that language may gesture toward but can never directly mediate. Some see this as opening up a distinctly theological role for the arts. They are richly meaningful yet stubbornly resist being reduced to language, which surely suggests a prime place for the arts among those who sense acutely both the reality of God and God's sheer inexpressibility. Where words fail God, the arts speak.

Undoubtedly, very often the backdrop to this intuition is an awareness of modernity's inflated confidence in the powers of language, in our capacity to seize and order the world through speech and writing. In theology this belief has all too regularly led to what Nicholas Lash calls a "cataphatic cockiness,"[73] a breezy assurance that our speech and writing can name and grasp the things of God with relative ease. Religious fundamentalisms typically expand their control base through implying that God is in some manner linguistically seizable. "Thus says the Lord. . . ." The tendency is symbolized by the hyper-Protestant male pastor, ensconced in his book-lined office, crafting glittering orations for the pulpit, deeply grateful that most members of his congregation have not reached his level of linguistic competence; or by the theologian, graced with the dazzling verbal dexterity to ensure a senior appointment but whom even her colleagues struggle

---

a member of the audience asked: "Do you believe Barth would be the man to give a novice Christian artist the theology he or she needs?" I didn't answer well at the time. Now I think I would reply as follows: No one theologian can give any artist the theology he or she requires, and many questions can and should be asked of Barth's (limited) account of the arts. Barth's inestimable contribution comes not principally from the specifics of what he says about any particular facet of culture but from the way he repeatedly orients his readers to the energizing center of the Christian gospel, namely, Jesus the Messiah as attested in Scripture, and the way he repeatedly makes us sense the wonder and limitless ramifications of all that has been opened up in Christ. No theologian of the last hundred years has done this more consistently, resolutely, and joyfully. Insofar as every artist requires this constant life-giving orientation (and it is hardly an option), it is difficult to think of a modern theologian who will prove a more inspiring and fruitful companion.

72. The original wording, "Where words fail, sounds can often speak" (popularly abridged to "Where words fail, music speaks") is from "What the Moon Saw," in Hans C. Andersen, *What the Moon Saw: And Other Tales*, trans. H. W. Dulcken (London: George Routledge & Sons, 1866), 38.

73. Nicholas Lash, *The Beginning and the End of "Religion"* (Cambridge: Cambridge University Press, 1996), 170.

to understand. The Reformed churches are hardly innocent here, as Edwin Muir reminds us.

> The word made flesh here is made word again
> A word made word in flourish and arrogant crook.
> See there King Calvin with his iron pen,
> And God three angry letters in a book,
> And there the logical hook
> On which the Mystery is impaled and bent
> Into an ideological instrument.[74]

Straining against this hubristic attempt at control through words lies a reverse current moving in the opposite direction, intensely sensitive to the limits of language, not least when it comes to the "Mystery" Muir identifies in his lament. Words are marred not only by finitude but by corruption— "bent," as Muir puts it. From this perspective God-talk is seen as a kind of forced entry, a desecration of transcendence, a raid on sacred infinity, and to that extent will almost inevitably lead to some kind of violation of others in the name of the divine we have supposedly attained and whose name we all too effortlessly utter. The widespread appeal today of various brands of so-called negative theology is perhaps hardly surprising.

It is just here that some call in the arts to assuage the anxiety. I have lost count of the number of times I have been told at conferences that the church has been hidebound for too long by its fixation on language and conceptual abstractions, entwined with corrupting power ploys; that it is time to renounce the iconoclastic drive of (Reformed) Protestantism and recover a sense of the infinitely "unsayable" through a rehabilitation of the (nonverbal) arts. Although certain types of visual art are often appealed to here, the art that is probably favored most to deal with our embarrassment with language is music. This appeal finds its most sophisticated and potent expression in the early German Romantics of the late eighteenth and early nineteenth centuries. Wordless music, long regarded by their forebears as inferior to music set to texts (because of language's capacity for representative precision), now becomes exalted not only as the highest form of music but as the highest form of art. J. N. Forkel claimed in 1778 that music "begins . . . where other languages can no longer reach,"[75] and Wilhelm Heinse has declared, "Instrumental music . . .

---

74. From "The Incarnate One," in Edwin Muir, *One Foot in Eden* (London: Faber & Faber, 1956), 47.

75. Quoted in Andrew Bowie, *Music, Philosophy, and Modernity* (Cambridge: Cambridge University Press, 2007), 54.

expresses such a particular spiritual life in man that it is untranslatable for every other language."[76] Music grants immediate access to that dimension of being in the world that underlies and makes possible all linguistic, conceptual, cognitive, and representational activity; indeed, music can mediate the infinite, surging, sacred spirit that courses through all things. The quasi-divine power of music is famously celebrated in a review of Beethoven's Fifth Symphony by E. T. A. Hoffmann in 1810, probably the most influential piece of music criticism ever written:

> Music discloses to man an unknown realm, a world that has nothing in common with the external sensual world that surrounds him, a world in which he leaves behind him all *definite* feelings to surrender himself to an inexpressible longing [*unaussprechlichen Sehnsucht*].[77]

In these circles, typically the ineffable spirit of the "unknown realm" is seen as coming to its most concentrated expression in the inner struggles and strivings of the human heart, supremely the heart of the composer, a sanctuary we are privileged to enter through his music. As Carl Friedrich Zelter wrote to the composer Joseph Haydn in 1804: "Your spirit has penetrated into the sanctity of divine wisdom; you have brought fire from heaven, and with it you warm and illuminate mortal hearts and lead them to the infinite."[78]

We might be tempted to dismiss all this as the quirky hyperbole of a historically remote corner of European modernity struggling with the challenges of disenchantment. But these ideas were to have massive purchase in the nineteenth century, and it is not hard to find them today—not least in the church. There are, for example, "contemporary worship" streams I have worked with that show an extraordinary confidence in music's power to mediate God's saving power directly, without words, and where the singer/ songwriter/worship leader is revered in ways that bear more than a passing resemblance to Romantic depictions of the priest-like artist—photographed on album covers against the background of some vast sublimity of the natural world or else lost in the silent contemplation of the heart (the haven

76. Quoted in Bowie, *Music, Philosophy, and Modernity*, 54.
77. As translated in W. Oliver Strunk, *Source Readings in Music History: The Romantic Era*, 5 vols. (London: Faber & Faber, 1981), 5:35–36 (italics mine). Andrew Bowie paraphrases Hoffmann thus: "What music expresses is the essence of Romanticism . . . precisely *because* it cannot be said in words." Bowie, "Romanticism and Music," in *The Cambridge Companion to German Romanticism*, ed. Nicholas Saul (Cambridge: Cambridge University Press, 2006), 243–55, here 245 (italics mine).
78. Quoted in Mark Evan Bonds, *Music as Thought: Listening to the Symphony in the Age of Beethoven* (Princeton: Princeton University Press, 2006), 16.

into which we are invited to delve). As Roger Lundin has often pointed out (though with relatively little recognition), many evangelicals at work in the arts seem deeply attracted to sentiments that owe more to Romanticism than to the New Testament.[79]

A full response to these currents is impossible here, and I certainly have no wish to decry them wholesale. Again I offer only some brief comments. The first simply reiterates a commonplace of biblically grounded confessional Christianity, namely, that *human language has been incorporated directly into the momentum of God's self-communication* in such a way that it is irreplaceably *intrinsic* to that momentum. This finds its climactic focus in the incarnation: the Word becomes flesh, and our fallen language is integral to that flesh so assumed.[80] Our speech, no less than any other dimension of our humanity, has, in this speaking person, the Word-made-Word-user, been purged and renewed, reforged and reshaped. As a result, through the Spirit, a fresh form of communally embedded speech has been set in motion and in due course inscribed as authoritative text. Christians are those baptized into a new community of speaking, a speaking that, through the Holy Spirit, shares by grace in the language-renewing event of Jesus Christ.

Obviously, my case here would take far more space than I have to develop and defend adequately. But in a sense I do not need to, for a steady stream of highly sophisticated Reformed writing along these lines has appeared in recent decades, for example, from T. F. Torrance,[81] Alan Torrance,[82] James

79. See, e.g., Lundin, *Believing Again*, 24–39.
80. It is telling that those at the theology-arts interface who advocate a recovery of "the sacramental" seem reluctant to talk about the sacramental role of Christian proclamation. Commenting on David Jones, Wolterstorff remarks: "It is characteristic of someone working within the medieval concept [of sacrament], as Jones does, to ignore the sacramental quality of proclamation entirely." Wolterstorff, "Evangelicalism and the Arts," 460. Or again, it is significant that those who speak most fervently about recovering a eucharistic sensibility rarely acknowledge that among the Eucharist's physical elements and actions are words. "*Contra* Marion . . . the 'real presence' of the Eucharist depends not only on iconic items and gestures but also on the words of institution ('This is my body. Do this in remembrance of me.'). . . . The personalizing of the divine self-giving does not mean its de-verbalizing." Vanhoozer, *Re-mythologizing Theology*, 103.
81. Thomas F. Torrance, *Theological Science* (Oxford: Oxford University Press, 1969); T. T. Torrance, *The Ground and Grammar of Theology* (Charlottesville: University Press of Virginia, 1980); T. T. Torrance, *Transformation and Convergence in the Frame of Knowledge: Explorations in the Interrelations of Scientific and Theological Enterprise* (Belfast: Christian Journals, 1984).
82. Alan J. Torrance, "*Auditus Fidei*: Where and How Does God Speak? Faith, Reason, and the Question of Criteria," in *Reason and the Reasons of Faith*, ed. Paul J. Griffiths and Reinhard Hütter (London: T&T Clark, 2005), 27–52; A. J. Torrance, *Persons in Communion: An Essay on Trinitarian Description and Human Participation* (Edinburgh: T&T Clark, 1996).

Smith,[83] Nicholas Wolterstorff,[84] and Kevin Vanhoozer.[85] There are important differences between these writers, but neither their common commitment to the "intrinsicity" of human language to God's redemptive ways with the world, nor their acute awareness of the baleful effects of modernity's over-confidence in humankind's linguistic powers is ever in doubt. What is disappointing is that none of this material seems to have found its way into current Christianity and arts discussions. There, all too often, theological language is treated as if it could be entirely abstracted from and is only extrinsically related to God's reconciling engagement with humanity in Jesus Christ (as if it were merely a humanly originated commentary on or witness to that engagement), whereupon the (nonverbal) arts are appealed to as alternative communicative media—perhaps as even superior media with the power to generate fresh norms of theological truth.

A second comment: just because language has been assumed into the reconciling purposes of *this* God, *it can never be thought capable of encompassing, circumscribing, or in any manner controlling the divine.* A concern for divine freedom vis-à-vis language is, I think, a large part of what drives the suspicion or even fear of language among many Christians at work in the arts, perhaps most of all among evangelicals (and "post-evangelicals"), some of whom have been reared on what is undoubtedly a highly constrictive view of theological speech and writing, in which a certain kind of declarative proposition and a certain kind of representative view of language are assumed to be definitive of "meaningfulness." In the midst of what feels like an overly secure, oversystematized, word-imprisoned Protestantism, it is not surprising that many will run to the arts for refuge, for they appear to promise a semantic freedom, an allusiveness and openness that the discourses of doctrinal orthodoxy seem to disallow.

Part of the response to this will be along the lines of the comment I have just made, about language being intrinsic to the momentum of divine grace. But left on its own, that will likely result in the very thing that many understandably want to avoid: an overconfidence in language's grasping powers. Thus we also need to recognize that the God who appropriates human language directly into his purposes is the God of gracious freedom, who exceeds all that can be spoken or thought, all that can be said or conceived. Today, a stress on the linguistic uncontainability of God is usually associated with

83. James K. A. Smith, *Speech and Theology: Language and the Logic of Incarnation* (London: Routledge, 2002).

84. Nicholas Wolterstorff, *Divine Discourse: Philosophical Reflections on the Claim That God Speaks* (Cambridge: Cambridge University Press, 1995).

85. Vanhoozer, *Remythologizing Theology.*

the post-structuralists and with premodern theological traditions on which they regularly draw. But that the finite cannot contain the infinite has always been near to or at the heart of the Reformed tradition. It is especially distinctive of its Christology[86] and to a significant extent drives its anxieties about constructing visual images of God. Divine self-*dis*closure prohibits divine self-*en*closure. And this applies to any language appropriated in the process. To be sure, Reformed theology has not always articulated divine freedom in ways that head off the danger of reducing God to an arbitrary will, a deity of abstract, absolute power (*potentia absoluta*). At its strongest, however, the tradition, in taking its bearing from God's positive engagement *with* language, can celebrate God's uncontainability *by* language, which is to say, the free uncontainability of God's covenant commitment.[87]

A third comment: it is a commonplace of most linguistic theory that by its very nature language is embedded in and relies on a host of nonverbal means of interaction with the world (bodily movement and gestures, symbol making, rituals, and so forth), and that these things cannot be dismissed as meaningless simply because they are not reducible to verbal articulation. It is in this context that the nonverbal arts' relation to language, and theological language in particular, needs to be set. The struggle is to hold at one and the same time that the church is called to be faithful to the discourse God has graciously appropriated *and* that *other communicative media—such as the nonverbal arts—will possess their own distinctive capacities to mediate dimensions of the very realities of which this discourse speaks and in which this discourse is caught up.* The arts do their own kind of work in their own kind of way, articulating depths of the Word of the gospel and our experience of it that are otherwise unheard or unfelt, while nonetheless being responsible and faithful to the normative texts of the faith. A major research agenda opens up here,

86. This is enshrined in the so-called *extra Calvinisticum*: the Son of God became human without abandoning heaven. See Myk Habets, "Putting the 'Extra' Back into Calvinism," *Scottish Journal of Theology* 62, no. 4 (2009): 441–56.

87. From a very different (Roman Catholic) perspective, Nicholas Lash deftly writes:
Why is it so difficult to speak sensibly of God? From the deist standpoint that defines and dominates the modern imagination, it seems obvious that the reason is that God is *so far away* from us. . . . But suppose we come at it from a different angle, from a Christian angle; from, that is to say, a standpoint shaped by recognition of God's uttered Word and outpoured Spirit. When some Romeo starts stammering, unable to find words that will do justice to his love, it is not because the beloved is *unknown* to him. . . . It is because she has become too *well* known for glib description to be possible. . . . God is not far from us. God's self-giving constitutes our very being, intimates each element and movement of our heart. *It is not those who know not God who find God difficult to talk about, but those who know God well.* (Lash, *Beginning and the End of "Religion,"* 170–71, italics of last sentence mine)

as well as a major practical challenge to all who care about the arts in the church. The New Testament scholar N. T. Wright has written: "If all theology, all sermons, had to be set to music, our teaching and preaching would not only be more mellifluous; it might also approximate more closely to God's truth, the truth revealed in and as the Word made flesh, crucified and risen."[88]

In my teaching in the United States and the United Kingdom over many years, I have often met students who long to find one theologian who will provide all the answers to their struggles and quandaries or one tradition into which they can sink and be released from the frantic but paralyzing sense that they need to read everything. It would be foolish in the extreme to claim this of the Reformed tradition or of any Reformed theologian, as it would be of any movement or figure in theology. My claim in this essay is more modest, namely, that as the theology and arts conversation continues to unfold apace, resources from the Reformed world—so often buried beneath an understandable but exaggerated shame—have considerably more to offer than is often supposed, especially if we are seeking to delve more deeply into the plotlines and harmonies of a scripturally rooted and vibrant trinitarian faith.

88. N. T. Wright, "Resurrection: From Theology to Music and Back Again," in Begbie, *Sounding the Depths*, 193–212, here 210–11.

Index

active process of making,
142–43
Adams, Byron, 104–5
aesthetic excellence, 185n11
aestheticism, 187
aesthetics, 186
aesthetic theology, 40
agape, 12
alternative worship, 142
Amadeus (Shaffer play), 180
Andersen, Hans Christian, 202
animal nature, 53
Anselm, 39
anti-emotionism, 76
anxiety, 99
apartheid, 45
Aquinas, Thomas, 182, 184
Arianism, 158
arousal theories of music,
65n38, 71–72
artist, as priest, 204
artistic creativity, as real presence of God, 134
arts, the
and beauty, 23, 185
church stifling, 139
fictionalize reality, 35n35
and Holy Spirit, 113, 127–28
and natural theology, 130,
135
and orthodoxy, vi–viii, 139,
206
physicality of, 191
and Protestantism, 182
as sacramental, 190–201
and Scripture, vi, 127
and theology, v–vi
and the Trinity, ix
voice creation's praise, 187

assurance, 108–9, 155n20
Augustine, 39, 182, 184, 200n67
aural space, 125, 143, 165–66
Auschwitz, 34, 47
autonomy, 152

Bach, C. P. E., 15
Bach, J. S., 83, 89–91, 133,
140, 142–43
and created beauty, 13–24
improvisation in, 19
as Lutheran, 20–21
openness and consistency
in, 18
Baker, Gordon, 147n3
Balthasar, Hans Urs von, 4n4,
5, 13n28, 39, 88, 179, 182,
184, 186, 189–90, 190n30,
201
Barber, Samuel, 73
Barclay, John, 172–73
Barth, Karl, 3n3, 43, 88,
151n12, 174n72, 175n75,
186–87, 188, 194n46, 201
Basil the Great, 10
Beardsley, Monroe C., 21n57
beauty, 184–90
created, 2, 7, 17, 23, 24
criteria of, 3
and desire, 12–13
distracting from moral responsibilities, 44–45
fostering a lie, 44
generated, 2, 23–24
as opiate of the people, 38
and outgoing love, 4–5
promise of, 190
re-creation of, 9
and sentimentality, 26, 26n2,
37–40

vs. sublime, 5–6
theological account of, 2–13
and Trinity, 3–4, 17, 26,
187n19
beauty-truth-goodness triad,
ix
Beckman, Max, 185
Beecham, Thomas, 162
Beethoven, Ludwig von, 38n43,
83, 99, 103, 135, 204
belief, and evaluation, 54n15,
60
Benedict XVI (Pope), 43,
109–10, 194n45
Berger, Karol, 90
Bible, the. *See* Scripture
binaries, 198
Birnbaum, J. A., 21n61
Blackwell, Albert, 193
Blake, William, 10
Blond, Philip, 192–93, 198
Blow, John, 124
bodily behavior, 65, 75
Boersma, Hans, 192, 198n62
Bonhoeffer, Dietrich, 37, 48,
173n71
Botstein, Leon, 94n2
Bouguereau, Adolph, 29
Bowden, Sandra, vi
bowels, 124
Bowie, Andrew, 204n77
brightness, 3
broken beauty, 188–89
Brown, David, 79–89, 91,
131–36, 139, 191n36
Brown, Frank Burch, vi
Bruckner, Anton, 81, 83
Burrell, David, 153n18
Butt, John, 21n61, 90–91

Calvin, John, 9n18, 118, 199
Campbell, Douglas, 154
Catherine of Genoa, 98
Chalcedon, 156–57, 158,
    173n71
Chaplin, Adrienne Dengerink,
    198
cheerful music, 66
chords, 68–70, 170
Christ. *See* Jesus Christ
Christian beauty, paradox
    of, 23
Christian kitsch, 35–36
Christology, 156–59, 174–75
chromaticism, 101–2
church, stifling of the arts, 139
Clark, Stuart, 159n32
Clarke, Elizabeth, 118n12, 121
classical music, 83, 132–33
Coakley, Sarah, 155, 157,
    157n27
cognitive accounts of emo-
    tions, 52–54
collective effervescence, 34
Colwell, John E., 200n66
coming from–coming toward,
    165, 167, 168, 169, 175
communal culture, 141–42
communion of saints, 96
compassion, conspicuous, 34
concentration, 72–73, 75
conscious experience, 51
consonance, 3–4, 10, 70
contemplation, 197n61
contemporary worship, 204
contingent order, 11
contour theory, 65–71
contract, 154, 173, 198n62
contrastive transcendence,
    149–50, 151n10
Cook, Nicholas, 64
Corresponding Society of the
    Musical Sciences, 22n61
costly action, 32–35, 37
covenant
    vs. contract, 154, 173, 198n62
    and creation, 200–201
covenantal soteriology, 154
covenant ontology, 193–94,
    198n62
creation, 140, 142, 200–201
    contingency of, 11

corruptions and distortions
    of, 8
    as testimony to God's beauty,
    7–8
Creator-creature differentia-
    tion, 200
Creator-creature relation,
    168–70, 176, 200
Cross, Ian, 141
crucifixion, 109
    beauty interpreted through,
    189–90
    torture of, 42–43
cultural endeavor, integrity
    and particularity of,
    81–82, 86–87, 130, 139
culture, 137, 142
Cunningham, Conor, 151n11
Cunningham, David, 145

Damasio, Antonio R., 55n18
dance, 72–73
Dante, 7
Danto, Arthur C., 25
Darwin, Charles, 53n10, 66n46
Darwinism, 28
Davenport, Anne, 151n11
Davies, Stephen, 64n40,
    65–66, 67, 69n56, 71
decoratio, 16
de Gruchy, John W., 45, 198
deism, 158, 198n62
depression, 57–58
Descartes, René, 52n9, 149n8
desire, 12–13
Deutsch, Diana, 162n44
Diana, Princess, 34
diatonicism, 101
Dickens, Charles, 31n16
Dillenberger, Jane and John, vi
Dionysius, 182
directional time, 90–91
disenchantment, 191–92, 204
dispositio, 16
dissonance, 20, 70
diversity of particulars, 10–11,
    18
divine and human agency,
    122–23, 125, 144, 152–53,
    171–75, 177–78
divine grief, 118
divine presence, 88–89, 194–201

divine self-disclosure, 207
divine sovereignty, prone to
    domestication, 155n20
doctrine, resistance to, vii–viii
Dostoyevsky, Fyodor, 39–40
double agency, 174n72
Dream of Gerontius, The
    (Elgar), 93–111
"Dream of Gerontius, The"
    (Newman poem), 95
Dreyfus, Laurence, 14, 15, 18,
    19, 21n57, 22n61
Duns Scotus, 151n11
Durkheim, Émile, 33
dynamic transcendence, 168
Dyrness, William A., vi,
    188n27, 197n61

"Easter" (Herbert poem),
    126–27
Easter, three days of, 40–42,
    44–45, 46–48
Easter Day, 26, 41
Edwards, Jonathan, 5n5,
    187n19
elaboratio, 14–16, 18, 22, 140,
    142
Elder, Mark, 104
Elgar, Edward, 93–111
    confidence and anxiety in,
    95, 106–11
    decadence of, 105–6
    hope in, 103–4
    modernism of, 99, 102
emotional self-indulgence,
    30–32, 37, 48, 76
emotions, 51
    appropriate and inappropri-
    ate, 58
    and decision-making, 59
    inappropriate, 76
    as individual, 52
    intrinsic and extrinsic sources
    of, 63n38
    as motivators to action, 60
    and music, 62–74
    oriented to objects, 56–58
    as private mental states, 52
    proto-emotion, 63
    reaction triad of, 51n4,
    55n18, 66
    reflex, 56
    tender, 26n2

transformation of, 62
without price, 33
and worship, 60–62, 76
enabling resonance, 144
Enlightenment, 22n61, 23,
    89–90, 139
entrainment, 141
"Ephes. 4. 30" (Herbert poem),
    114–24
eros, 12
evaluation (appraisal), 54–55
evil
    evasion or trivialization of,
        27–30, 46, 48
    harmonizing away of, 38–40,
        45
excess, 11
expression, 71–72
expressive bodily behavior, 51
expressive theories of music,
    65n38
extra Calvinisticum, 158,
    207n86

faithful improvisation, 143
fall, the, 30, 37, 123, 186
Farley, Edward, 184
feelings, 58
felicitous culture, 142
Feuerbach, Ludwig, 152
fiction, as deeper appreciation
    of reality, 35n35
fideism, 3
film, 64
Fish, Stanley E., 122n29,
    123n31
Forkel, J. N., 203
freedom, 144, 149–51, 171–72.
    See also divine and human
    agency
    and musical perception,
        176–78
Frijda, N. H., 60
Fujimura, Mako, vi

general revelation, 135
German Enlightenment, 22n61,
    23
German idealism, 39
gesture, 66–68, 71, 72, 73
God
    allure of, 13
    beauty of, 11, 17, 186–87

and creation, 200–201
and evil, 39–40
extravagance of, 11
of the gaps, 150
infinity of, 151, 170
intratrinitarian life of, 7n15,
    11, 144
kenotic embroilment of, 85
as linguistically uncontain-
    able, 206–7
power and love of, 118
saving love of, 43
self-disclosure of, 40
and time, 91
transcendence of, 149–51
and ugliness, 43
Goldberg Variations (Bach),
    1–2, 17, 18, 20, 24, 90,
    91n45, 143
Good Friday, 26, 41–42, 44, 47
goodness, and beauty, 38
gospel, ungainliness of, 43n58
grace, in contractual soteriol-
    ogy, 154
greeting cards, 29
Gregory Nazianzen, 61
Gregory of Nyssa, 170
Grimley, Daniel M., 104n28
Gunton, Colin E., 37, 140n31,
    149n7, 200n67
Gurney, Edmund, 106n39

Hamilton, Andy, 162
Hanslick, Eduard, 63n39
happy music, 67
harmony, 29, 68–69, 83
Harper-Scott, J. P. E., 99–101,
    102–3
Harries, Karsten, 30n15
Hart, David Bentley, 4n3, 6n11,
    6n13, 14, 18, 152–55, 186
Hart, Trevor, 183
Haydn, Joseph, 81, 204
Hegel, G. W. F., 39
Heidegger, Martin, 156n24
Heinse, Wilhelm, 203–4
Herbert, George, 114–28
Hick, John, 39
Higgins, Kathleen, 37n40
Hodgkins, Christopher, 123n31
Hoess, Rudolf, 34
Hoffmann, E. T. A., 204

Holy Saturday, 26, 41–42
Holy Spirit, 91
    and the arts, 113, 127–28
    as beautifier in God, 187
    and beauty, 5, 9–11, 190
    and Eucharist, 199
    grieving of, 116
    Herbert on, 127
    and music, 124–27
    and ordering of desires, 13
    and poetry, 128
    and Scripture, 119–20
    unpredictable improvisa-
        tions of, 19
homoeroticism, 105
hope, 101, 103–4, 107, 110, 111
Hopkins, Gerard Manley, 10
Hull, John, 166n53
humanity, and natural
    theology, 137
human reasoning, and natural
    theology, 137–38
Hunsinger, George, 174n72
hyper-space, 149
hypostatic union, 176

image of God, 44
imagination, and tradition,
    82–83
imaginative theology, 134
immanence, 149, 169
immuring-immured tonal
    structure, 99–101
impatience, of sentimental-
    ity, 33
improvisation, 12, 19, 91,
    107, 143
incarnation, ix, 85–86, 133,
    158, 193, 205
infinity, 151, 170
Inge, John, 196n53
injustice, 38, 45, 198
instrumentalism, 82, 86–87
instrumental rationality, 82, 132
intentional fallacy, 21n57
intermediate state, 109
interpenetration, 164, 167,
    168, 169, 173, 175
interpersonal agency, 144, 171,
    173
inventio, 14–16, 18, 22, 142
Irwin, Joyce, 21

James, William, 34, 52n9
James-Lange theory, 53n9
Jasper, David, 114, 119
Jefferson, Mark, 27n2
Jenkins, John, 124
Jenson, Robert, 4n3
Jesus Christ
  "in Christ," 108
  as eschatological goal of
    creation, 9
  as primordial sacrament,
    194n46
  redemptive emotion of, 75
  vicarious humanity of, 61–62
  visual portrayal of, 195
Johnson, Keith, 201
Jones, David, 195n53, 205n80
joy-as-resolution, 69
Jüngel, Eberhard, 140, 190
Juslin, Patrik N., 63n38, 64n41
justice, beauty of, 44–45

Kandinsky, Wassily, 131
Kant, Immanuel, 5–6
Kantian tradition, 12
Keble, John, 191n35
kenotic Christologies, 155, 156
Kinkade, Thomas, 37
kitsch, 30–31, 35–36
Kivy, Peter, 64n40, 65–66, 71
Klee, Paul, 131, 164n49
Knight, Deborah, 27n5
Kundera, Milan, 30–31

Lange, Carl, 53n9
language, 146–47
  as fallen, 123
  as finite, 123
  and God's self-
    communication, 205–6
  infirmities of, 202–8
  and nonverbal interaction,
    207
  overconfidence in, 202, 206
Lash, Nicholas, 28, 202, 207n87
Lazarus, R. S., 54n15, 56n20
Leibniz, Gottfried, 22n61
Lewis, Alan F., 41
Lewis, C. S., 57
liberal Protestants, 182
libertarian freedom, 153n18,
  155

likeness of Christ, 61
Lindbeck, George, 157n26
Liszt, Franz, 19
literature of tears, 116–17
longing for God, 13
Lowe, Walter, 152n12
Lubac, Henri de, 182, 192
Lundin, Roger, 156n24, 191,
  205
Luther, Martin, 89
Lutheranism, of Bach, 20–21
Lyons, William, 54n15, 55,
  57n21

Mackenzie, Ian, 175n75
MacMillan, James, 46–47, 190
Madell, Geoffrey, 68n54
Mahler, Gustav, 81, 83
major chords, 69, 71
Malevich, Kazimir, 192
Maritain, Jacques, 182, 185
mathematics
  of Bach, 90
  in Barth, 16–17
Maundy Thursday, 47
McColley, Diane Kelsey, 125–26
McFadyen, Alistair I., 147n2,
  196n53
melancholy music, 66
Mendelssohn, Felix, 73n63
Menorah (Wagner painting),
  195
Merleau-Ponty, Maurice,
  167–68
Messiaen, Oliver, 83
Mestrovic, Stjepan, 33–34
Meyer, Leonard B., 69n57
Midgley, Mary, 30n15
Milbank, John, 5–6, 17n46
mind-body dichotomy, 52
minor chords, 68
Mission, The (film), 64
modalism, 159
modernism, 28, 99, 102
modernity
  confidence in language, 202
  on freedom, 146, 153
  on generated beauty, 23
  on sublime, 5
  visual space of, 157, 159
Moltmann, Jürgen, 46n62,
  147n4, 151n10

Mondrian, Piet, 131
Mondzain, Marie-José, 178
Monti, Anthony, 134–36
moods, 58
Morley, Iain, 71n60
Mozart, W. A., 135, 188
Muir, Edwin, 203
music
  cheerful, 66
  classical, 83, 132–33
  as created beauty, 13
  discloses unknown realm, 204
  and emotion, 49–50, 62–74
  floating intentionality of,
    141–42
  and freedom, 146
  happy, 67
  and Holy Spirit, 124–27
  illuminates and enriches
    theology, 76
  and language, 203
  melancholy, 66
  and natural theology, 89, 92,
    129–40, 144
  and poetry, 128
  popular, 133
  and sacraments, 83, 132
  sad, 67
  and social cohesion, 141
  and worship, 36–37, 75–77
musical space, 143–44, 168
musical tones, 162
Myers, David, 67n50
mystery, 203

natural religion, 80, 131
natural sciences, 137
natural theology of music,
  89–92, 129–40, 144
Neo-Calvinism, 182, 185
New Calvinism, 183n4
Newman, John Henry, 93,
  95–98, 107, 108, 110
Newton, Isaac, 150n8
Nietzsche, Friedrich, 43n58
noise, 162
noncognitive accounts of
  emotion, 52–54
nongodforsakenness of the
  world, 130, 139, 140
Norris, Richard, 157
nostalgia, 37n42

number symbolism, 16–17
Nussbaum, Martha, 55n18,
    56n20, 59

objectivism, 83
objects of emotion, 56–58,
    63–64
occurrent emotion, 52, 56,
    63n38, 71
octave illusion, 162n44
O'Hear, Anthony, 34n31
optocracy, 178
orthodoxy
    and the arts, vi–viii, 139, 206
    peculiar, vii–viii
    and poetic virtuosity, 127
Orwell, George, 33
O'Siadhail, Micheal, 47–48

Pahlka, William, 123
pain, 31
Pannenberg, Wolfhart, 7n15
participation, 8–9, 176n78
particularities and integrities
    of the world, 130, 139
particulars-in-relation, 11
Patel, Aniruddh, 68n51
peculiar orthodoxy, vii–viii
penance, 97–98
perceived property, 65
perfection, 3, 22n61
perichoresis, 176
physiological activation, 51
Pirie, Peter, 95
Placher, William, 150n8, 154–55
Platonism, 8, 9n18, 191
pleasure upon contemplation,
    3, 4
poetry, 120–22, 127–28
Polanyi, Michael, 59n30
Polkinghorne, John, 135
polyphony, 173n71
popular music, 133
postemotionalism, 33–34
postmodernity
    on generated beauty, 23
    as postemotional, 33
    on sublime, 5
Poulenc, Francis, 83
prayers for the dead, 109n42
presence, 194–95
Prestcott, Ted, 44

primordially human, 137, 141
principalities and powers,
    42, 45
progress, 28
promise, of beauty, 190
proportion, 3–4, 10
propositional language, vii
proprioceptive feedback, 67
Protestantism
    and the arts, 182
    neglect of beauty, 185
    as oversystematized and
        word-imprisoned, 206
    on purgatory, 107
    and visuality, 178–80
proto-emotion, 63
purgation, 108, 109
purgatory, 94, 97–98, 107–10
purification, 97–98
Pythagorean tradition, 193

Quash, Ben, 12n26, 179

Radical Orthodoxy, 8n16,
    191–92, 198
Rae, Murray, 175n75
Rahner, Karl, 171, 182
rationalism, 53
rationality, 137–38
Ratzinger, Joseph, 43, 109–10,
    194n45
receptacle philosophies, 158
reconciliation, 173
reflex emotions, 56
Reformed Protestantism, and
    the arts, 182, 188n27, 208
religious experience, 80, 114,
    134
Rembrandt, 42
renewed rationality, 143
Reno, R. R., 7
representation, 23, 73–74
representational theories of
    emotion, 63n38
resonance, enabling, 144
resonance, sympathetic, 144
resonant order, 165–67, 168,
    170
resplendence, 3
resurrection, and re-creation
    of all things, 45
resurrection life, as defiant, 48

revelation, and human imagi-
    nation, 132
rhythm, 67–68, 83
Riesman, David, 33
Riley, Matthew, 95, 101–2
Ritzer, George, 33
Robinson, Jenefer, 56
Roman Catholicism, 105, 182
Romanticism, 53, 203–5
Rookmaaker, Hans, 182–83
Rowell, Geoffrey, 96, 107n40
"rumours of transcendence,"
    88

sacrament, 122, 194n46
    art as, 190–201
sadism/sadomasochism, 43
sad music, 67
Said, Edward, 24n65
salvation, and freedom, 154
sanctification, 123
Savile, Anthony, 28
Schoenberg, Arnold, 83
Schoot, Henk J. M., 169n61
Schubert, Franz, 83
Schwartz, Regina, 122
Scripture
    and the arts, vi, 127
    and Holy Spirit, 119–20
    polyphonic texture of, 179
    scriptural imagination, vi
    theological interpretation
        of, viiin4
    and tradition, 82, 84–86,
        131–32
Scruton, Roger, 68, 160–63, 165
Seerveld, Calvin, vi, 182–83,
    185, 189n27
sentimental emotions, 30–32
sentimentality, 26–35, 76, 189
    and beauty, 26, 26n2, 37–40
sentimental solipsism, 36
Shaffer, Peter, 180
shame, 108–9
Shults, F. LeRon, 151
Sibbes, Richard, 116n7
Sidney, Philip, 121
simplicity, as elaborated sim-
    plicity, 18
Simpson, O. J., 34
Sloboda, John A., 63n38, 64n41
Smit, Laura, 32, 199n64

Smith, C. A., 54n15
Smith, James K. A., 205–6
social Trinity, 159
sola gratia, 118
solipsism, 36
Solomon, Robert C., 26n2, 29–30
sounds
  physicalist accounts of, 161n41
  as pure events, 160–62
  as secondary objects, 160–62
  space of, 160–64
South Africa, 45
space, 147n2, 147n4
  and freedom, 152, 155
  and language, 178
  receptacle notions of, 158
  of sounds, 163–64
  and Trinity, 175–76
Spackman, Betty, 35
spatiality, 148
Spe Salvi (Benedict XVI), 110n46
Stapert, Calvin, 16n43
Steiner, George, 30, 130, 143n40
Sting (singer), 114
Stravinsky, Igor, 83, 185
subjectivism, 83
sublime, 5–6
suffering, 28–29, 32
  irrationality of, 46
supernatural, present with and within ordinary, 192
sympathetic resonance, 144

Tanner, Kathryn, 84, 133, 149–51, 157, 168–69, 171
Tatarkiewicz, Wladyslaw, 3, 3n2
Tchaikovsky, 32, 73
telos, and freedom, 153n18
temporality, in Bach, 90–91
tension-resolution pattern, 69–70
theodicy, 29, 39
theological aesthetics, 40, 184, 186
theological interpretation of Scripture, viiin4

theology
  and the arts, v–vi
  and music, 76, 87–88
  tragic, 46
Third Reich, 35
thirst for God, 13
Thomas Aquinas, 182, 184
three days of Easter, 40–42, 44–45, 46–48
Tillich, Paul, 182
time, 91, 147n4, 158
tones, 170
Torrance, Alan J., 9n18, 154, 205
Torrance, Thomas F., 150n8, 158, 205
totalitarianism, and sentimentality, 34
tradition, 82–83, 88
  and Scripture, 82, 84–86, 131–32
transcendence, 6, 88, 149–51, 168–69
transparency, 23
Tree of Life, The (sculpture), 190
Triduum (Paschal), 41, 47
trinitarian imagination, ix
Trinity, 134, 136
  and the arts, ix
  and beauty, 3–4, 17, 26, 186n16
  ceaseless flow of self-giving, 11
  and creation, 140, 142
  in Herbert, 118
  rendered in visual art, 159
  and space, 175–76
truth, found in the resurrection of Christ, 44

U2, 167
ubiquity of Christ's humanity, 158
uncontainability, 11
union with Christ, 36, 199
unknown realm, 204
Updike, John, 188n24

Valdés, Juan de, 119–20
Vanhoozer, Kevin J., 206
Velez, Juan, 98

Verdi, Guiseppe, 167
Vernazza, Ettore, 98
Viladesau, Richard, vi, 189
visible and invisible, 198
vision, unreliability of, 159n32
visual perception, 143, 160
vocalization, 66, 68, 70, 71, 72, 73
Volf, Miroslav, 62
voluntarism, 153n18

Wagner, Richard, 105, 106
Wagner, Roger, 195
Walford, John, 188
Webster, John, 8–9, 175n75
Well-Tempered Clavier, The (Bach), 22, 142
West, Patrick, 32n20
Western doctrine of progress, 28
Wilde, Oscar, 31, 105, 106
Williams, Peter, 1–2, 17n45, 18
Williams, Rowan, 36, 194n45, 195–97
Wimsatt, William K., 21n57
Wittgenstein, Ludwig, 146–47
Wolfe, Gregory, vi, 37n42
Wolff, Christoph, 15–16, 22n61, 23n64
Wolterstorff, Nicholas, vi, 3, 3n2, 35n35, 87n30, 182, 185, 189n27, 191n35, 195n53, 199n65, 205n80, 206
Wood, David, 149n6
world, reconciliation of, 45
worship
  and emotion, 60–62
  and music, 36–37, 75–77
  sentimentality in, 35–37
Wright, N. T., 208

Yates, William, vi
Yeats, W. B., 95

Zajonc, R. B., 56n20
Zelter, Carl Friedrich, 204
zero-sum game, divine and human freedom as, 122, 125, 143, 153, 172
Zuckerkandl, Victor, 135, 146, 164–65, 175